Clinical Dilemmas
in Psychotherapy

Clinical Dilemmas in Psychotherapy

**A Transtheoretical Approach to
Psychotherapy Integration**

Douglas J. Scaturo

American Psychological Association • Washington, DC

Published by
American Psychological Association
750 First Street, NE
Washington, DC 20002
www.apa.org

To order
APA Order Department
P.O. Box 92984
Washington, DC 20090-2984
Tel: (800) 374-2721; Direct: (202) 336-5510
Fax: (202) 336-5502; TDD/TTY: (202) 336-6123
Online: www.apa.org/books/
E-mail: order@apa.org

In the U.K., Europe, Africa, and the Middle East, copies may be ordered from
American Psychological Association
3 Henrietta Street
Covent Garden, London
WC2E 8LU England

Typeset in Goudy by Stephen McDougal, Mechanicsville, MD

Printer: Sheridan Books, Ann Arbor, MI
Cover Designer: Naylor Design, Washington, DC
Technical/Production Editor: Devon B. Bourexis

The opinions and statements published are the responsibility of the authors, and such opinions and statements do not necessarily represent the policies of the American Psychological Association.

Library of Congress Cataloging-in-Publication Data

Scaturo, Douglas J.
   Clinical dilemmas in psychotherapy : a transtheoretical approach to psychotherapy integration / Douglas J. Scaturo. — 1st ed.
      p. cm.
   Includes bibliographical references and index.
   ISBN 1-59147-229-6
   1. Eclectic psychotherapy. 2. Cognitive therapy. 3. Psychotherapists—Professional ethics.
4. Psychotherapist and patient. I. Title.

   RC489.E24S28 2005
   616.89'14—dc22   2004022391

British Library Cataloguing-in-Publication Data
A CIP record is available from the British Library.

Printed in the United States of America
First Edition

For Janis, my wife, love, and closest friend,
and our son, Michael, the joy of our lives.

CONTENTS

ACKNOWLEDGMENTS

A book such as this is a journey and, as such, it cannot be written without the contributions, direct or indirect, of many. Most of all, I would like to express my deepest gratitude to my wife, Janis, whom I have been blessed with as a lifelong love and companion. Also, I wish to thank our dear son, Michael, who has been the joy of my life and hope for the future. From them I have learned the most important lessons of life and of relationships.

I am also fortunate to have learned from the professionalism, clinical wisdom, experience, and compassion of many colleagues, mentors, and friends. Of special note have been Robert W. Bell, Gerald J. Mozdzierz, Frank J. Macchitelli, L. Garth Turner-Harrington, and John J. Huszonek. Most important, I would like to thank the truest of all my mentors, Neal S. Smalley, whose warmth, support, and friendship have been ever present throughout my professional lifetime. I was also most especially blessed to have as a loyal friend and colleague Robert P. Sprafkin, whose wit, good humor, and incisive thinking have been with me down the longest portion of my professional road thus far. I would like to thank my dear friend and colleague David V. Keith for his warmth, friendship, creativity, and perspective on the clinical situation. I have been grateful for the warmth, inspiration, and support of Barbara H. Fiese, an outstanding exemplar of academician, researcher, and clinician. A special note of tribute belongs to my colleague William R. McPeak, who, as my copresenter in a number of professional workshops, served as a catalyst to refine my thinking about the dilemmas inherent in the clinical situation. I would also like to thank the many patients whom I have had the honor to treat over a good number of years for sharing with me the pain and resilience of their lives. I would like to thank the many interns and graduate students over the years whom I have had the privilege to supervise and from whom I have had the indispensable opportunity to learn by teaching. Finally, I wish to thank my dear colleague, Damien S.

Vallelonga, without whose support and encouragement this book would not have been written.

Navigating the dilemmas along the long and arduous path to clinical wisdom is, as the Katha-Upanishad[1] teaches of the narrow path to enlightenment, as difficult to walk as a "razor's edge."[2] It has been, however, a fascinating road, well traveled with good and worthy companions.

---

[1]Nikhilananda (Trans.). (1949). *The Upanishads: Katha, Isa, Kena, and Mundaka* (Vol. 1). New York: Harper & Brothers Publishers.
[2]Maugham, W. S. (1944). *The razor's edge*. London: William Heinemann.

I

CLINICAL DILEMMAS:
AN INTRODUCTION

1

FUNDAMENTAL CLINICAL DILEMMAS IN PSYCHOTHERAPY: INTRODUCTION TO A TRANSTHEORETICAL CONCEPT

Dilemmas and emotional conflicts are endemic to the human condition and to life itself. Throughout history and literature, personal conflicts have been a recurring theme in amassed evidence to the ubiquity of this problem in daily living. When Shakespeare's *Hamlet* posed the question, "To be or not to be," he was fundamentally confronting the question about which avenue was more intolerable to him at that moment in time: continued life with his suffering of the "slings and arrows" of his particular "outrageous fortune" or the finality of death. On what bases are important choices in life to be made?

The notion of intrapsychic conflict has been basic to psychological theorizing since its early beginnings (Kendler, 1968). Freud (1940/1964b) saw conflict as the basis of neurotic disturbances and anxiety-based behavior. In

This chapter is an adaptation of "Fundamental Dilemmas in Contemporary Psychotherapy: A Transtheoretical Concept," by D. J. Scaturo, 2002, *American Journal of Psychotherapy*, 56, 115–133, copyright 2002 by the Association for the Advancement of Psychotherapy; and "Fundamental Dilemmas in Contemporary Psychotherapy: An Overview," by D. J. Scaturo, 2003, *Ethical Issues in Mental Health Counseling*, 6(1), 1–11, copyright 2003 by The Hatherleigh Company. Adapted with permission.

parallel fashion, Pavlov (1927) demonstrated that dogs in a laboratory setting displayed behaviors that could be described as "neurotic" if they were continuously subjected to discrimination learning tasks that were increasingly difficult to perform. The dogs were trained to salivate and expect food in response to the stimulus of a circle and not so to the stimulus of an ellipse. As the ellipse was gradually changed to be increasingly like the form of a circle in which discrimination was difficult (i.e., on what basis is a choice–expectation with reasonably predictable consequences to be made?), the previously calm animal demonstrated increasingly agitated behavior. Also, social psychological field theory (Lewin, 1935) viewed conflict as the effect of the bipolar opposites of *attracting* and *repelling* aspects of an organism's environment, yielding a classic threefold categorization of conflict in approach–approach, avoidance–avoidance, and approach–avoidance terminology.

A *dilemma* is defined as "a situation involving choice between two equally unsatisfactory alternatives" (Merriam-Webster's Collegiate Dictionary, 1986, p. 355). Synonyms include predicament, quandary, and impasse, as well as the colloquial expressions of "catch-22" (Heller, 1961) and a "tight spot." In social psychological terms, such a scenario would be classically described as an *avoidance–avoidance conflict* (Lewin, 1935). An individual caught in an avoidance conflict, or dilemma, might describe him- or herself as "caught between the devil and the deep blue sea" or "caught between a rock and a hard place." Avoidance conflicts have been described as having a "damned if you do, damned if you don't" quality (Coon, 1980). Because such conflicts are highly stressful and rarely resolved fully, they are a source of anxiety. The psychotherapy patient faced with such alternatives frequently "freezes" and finds it difficult to make a decision or take any action whatsoever. Such a life impasse is often the precipitant for the patient to seek therapy. The psychotherapist, however, is generally not seeking a full resolution to an unsolvable conflict, knowing that complete resolution rarely, if ever, exists. The experienced therapist also knows that inaction is rarely a viable or desirable solution.

Why are dilemmas critical to the practice of psychotherapy? The answer to that question is in part related to the nature of avoidance–avoidance conflicts. In contrast to avoidance conflicts, *approach–approach conflicts* are typically resolved more easily. For example, "Shall I see a drama or a comedy when I go to the movies this weekend?" Approach–approach conflicts are often resolved so rapidly that people are frequently not cognizant of the momentary conflict that they produce (Kendler, 1968). Rather, patients are prone to request help in dealing with consequences that are more substantial. However, even while approach conflicts such as "Shall I respond to the acceptance that I received from Harvard or from Yale?" may result in seeking advice from family and friends, they tend to be resolved without seeking professional help. People typically do not need to seek such assistance in resolving conflict between two positive alternatives. We know from basic psychological learning research (Miller, 1959) that aversive consequences entail a much greater valence than a choice between positive alternatives. We, therefore, might conclude that the avoidance of severely negative alternatives carries with it a certain survival value in an evolutionary sense (Buss, 1999).

The *approach–avoidance conflict* tends to be prevalent in life and is therefore more difficult to circumvent than the avoidance–avoidance conflict. In this situation, the person is both attracted and repelled by a given selection (Kendler, 1968). For example, "Shall I go swimming (which I enjoy) in the cold water (which I detest)?" A central characteristic of an approach–avoidance conflict is the experience of *ambivalence*, or the mixture of positive and negative feelings about the same event. Furthermore, many of life's more important decisions are characterized by approach–avoidance conflict, such as wanting to eat when overweight, or wanting to marry someone of whom one's parents strongly disapprove (Coon, 1980). Such concerns may entail sufficient emotional distress to bring one to engage the services of a skilled psychotherapist.

Dilemmas, or avoidance–avoidance conflicts, however, are truly the "sticking points" of life. They may, fortunately, be experienced less frequently, in part, because of the person's tendency to "leave the field" of conflict to escape the aversive nature of the consequences of choice. In questions of responsibility for actions, one way to leave the field is commonly known as "passing the buck." Hence, President Harry Truman accepted the responsibility of the presidency and committed himself to not leave the field, with the sign on his desk that read, "The buck stops here." In situations in which escape is not possible, indecision, inaction, and freezing are common responses. Even when not choosing carries with it its own undesirability, it may be preferable to electing one of two severely negative choices. Such inescapable situations are frequently the precipitants of psychological trauma, even after a choice has been made on whatever grounds. A poignant example of such trauma is *Sophie's Choice* (Styron, 1979) in which a young woman in a concentration camp is forced by a sadistic Nazi officer to choose which of her two children will live or die, when it is the civilized obligation of a parent to equally ensure the survival of all of his or her children. People who have undergone such traumatic life experiences almost always find benefit from the assistance of professional help to achieve a personal understanding of the event, even if only partial resolution or accommodation of the event is possible.

CLINICAL DILEMMAS AND THE PSYCHOTHERAPIST

The concept of the *clinical dilemma* (e.g., Dryden, 1997; Horowitz & Marmar, 1985; Ryle, 1979; Scaturo & McPeak, 1998) is one of the ubiquities in the practice of psychotherapy, for not only the psychotherapy patient but also the psychotherapist. The process of psychotherapy itself can be viewed as a constant series of clinical choices and recurring dilemmas for the psychotherapist. For the practicing clinician, such decision making is a part of everyday occupational life. It is often said that one may find oneself "on the horns of a dilemma," that is to say, somewhere between two points, hoping not to get stuck on or by either. It requires of the therapist substantial tolerance for ambiguity. It is no wonder that an ability to think and function within the finer gray hues of life, rather than either the black or white polarities, tends to be a requirement of the job. The ability to clearly conceptualize such dilemmas is perhaps best captured by the term *clinical judgment* or *clinical reasoning*.

An undercurrent throughout this volume is that the clinical dilemmas discussed herein, and the corresponding demands for sound professional judgment and comprehensive clinical reasoning, will be readily recognizable to clinicians of all theoretical orientations to treatment. The substantial trend in the fields of psychology and psychotherapy, which began to escalate over the past decade, has progressed toward greater integration among theoretical approaches and treatment modalities and is likely to continue (e.g., Arkowitz, 1992b; Norcross & Goldfried, 1992; Scaturo, 1994; P. L. Wachtel, 1977, 1991). The notion of *psychotherapy integration* and the transtheoretical concept of clinical dilemmas go hand in hand throughout the everyday lives of psychotherapists who practice from a wide range of clinical perspectives and for whom this volume is intended to provide clinical utility.

Hospitalization of the Suicidal Patient

When dilemmas present themselves clinically, the psychotherapist, like the psychotherapy patient, is susceptible to anxiety—sometimes intensely so. No doubt the degree of anxiety varies according to a number of factors, at least two of which are (a) the importance or criticality of the consequences in a given dilemma and (b) the increased difficulty in making a discrimination between the most favorable and most unfavorable option. When the consequences of a mistake in judgment are severe, and the stakes are high, the anxiety of the clinician is at its peak. There are, perhaps, few judgment calls that produce the feeling of anxiety and agitation in the clinician as that of the suicidal patient. When a seriously suicidal patient presents to the clinician and the question of psychiatric hospitalization is broached, intense consternation fuels clinical thoroughness. Concern for the patient's well-being and the costs of a potential misjudgment both personally and professionally take their toll. If the patient is particularly reluctant to be hospitalized, and especially if the hospitalization will be a first admission for a given patient, then alternatives to admission (e.g., medication consultation, increased frequency of outpatient contacts) are likely to be even more thoroughly considered by the clinician. Hospitalization is approached with such caution, in part, because the well-documented social consequences of psychiatric hospitalization (e.g., stigmatization, feelings of shame) are still very present (e.g., Corrigan, 2005; Goffman, 1961, 1986; Szasz, 1970), even in this new millennium. Furthermore, men often find the experience of a psychiatric hospitalization emasculating. Therefore, the prudent clinician does a thorough review of the risk factors, indices of lethality (e.g., Drowns-Allen, Allen, & Larson, 1980), consultation with colleagues when possible, and the recollection of clinical wisdom offered by almost every preceptor ever given on this topic, in an attempt to ensure proper clinical judgment in this critical situation. If the judgment call is close, and the feeling is that of a coin toss, then the criticality of the situation often lends clarity to the decision. If an error is to be made, the prudent clinician is likely to err on the side of safety, wishing of course, first of all, if possible, to do no harm (e.g., Greenblatt & Levinson, 1967) in accordance with the long-held principle of nonmaleficence in medical ethics (Beauchamp & Childress, 1994). In such a scenario, hospitalization is likely to occur or at least be strongly recommended, although the other factors arguing against hospitalization in a given instance are likely to remain.

Compliance With Reporting Requirements

Another "difficult call" in psychotherapy in a critical situation concerns the sense of divided loyalties that an individual therapist may feel. At stake is the balance between the individual needs of the patient (e.g., preserving the patient's confidentiality) and the therapist's desire and obligation to, for example, protect the welfare of the patient's child in the case of suspected child abuse, by complying with mandated reporting requirements to child protective services (e.g., Keller, 1999).

ATTEMPTS AT TAXONOMY: TECHNICAL VERSUS ETHICAL DILEMMAS

One basic distinction in the array of dilemmas in the practice of psychotherapy is that of courses of clinical action that have predominantly *technical versus ethical* consequences on the treatment process and the patient. Although there is a substantial literature of ethical dilemmas in psychotherapy (Clarkson, 2000), there exist myriad daily decisions in treatment that are essentially matters of psychotherapeutic technique and cannot readily be answered by decision trees, empirically supported therapy manuals, and "best practices" guidelines. And, although consulting such sources is indeed part of what a prudent and competent practitioner does in this process in attempting to resolve technical questions and dilemmas, manualized answers are only variably sufficient.

What distinguishes ethical dilemmas from technical dilemmas? Because the psychotherapeutic relationship and alliance (Safran, 1993) are critical to any method of psychotherapy, a considerable gray area exists between technical and ethical dilemmas in treatment. This may be represented visually by the simple Venn diagram of the relative intersection of technical and ethical dilemmas in Figure 1.1a. Precisely how much of the variance is shared between the technical and ethical struggles of the field differs in perspective from professional to professional. Indeed, there are therapists (e.g., Kaschak, 1999) who reasonably argue that all psychotherapeutic decisions can only exist within a moral framework, as does each and every human relationship.

Technical Dilemmas: Decisions Regarding Psychotherapeutic Technique

The process of clinical reasoning to establish even seemingly minor clinical decisions on a minute-to-minute basis can cause some consternation in the conscientious and reflective clinician but may not necessarily take on the magnitude of ethical overtones or implications. For example, how much confrontation of defenses is needed and tolerable for a given patient in insight-oriented psychotherapy with a given history at a given point in treatment (Scaturo & McPeak, 1998)? An error in judgment on this score may have ethical implications. However, such an error in psychotherapy may not have any more ethical implications than, by analogy, the degree of misjudgement in surgery regarding the needed length of an incision during an operation. Most prudent clinicians would likely regard such daily decisions as more a matter of clinical technique than a matter of neglect or questionable competence or ethics. Thoughtful clinicians, substantial in number, are likely to feel that the degree of shared variance between the technical and the ethical in psychotherapy is predominant, but not a complete one-to-one correspondence. Such thinking is likely to be reflected diagrammatically in the Venn diagram of Figure 1.1b.

In trying to consider what constitutes a chiefly technical dilemma, it may be helpful to consider an example of what might constitute a *technical error* in clinical judgment in the area of "known contraindications" in psychotherapy. The treatment of psychological trauma has formed one of the cornerstones of the mental health professions since their inception. Patients who have experienced severe, emotionally traumatic events, from either natural disasters (e.g., flood victims), technological catastrophes (e.g., auto accident survivors; Blanchard & Hickling, 1997), or traumas of intentional human design (e.g., combat veterans; Scaturo & Hardoby, 1988; Scaturo & Hayman, 1992), are likely to suffer from the intrusive memories of the traumatic event and disruptive symptomatology of posttraumatic stress disorder (PTSD; American Psychiatric Association, 1994). Cognitive–behavioral exposure treatments, which gradually expose patients to their fearful recol-

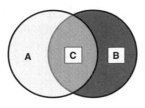 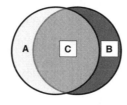 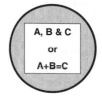

a. *Equi-Proportionate Intersection*   b. *Predominant Intersection*   c. *One-to-One Correspondence*

A = Technical Dilemmas

B = Ethical Dilemmas

C = Their Intersection

Figure 1.1. Technical versus ethical dilemmas in psychotherapy: (a) relatively equiproportionate distribution of technical and ethical dilemmas and their intersection; (b) predominantly shared variance between technical and ethical dilemmas; (c) one-to-one correspondence between technical and ethical dilemmas. From Fundamental Dilemmas in Contemporary Psychotherapy: A Transtheoretical Concept, by D. J. Scaturo, 2002, *American Journal of Psychotherapy, 56*(1), p. 119, copyright 2002 by the Association for the Advancement of Psychotherapy; and Fundamental Dilemmas in Contemporary Psychotherapy: An Overview, by D. J. Scaturo, 2003, *Ethical Issues in Mental Health Counseling, 6*(1), p. 3, copyright 2003 by The Hatherleigh Company. Reprinted with permission.

lections with either imagery or in vivo techniques, have come to be accepted as one of the major, empirically supported treatments for PTSD (Foa, Keane, & Friedman, 2000). However, despite the demonstrated effectiveness of exposure-based treatment, Meichenbaum (1994) has reviewed a long list of contraindications for this otherwise highly recommendable form of treatment. These clinical considerations include a history of impulsivity, suicidality, inability to tolerate intense emotional arousal, and the presence of other comorbid diagnoses (Allen & Bloom, 1994; Litz, Blake, Gerardi, & Keane, 1990). In addition, in some instances, exposure-based treatments have been found to have deleterious effects on patient functioning (Davidson & Baum, 1993; Pitman et al., 1991), including the augmentation of shame and guilt associated with the traumatic event.

It is incumbent on the clinician to have not only a working knowledge of these contraindications but also an ability to assess them accurately in the PTSD patient with considerations given to potential treatment recommendations, particularly if direct exposure therapy is being considered. Overlooking treatment contraindications would minimally constitute a technical error, and more glaring deviations would likely bring forth questions concerning the clinician's competencies. However, a technical dilemma, largely separate from that of an ethical dilemma, would nevertheless exist for the cautious, caring, and prudent clinician, who thoroughly evaluates all known contraindications before providing treatment recommendations and is left with an unclear judgment call. On the horns of this particular dilemma, the choice might be characterized as (a) providing less-than-effective supportive therapy for someone who may potentially benefit from the alternative versus (b) providing a more aggressive exposure-based therapy that has the potential for deleterious effects in a patient with an unclear mix or moderate degree of contraindications (Dryden, 1997).

Such decisions exist universally for practicing clinicians, regardless of theoretical persuasion. Similar contraindications exist, for example, in intensive short-term dynamic psychotherapy (Davanloo, 1978) that utilizes intense confrontation of the patient's defensive structure to facilitate the treatment process. Many contraindications for these approaches, including fragile ego structure, major affective disorders, bipolar disorders, psychosis, borderline disorders, and substance abuse, are among the many diagnostic elements that require a rule-out (Davanloo, 1988).

Ethical Dilemmas: Decisions Regarding the Overall Welfare of the Patient

What then distinguishes an ethical dilemma from a technical dilemma? In effect, what distinguishes a given treatment decision as an ethical dilemma generally involves the question of proper professional conduct concerning the patient's well-being. Are there technical dilemmas that exist apart from an ethical implication? To be sure, the gray area of overlap between them is a substantial one, and the identification of discrete categories is by no means definitive. In addition, there is reasonable concern over the tendency of dilemmas that are fundamentally ethical in nature to masquerade as problems of clinical technique (e.g., boundary management in the therapeutic relationship; Scaturo & McPeak, 1998). There are, however, several general principles that guide decision making and clinical reasoning in the area of professional conduct in health care. The traditional principles of biomedical ethics generally include those of (a) nonmaleficence, (b) beneficence, (c) justice, and (d) patient autonomy.

Nonmaleficence requires that the health care professional not intentionally, or through neglect, create needless harm or injury to the patient. It is that tenet of the physician's Hippocratic Oath that requires that we first, and above all, do no harm to the patient. Meeting requisite clinical competencies is a fundamental necessity in order to be able to hold true to this value. Avoiding potential harm to the patient is considered to be "self-evident," that is, a prima facie duty of the health care professional. *Beneficence,* also a prima facie duty, means that the practitioner's treatment efforts are always intended to be of benefit to the patient. Beneficence is, however, a more limited duty of the clinician in that it is restricted to those people with whom the practitioner has a treatment agreement and a practitioner–patient relationship. Third, *justice* in health care encompasses the notion of fairness in allocating valuable medical resources among the various members of a society, which has increasingly become an issue within a managed health care system. Finally, the *autonomy* of the patient to make health care decisions in a fully informed and genuinely voluntary manner is an operative value throughout. It presupposes that the patient has the capacity to understand the decisions that are to be made and, therefore, becomes the basis for the process of informed consent for proposed treatment interventions.

Against this backdrop of ethical principles in health care, the more specific types of dilemmas that fall into the category of ethical conflict for psychotherapists are several. Survey research studies in both the United States (Pope & Vetter, 1992) and the United Kingdom (Lindsay & Clarkson, 1999) among psychologists found common localized areas of ethical concern. In order of most frequently identified were the following categories of concern for professional ethical dilemmas: confidentiality, dual relationships, colleagues' conduct, sexual issues, academic/training issues, and professional competence.

The largest category of ethical concerns surrounded events that might require the suspension of the time-held obligation of confidentiality of the patient. Such instances involve the possible risk to third parties (i.e., reporting child or sexual abuse), risk to the patient (i.e., suicidality), disclosure of information to other third parties even with written consent of the patient (e.g., to the patient's significant others, as well as other health care providers and insurance agencies), and the possibility of careless or inappropriate disclosures without written consent.

A second area of concern consisted of the possibility of dual relationships with a patient, excluding those involving sexual behavior. These include other types of social relationships with patients (e.g., providing treatment for colleagues and their families) or working with two separate patients who have a relationship with one another (e.g., a patient who refers his or her coworker). Third, a significant number of ethically troubling events concerned the professional conduct of their colleagues, including concerns over the professional competence of a colleague, unprofessional comments by colleagues, professional conflicts regarding referrals, and inappropriate disclosure of clinical information. Fourth, there arose a considerable number of issues surrounding the sexual relationship between a psychotherapist and a patient; these included (a) the mere existence of a sexual relationship with a patient, (b) the time of onset of the relationship (i.e., during or after treatment), (c) who initiated the relationship, (d) the vulnerability of the patient, and (e) sexual relationships between supervisors and trainees. Fifth, a number of ethical dilemmas surrounded academic training that involved the supervision of trainees whom they consider either unready or unsuitable to practice for any of a number of reasons. Finally, there were general questions about competence of self and others at the outset of one's career in dealing with cases of exceeding complexity, as well as questions concerning impaired providers (e.g., knowledge of a colleague's alcohol problem).

Clinical Dilemmas Identified by Master Psychotherapists

Another approach that has been taken to identify the salient dilemmas, both technical and ethical, in psychotherapy has been to consult an array of master therapists regarding the dilemmas that they have experienced in their own clinical practices. Dryden (1997) conducted 14 interviews with different psychotherapists in the United Kingdom and the United States. The 14 dilemmas discussed were classified into six overlapping categories, or themes, with some discussions being relevant to more than one category.

Compromise dilemmas involved the therapist's struggles between the ideal and the pragmatic in psychotherapy, such as accepting more limited and traditional therapeutic goals for a patient versus striving for more radical (but perhaps riskier) goals. Another category consisted of *boundary dilemmas* in which the therapist is confronted by a choice as to whether he or she should cross the boundaries of a given technical framework, such as how much the therapist should reveal about him- or herself. Third, there were *dilemmas of allegiance* in which a therapist may struggle to maintain a certain allegiance to a particular school of thought versus branching out into new avenues of therapeutic intervention and the potential loss of support that one receives from one's primary collegial reference group. The fourth grouping was that of *role dilemmas* such as the conflict between educator and healer or scientist and practitioner. The fifth theme concerned *dilemmas of responsibility* in which the psychotherapist struggles between accepting a certain degree of responsibility for a given patient's welfare and respecting the patient's autonomy for his or her own life choices, given the varying degrees of functionality exhibited by different patients. Finally, there was the class of *impasse dilemmas* in which the therapist confronts varying avenues of response when a certain course of treatment has become intractable or reaches a limited plateau.

P. L. Wachtel (1997) exemplified the impasse dilemma associated with what he termed the *nonimproving patient*. He aptly noted that no psychotherapist is universally effective. Yet, there are many patients who seem to form an important bond with their psychotherapist, despite a prolonged absence of symptomatological improvement. In a fee-for-service model, Wachtel talked of the ethical misgivings that the therapist has in such a circumstance about the patient paying for services in which he or she appears to derive no symptomatic benefit. However, he noted great concern about the patient experiencing serious relational rejection by even addressing this topic in treatment. This situation may be further complicated by managed health care. Frequently, it may be expected that third-party reimbursement for treatment will be terminated for lack of symptom improvement, despite the patient's potential sense of rejection and any emotional harm that may result from that scenario. Often, behavior change is the patient's "calling card" for treatment, although some sense of self-acceptance for one's life in the absence of any behavioral alterations may well be what many patients are seeking. Admittedly, in many cases of dysthymia, for example, one might reasonably expect some abatement of depression when self-acceptance is enhanced, but not in all cases. Is there a place for palliative psychological care for chronic depression in the current health care lexicon? This may be less of a dilemma in circumstances in which the patient's condition is, in fact, worsening despite the best effort of a given clinician (P. L. Wachtel, 1997). In such instances, it may be very clear to both the patient and the therapist that a referral to another clinician or another form of treatment is indicated and is, thereby, experienced as less rejecting to the patient. Unfortunately, however, much like Pavlov's (1927) experiments in which it is increasingly difficult to discriminate between the circle and the ellipse, cases in the gray area of intractable, but nonworsening depression frequently exist. It is clear that grappling with clinical dilemmas is not designed for clinicians who may be seeking an array of manualized answers to what are invariably exceedingly complex questions (Dryden, 1997). The examination of psychotherapeutic dilemmas remains an area in which the concept of clinical wisdom continues to have relevance (Karasu, 1992; Scaturo & McPeak, 1998).

Dilemmas Relevant to Circumscribed Areas of Psychotherapy

Another method of attempting to circumscribe the broad array of dilemmas that occur in the process of psychotherapy has been to delimit a given discussion to a specifically defined subarea of psychotherapy. A sampling of four such circumscribed areas of psychotherapy would include the dilemmas that clinicians have encountered in (a) brief therapy, (b) managed behavioral health care, (c) sexual issues in treatment, and (d) feminist therapy.

Dilemmas of Brief Therapy

The fundamental question for brief psychotherapy is "whether it can be more than shallow?" (Gustafson, 1995, p. vii). The main task of brief psychotherapy is to select a focus for the episode in which the patient has sought treatment and adhere to it (Gustafson, 1995; Ryle, 1979; Schacht, Binder, & Strupp, 1984). Whether this involves a focus on target behaviors for change as in classical behavior therapy, centering attention on the modification of the patient's thought processes and maladaptive self-statements as in cognitive–behavioral therapy (e.g., Meichenbaum, 1977; Meichenbaum & Cameron, 1974), a psychodynamic focus as in time-limited psychodynamic psychotherapy (e.g., Scaturo, 2002c; Schacht et al., 1984), or the central relationship dynamic in brief marital and family therapy (e.g., Budman & Gurman,

1988; Scaturo, 2002a), the clinical focus of psychotherapy necessarily favors one area of exploration and change while neglecting others.

In considering this dilemma, Gustafson (1995) provided the useful analogy of acute versus peripheral vision. The acute vision from the fovea of the retina is excellent in the singular task of providing detailed focus but dangerous in the broader task of living unless balanced by the qualities of peripheral vision. Although it is essential for the psychotherapist to explore what the patient is consciously seeking in any given hour of treatment, it is also the responsibility of the therapist to consider what the patient may have omitted unconsciously in his or her narrative that may pose a contributing factor to expressly verbalized concerns. Even interpersonal therapists like Harry Stack Sullivan, who maintained less of an emphasis on unconscious processes, believed that the patient always leaves out the most important part of his or her story (Gustafson, 1995).

The ability to grapple with and identify possible unconscious and related factors in interpersonal difficulties are partly why the mental health consumer seeks out a professionally trained psychotherapist instead of accepting "good advice" from friends. It is incumbent, therefore, on the psychotherapist—even the brief psychotherapist—to have the capability of conceptualizing the patient's problems broadly, even though he or she may choose to intervene in a more focused manner in a given phase of treatment. Generally, such broad case conceptualization involves the ability to view the case material from a behavioral/symptomatic level of understanding, an intrapsychic/psychodynamic level of abstraction, and a multigenerational family systems perspective (Scaturo, 2001).

Dilemmas of Managed Health Care

Another broad subarea of rapidly emerging dilemmas in contemporary psychotherapeutic treatment, in part related to and extending the previously noted dilemmas of brief therapy, is the advent of managed health care. Managed care has affected the practice of medicine and its impact on traditional medical ethics (LaPuma, 1998), as well as the practice of psychological and behavioral health care (Sperry & Prosen, 1998). Prior to the age of managed behavioral health care in which constraints on clinicians impelled them to work within increasingly shorter time limits, the vast majority of clinicians were aware of their ethical obligation to alleviate patient suffering in a time-efficient manner. This concern, however, was always counterbalanced by the concern about thoroughness in treatment (i.e., Gustafson's admonishment for the clinician not to overlook what the patients themselves may do unconsciously) and the concern with the substance and durability of the changes made in therapy. Whether the duration of treatment is conceptualized as 2 weeks, 2 months, or 2 years, clinicians know that it is incumbent on them to work to eventually make themselves increasingly obsolete in the patient's life. In the age of the fee-for-service model, the responsible clinician was always aware that extending the duration of treatment for the purposes of his or her own financial gain was a clear infraction of his or her ethical duty. In the age of managed health care, where the conservation of health care resources is primarily concerned with shortening and imposing limits for reasons other than the alleviation of the patient's suffering, it now becomes the clinician's ethical obligation to make certain that limiting treatment does not sacrifice the thoroughness of care for the purposes of the managed care company's financial gain.

Sperry and Prosen (1998) provided a number of examples of newly emerging ethical dilemmas surrounding psychotherapy and managed mental health care. These include managed care's pervasive use of serotonin reuptake inhibitor (SSRI) antidepressant medications because of the reduced cost of such treatment in comparison with even brief courses of psychotherapy with limited regard for the patient's treatment preferences. Paradoxically, they noted that the use of SSRI medications is also being encouraged for subclinical or normal variant mood conditions in a practice that they have termed *cosmetic psychopharmacology*. In addition, they noted concerns over breaches of confidentiality to supply patient information to managed care's administrative personnel, and the potentially damaging effects on the therapeutic alliance. Finally, they also cited concerns about limitations of treatment to patients with serious chronic conditions, and the clinicians' concerns over not abandoning such patients. These dilemmas constitute severe challenges to the time-honored values of many clinicians.

Dilemmas Involving Sexual Emotions in Psychotherapy

If the anxiety surrounding psychotherapeutic dilemmas were exclusively limited to the difficulty in discriminating a course of action in a close judgment call, then the question of sexual intimacy with patients (Pope, Lief, & Bouhoutsos, 1986) could not be considered a dilemma by this criterion. The ethical guidelines in all of the psychological helping professions (psychiatry, psychology, social work, and marriage and family therapy) are quite clear on this point: Dual relationships (i.e., the intimately personal and the professional) are never acceptable in practice and always compromise treatment in some fashion and to some degree. So, the notion of a viable sexual relationship is never a question of a judgment call and is never an option for the helping profession. No doubt, the same standard must hold true for other professional relationships as well, including academia and the teaching profession, the medical profession, the clergy, and the legal profession. Is this, however, the end of the discussion of this topic as a dilemma? From a behavioral standpoint (i.e., professional conduct) certainly, but the topic of sexual feelings in psychotherapy (Pope, Sonne, & Holroyd, 1993) is a broad topic worthy of extensive discussion and beyond the scope of this overview. Although it is incumbent on psychotherapists to behave in a manner that observes and respects appropriate professional boundaries consistently, it would be a mistake to conclude that the dictates of one's professional guidelines cease to make this a dilemma for people working in this complex human endeavor.

To the contrary, most authorities that work in this area of study feel that "a repressive, punitive attitude toward normal personal feelings" (Edelwich & Brodsky, 1991, p. xv) is nothing less than disastrous for the practicing clinician. For preceptors in our clinical training programs to behave as if the discussion of interpersonal attraction in the therapist–patient relationship is necessarily dangerous and countertherapeutic and is, therefore, to be shunned does a grave disservice to our trainees and future practitioners (Pope et al., 1993). In such instances, our interns, residents, and trainees are likely to feel a lack of preparedness to conduct competent, let alone sophisticated, clinical work. A serious danger is to accept confusing transferential and countertransferential emotional dilemmas to remain unexamined for the clinician (Edelwich & Brodsky, 1991). Transferentially, these reactions then remain unavailable as important clinical data for effective psychotherapeutic intervention. Far worse, countertransferentially, such unaddressed emotions in the clinician carry the risk of being deleteriously acted out in treatment rather than being talked out and sorted out in the context of consultation and supervision.

Dilemmas in Feminist Therapy

One of the many contributions of clinicians and authors who practice psychotherapy from the standpoint of a feminist perspective (Feminist Therapy Institute, Inc., 1990) has been the prompting that psychotherapy is not a value-free profession. Kaschak (1999, p. 1) wrote the following: "No human relationship can exist outside a moral framework. . . . The psychotherapeutic relationship is no exception. Psychotherapy is as much a morality play as it is art or science." In its extreme form, this approach is an uncompromising systems theoretical perspective that believes that "context is everywhere" (Clarkson, 2000, p. 27). Ethicists remind us that ethicality permeates all human relationships, therapeutic and otherwise. Further, an increasing number of clinicians have argued that psychotherapists must take a more proactive stance in promoting moral responsibility among their patients and families in treatment (Doherty, 1995). These therapists are likely to view the intersection of technical and ethical dilemmas as a one-to-one correspondence that looks more like the Venn diagram shown in Figure 1.1c than the more proportionate diagrams depicted earlier in either Figure 1.1a or 1.1b.

Accordingly, psychotherapy is viewed as not only a cluster of behavior change techniques (e.g., cognitive restructuring or resolution of inner conflict) for behavior change and symptom relief but also an opportunity to live a more fulfilling life (Kaschak, 1999). In this broader perspective, the feminist principle of personal *empowerment* (Kaschak, 1999), viewed within a systemic context, is central to the practice of psychotherapy. In this regard, however, the concept of *justice* (Kaschak, 1999) among all of the participants of either an institutional or a family system is a critical component of the mental health and well-being of the patient in feminist therapy. Historically, family therapists were among the first to address this fundamental dilemma of human existence of what one owes to oneself versus others (e.g. Bowen, 1978; Bowlby, 1969; Framo, 1976), representing the need for independence and autonomy, on the one hand, and the need for attachment and affiliation, on the other. This worldview is also consistent with the integrative therapist's belief that "only in concert with others can we achieve the conditions for harmony within" (P. L. Wachtel, 1981, p. 15).

Included in this broadened context is consideration for the substance and personhood of the clinician as well as the patient. Carroll, Gilroy, and Murra (1999) discussed what they regarded as the moral imperative of the self-care of women psychotherapists. These authors echo concerns voiced earlier by Keith, Scaturo, Marron, and Baird (1993) from a family systems perspective that the self-care of all health care professionals, regardless of gender, is a critical prerequisite for adequate patient care. This notion can be somewhat "anticultural" to the espoused values of traditional medical education in which, quite understandably, "the patient comes first" (Keith et al., 1993). In the case of the impaired or beleaguered professional, however, these authors question whether this should always be so. Perhaps, making self-care for the professional a priority is putting the patient first. What emerges, then, from this feminist and systemic dialogue is the observation that our "rule books" and professional codes of ethics, although critically important, are not able to address all of the complex "uncodified decisions" that confront the clinician on a daily basis (Kaschak & Hill, 1999). Accordingly, the invisible decision-making processes of the psychotherapist become increasingly visible when the choices that confront the clinician are not readily classifiable into the expectable categories of our codebooks (Kaschak, 1999).

Technical Dilemmas Fundamental to the Psychotherapeutic Process

Scaturo and McPeak (1998) have articulated a number of clinical dilemmas that are fundamental to the processes of psychotherapy. These dilemmas are endemic to various interventions of psychological treatment (e.g., cognitive–behavioral therapy, family therapy) and various tasks of psychological practice (e.g., psychological assessments) by virtue of the foci that these various areas of practice encompass. For example, when conducting cognitive–behavioral therapy, psychotherapists may find themselves in some degree of dilemma in the assignment of behavioral homework and the directives that tend to be an integral part of such treatment. As many patients experience such directive treatment as confrontation, and thereby a withdrawal of the psychotherapist's support, the timing and magnitude of such assignments must be carefully judged by the therapist so as to not disrupt what may be at times a fragile therapeutic alliance (Safran, 1993). Such clinical reasoning and judgment become increasingly central to the conduct of psychotherapy, particularly with the trend and influx of manualized (i.e., empirically supported) treatments (Scaturo, 2001).

Family therapy, for example, has many problems that are unique to the expansion of the treatment system to include the marital couple or other family members (Scaturo & McPeak, 1998). E. F. Wachtel (1979) noted that these difficulties pose various dilemmas to the individually trained psychotherapist attempting to adapt his or her treatment approach to a family systems perspective. Most prominent among these dilemmas tends to be the question of "blame" for the presenting problems (Scaturo & McPeak, 1998). In individual psychotherapy, poor child-rearing practices (i.e., parents) have tended to be blamed for any dysfunctional behavior and emotional problems in the identified patient. In family systems treatment, by contrast, the responsibility for any given form of behavioral dysfunction does not reside exclusively with any one individual (i.e., either parents or spouse or identified patient) but rather with the complex interplay of interactions among the parties concerned. This reduces the tendency to blame (including excessive self-blame) and, thereby, paves the way for better interpersonal connectedness among significant others. Such a perspective, however, requires a more complex view of reality and relationships for both the psychotherapist and the patient.

As a final example, the process of psychological assessment can entail its own array of dilemmas for the clinician. One example involves the question of non-treatment-oriented psychological assessments. When an evaluation is done for the purposes of treatment, then, at least, the presumption of an intention to help the patient exists. In non-treatment-oriented assessments, no such presumption exists. To clarify, it becomes important to ask the question, "Who is the customer (i.e., the person or institution) paying for the evaluation?" in the current health care lexicon. When the answer to this question involves someone other than the patient, then there is the accompanying question, "For whose good is the evaluation being done—the patient or the institution?" (Scaturo & McPeak, 1998). Many such clinical scenarios exist; these may include child custody evaluations (Gardner, 1986), determinations of sanity for legal purposes, alcohol assessments for DWIs, and psychosocial evaluations for medical procedures. In such instances, the patient may rightfully question whether the results of the examination are intended for his or her benefit. In each instance, it is critical that the clinician be able to adequately articulate the dilemma from multiple perspectives, which include that of the patient or examinee, the particular institution involved, as well as the examiner.

CONCLUDING REMARKS:
THE TRANSTHEORETICAL NATURE OF CLINICAL DILEMMAS

The concept of clinical dilemmas in psychotherapy has been difficult to conceptualize because of their nondiscrete quality. The varieties and range of clinical dilemmas in psychotherapy challenge attempts at taxonomy and categorization. In part, because of the inseparable and inherently interpersonal character of psychotherapeutic treatment, clinical dilemmas are ever present within the psychotherapeutic context, regardless of the type of therapy or theoretical framework being used or the availability of a therapy manual for consultation.

The concept of the psychotherapeutic dilemma can be best seen as a transtheoretical experience (Prochaska & DiClemente, 1984). A transtheoretical approach is one that attempts to go beyond eclecticism in an attempt to form a higher order theory of psychotherapeutic processes that cuts across or transcends the major theoretical schools of treatment (Prochaska, 1979). In this way, Prochaska and DiClemente's (1992b) concept shares a similar theoretical goal with Wachtel's notion of integrative psychotherapy and cyclical psychodynamics (P. L. Wachtel & McKinney, 1992). The transtheoretical conceptualization has been most often associated with the concept of *stages of change* (Prochaska & DiClemente, 1992a), that is, the psychotherapy patient's readiness for change at any given point in time. The stages of the psychotherapy patient's preparedness for change involve precontemplative, contemplative, taking action, and maintenance of change. The notion of change-related readiness is essentially within the province of the patient, regardless of what form or orientation of therapy he or she seeks out. The concept transcends the various theoretical approaches to treatment, necessarily intersects with them all, and has broad applicability.

Other theorists have also postulated concepts that have transtheoretical relevance as well. When Bandura (1977a) first advanced the notion of *self-efficacy* in treatment, he viewed this as a potentially unifying concept in behavior change processes. He hypothesized that psychological treatment procedures (i.e., psychotherapy), "*whatever their form*" (Bandura, 1977a, p.191; italics added), that is, whatever their theoretical foundations, affect the level of the patient's self-efficacy (i.e., perceived control or mastery) in a given problem situation, to the extent that those methods are effective in bringing about behavior change. Thus, it may also be suggested that Bandura (1977a, 1997) was advancing a concept that was not only transtheoretical in nature but also transmethodological and transtechnical. Furthermore, it is a testament to the transtheoretical aspects of this concept that parallel notions appear in other writings on psychotherapeutic treatment. One such concept includes Seligman's (1990) notion of *learned optimism* that has been predicated on his classic and well-documented empirical research of its opposite concept, *learned helplessness*, and its role in the development of depressive disorders. Likewise, the transtheoretical nature of Bandura's self-efficacy in all forms of psychotherapy is corroborated by the feminist therapist's view of *empowerment* (Kaschak, 1999) in treatment noted earlier.

Similarly, the transtheoretical phenomenon of *therapeutic alliance ruptures* or breaches, that is, negative shifts in the quality of the therapeutic alliance or its establishment, also has applicability to psychotherapists from diverse theoretical orientations (Safran & Greenberg, 1993). Regardless of theoretical framework, a pattern of negative patient–therapist complementarity has been associated with treatment failures (e.g., Henry, Schacht, & Strupp, 1990). Different therapeutic approaches and the specific techniques that emanate from them, each, for different reasons, place the patient–therapist alliance at risk for rupture (Scaturo, 2003b).

In sum, like the concepts of stages of change, self-efficacy, or the therapeutic alliance rupture, the perspective advanced presently is that the notion of the clinical dilemma in psychotherapy, whether predominantly technical or ethical or admixture, transcends the particular mode of therapy being used by the clinician (Scaturo, 2002b). Psychotherapists, regardless of their particular theoretical persuasions, frequently find themselves grappling with similar judgment calls in the treatment of a given patient or family (Scaturo, 2001). The comprehension of this complex notion, in both its technical and ethical realms, likely differentiates the professional psychotherapist from the behavioral technician and may ultimately lead to the patient's improvement and betterment.

A COGNITIVE MAP OF THE BOOK

As is apparent from the foregoing discussion, there have been a number of attempts to classify the various dilemmas that psychotherapists experience during the course of their clinical day. These include the dichotomy between ethical and technical dilemmas, those dilemmas identified by master psychotherapists, dilemmas relevant to various circumscribed areas of psychotherapy, and technical dilemmas fundamental to the process of psychotherapy. All of these approaches have validity, although none seem to dominate the field. As a result, the approach taken in this book is to outline the major dilemmas that have been encountered in the field as various schools of psychotherapy have evolved as attempts to grapple with the complexity experienced in the clinical context over the past century of treatment.

The book is divided into four parts. Part I provides an overview of clinical dilemmas and of the major schools of theoretical thought—psychoanalysis, cognitive–behavioral and social learning theory, interpersonal and family systems theory, and humanistic psychology—and the dilemmas that have emerged as they each have confronted their respective limitations in addressing the complexity of human experience (chap. 2).

Part II discusses the dilemmas involved in five treatment modalities that have emerged from those theoretical approaches and the dilemmas that are particular to those forms of treatment (chaps. 3 through 7). A focus on how clinical dilemmas play out in the treatment modalities that have evolved from psychodynamic and insight-oriented approaches, through the behavioral and cognitive–behavioral treatments, to those involving more that just the individual patient (i.e., couple and family therapy, group therapy) is a logical extension of the theoretical conceptualizations of human psychological functioning and psychopathology from which they have emerged as discussed in Part I. In some instances, dilemmas that might initially appear to be exclusive to a particular approach often, on further examination, share the same struggle, but in different forms or terminology. For example, the psychodynamic psychotherapist's classic dilemma of confrontation versus support of the patient's defensive structure tends to entail the same risks to the therapeutic alliance faced by the behavior therapist in balancing the directive (i.e., behavioral homework assignments) and nondirective (e.g., empathic listening) aspects of treatment.

Part III describes a number of clinical dilemmas that emerge from the inherently interpersonal process that is at the heart of psychotherapy. These include unconscious processes in interpersonal behavior such as transference, countertransference, and resistances (chap. 8), as well as dilemmas involving where precisely to draw the professional boundary while still therapeutically engaging with the patient (chap. 9). These are common to all treatment approaches, regardless of specific differences in theoretical underpinnings, as the recent literature's recognition of countertransference in cognitive–behavioral therapy would attest.

Finally, Part IV concludes by proposing a three-phase learning-based theoretical model for integrative psychotherapy that incorporates a consideration of the therapeutic alliance and technical interventions in treatment that result in a relearning of more adaptive interpersonal behaviors in the patient's life space (chap. 10). In addition, an illustration of the management of various dilemmas in actual integrative practice is provided in the treatment of panic disorders with agoraphobia (chap. 11). Chapter 12 concludes the book with a discussion of the pervasiveness of dilemmas and dialecticism, as well as the importance of integration and synthesis, throughout the history of psychology, psychotherapy, and life itself.

2

THE EVOLUTION OF PSYCHOTHERAPY: THE DILEMMA OF INTEGRATION VERSUS MANUALIZATION

Isaac Disraeli, the 19th-century literary scholar and father of one of Great Britain's most eminent prime ministers, Benjamin Disraeli, was fond of quoting the old Latin proverb, "*Cave ab homine unius libri.*" In its translated form, Disraeli (1861) was admonishing his contemporaries to "Be cautious of the man of one book!" Likewise, the mental health consumer in the new millennium would do well to heed a modified version of Disraeli's admonishment: "Be cautious of the psychotherapist of one manual!"

In recent years, there has been a movement toward what has been termed the *manualization* (e.g., Garfield, 1992b) or the "textbook practice" (Scaturo & McPeak, 1998) of psychotherapy, and, in a somewhat less flattering light, a "cookbook" or "paint-by-numbers" approach to treatment (Silverman, 1996). The development of treatment manuals has emerged from a number

This chapter is an adaptation of "The Evolution of Psychotherapy and the Concept of Manualization: An Integrative Perspective," by D. J. Scaturo, 2001, *Professional Psychology: Research and Practice, 32,* 522–530. Copyright 2001 by the American Psychological Association.

of multistudy projects on psychotherapy from various academic research centers across the United States. Excellent examples include the behaviorally oriented work on anxiety disorders (e.g., Craske, Barlow, & Meadows, 2000) from Barlow's (1992) Anxiety Research Clinic, time-limited psychodynamically oriented psychotherapy (e.g., Strupp & Binder, 1984) from the Vanderbilt Center for Psychotherapy Research (Henry & Strupp, 1992), and interpersonally oriented psychotherapy (e.g., Klerman, Weissman, Rounsaville, & Chevron, 1984) from the New Haven–Boston Collaborative Depression Research Project. Therapy manuals differ not only in theoretical orientation but also in the degree of specificity and step-by-step, session-by-session procedural guidelines.

However, the multiplicity of clinical dilemmas replete in the complex practice of psychotherapy (e.g., Dryden, 1997; Scaturo & McPeak, 1998) is a reflection of the numerous situations encountered in this discipline in which there is a considerable amount of ambiguity. It is often difficult to select the best course of action among a range of clinically appropriate alternatives. A first step in any field dealing with human situations governed by ambiguous stimuli, which was incumbent on the early pioneers in the field of psychotherapy, is to construct a set of decision rules, in this case, clinical methods and techniques that serve to add structure to contexts that might be previously regarded as low in structure or without structure. This was particularly true with Freud's task in determining what was curative about a "talking cure" that had not yet been previously established or studied. Subsequent schools of psychotherapy also have been attempts to provide structure and decision rules predicated on various assumptions about what constitutes psychopathology and its treatment.

In this chapter, some historical perspectives on psychotherapy are examined that may help psychologists and psychotherapists who have been reading more about manualized treatments to make decisions about how to incorporate such information into their clinical practices. Even before the "age of manualization" and its attendant specificity, each of the major schools of psychotherapy suffered from the same limitations of being unable to be thoroughly exhaustive about each and every clinical circumstance, to the extent that the interpersonal sphere surrounding complex human problems is not subject to universal rules governing behavior. Historically, most clinicians, regardless of their particular theoretical orientation, have experienced the constraints of existing guidelines and standards of practice for certain patients. This chapter examines three of the major schools of psychotherapy—psychodynamic psychotherapy, cognitive–behavioral therapy, and family therapy—and the limitations that clinicians working within each theoretical framework have encountered in light of the recent trend toward treatment manualization. Perspectives on the role of manualized therapies in clinical practice, the role of nonspecific factors associated with the therapeutic alliance, and the respective roles of professionalism versus behavioral technology are discussed. In particular, the fundamental clinical dilemma of whether the manualization constitutes an asset or a liability to the professional practice of psychotherapy in general, and to psychotherapy integration in particular, is considered.

PSYCHOANALYTIC AND PSYCHODYNAMIC PSYCHOTHERAPY: THE THERAPEUTIC FRAME

If there were a Book of Genesis in the field of psychotherapy, it would probably start out something like this: "In the beginning, there was psychoanalysis, and it was without form and void." Freud had the formidable task of creating something from nothing and of structuring the structureless. He was endeavoring to determine what were the curative elements of the psychoanalytic method. Various *ground rules*, such as structuring the frequency and duration of sessions, confidentiality, patient–therapist boundaries, and technical neutrality, as well as various *interventions*, such as confrontation, support, interpretations, and silence in psychoanalytic technique, emerged over time predicated on psychoanalytic experience (e.g., Auld & Hyman, 1991; Langs, 1973). The resulting technique evolved into a more rigid form of therapeutic guidelines than Freud himself had ever intended (P. L. Wachtel, 1993). Often, there has been an overconcern by many psychoanalytically oriented clinicians about the "purity" of psychoanalytic technique to the exclusion of those parameters that make psychotherapy a uniquely human endeavor (Auld & Hyman, 1991).

The methods actually used by Freud in 43 of his psychoanalytic cases conducted in the mature years of his practice have been examined (Lynn & Vaillant, 1998). The results of this study showed that Freud's actual psychotherapeutic methods deviated from his own published recommendations in at least three vital areas of clinical practice. First, Freud (1912/1958c, 1913/1958b, 1926/1959b, 1940/1964b) recommended *anonymity* of the therapist such that the analyst not reveal his or her own emotional reactions to the material presented by the patient, and he viewed therapy with any prior acquaintance with the patient, or the patient's significant others, as problematic. Freud deviated from this tenet about treatment in all of the 43 cases reviewed. He frequently discussed his own attitudes and opinions on various matters, his own anxieties about issues in his family life, and his feelings about his analysands. Second, Freud (1912/1958c, 1917/1963, 1937/1964a, 1940/1964b) recommended *technical neutrality* for the analyst, such that he or she does not give the patient directions concerning the life choices confronting the patient and does not assume the role of educator for the patient. In actuality, directives, opinions, and self-reflections were present in 86% of the cases examined. Third, Freud (1913/1958b, 1917/1964a, 1940/1964b) recommended that the psychoanalyst technically and ethically maintain the *confidentiality* of the patient. Here, Freud broke confidentiality to people known to the analysands in 53% of the cases studied, and this figure did not include discussions with referral sources and consultants (Lynn & Vaillant, 1998). Further, Freud maintained significant extra-analytic social and professional relationships with his analysands in 72% of these cases.

Lynn and Vaillant (1998) aptly concluded that Freud's prescribed technique was not the technique that was tested in his practice. Thus, it is not possible then to conclude that rigidly following Freud's recommendations regarding psychoanalytic technique will be the operative elements in duplicating his successes. It is also not clear whether the variations from his subsequent recommendations contributed to any degree of failure in his cases. Nevertheless, these findings should not imply that Freud's above-noted recommendations are not good general guidelines for clinical practice. They do, however, imply that a certain degree of flexibility regarding these may be indicated guidelines (e.g., F. Alexander & French, 1946), especially with variations in technique that do not entail ethical considerations.

Psychoanalysts (e.g., Eissler, 1953) have used the word *parameters* to refer to clinically appropriate departures from classical psychoanalytic techniques. Some analysts (e.g., Langs, 1973) have considered all noninterpretive interventions to be relegated to the status of parameters (Auld & Hyman, 1991, p. 184), as opposed to "curative" methods of intervention (i.e., active ingredients of change). Much of what were regarded merely as parameters in Freud's treatment methods may have constituted active ingredients in promoting cure among his successes. It may have been Freud's own clinical intuition that resulted in the necessity to strain against the limitations of his theory and methods.

Yalom's (1980, p. 4) analysis of Freud's treatment of Elizabeth Von R. provides an instructive illustration of such parameters in psychoanalytic care that are not simply incidental to the patient's cure but possibly instrumental in bringing about curative results. Elisabeth was a young woman who presented to Freud with psychogenic problems in walking, and for whom Freud's sole explanation for her improvement was based on an abreactive process, that is, the derepressing of Elizabeth's unacceptable thoughts and wishes. However, in a review of Freud's notes, Yalom (1980) found a wide range of clinical activities, or parameters, undertaken by Freud that obviously were intended to address several social and interpersonal problem difficulties in Elizabeth's life.

Among these clinical maneuvers during Elizabeth's course in treatment, Freud first suggested behavioral homework assignments that included Elizabeth visiting her sister's grave and calling on a gentleman whom she found attractive (if one can envision Freud as a *behavior therapist*). Second, Freud reportedly interceded with the patient's family on her behalf, asking her mother to allow her daughter to speak more freely of her concerns at home (if one can see Freud as a *family therapist*). Third, Freud assisted the patient's family in overcoming their financial entanglement (if one can imagine Freud as a *social caseworker*). Finally, after Elizabeth's completion of treatment, Freud learned that she would be going to a private party. Accordingly, he obtained an invitation for himself so that he could observe that this young woman with a history of psychogenic difficulties in walking engage in a lively dance, thereby sacrificing anonymity for the curative powers of *transference* (and perhaps *countertransference*). Yalom (1980) could not help but wonder if Freud's parameters do not, in fact, constitute important clinical interventions, and excluding them from the "treatment package" is to "court error." The mindful and prudent clinician cannot help but agree.

THE LIMITATIONS OF PSYCHOANALYSIS: COMMON CRITICISMS

The Brief Therapist's Critique

The uncertainty about what was, in fact, curative in the psychoanalytic method and its accompanying length and cost brought forth attempts to improve on the method. Even before the advent of behavior therapy in the 1950s, psychotherapists within the psychoanalytic community itself were greatly concerned that psychoanalysis, as a treatment modality, was not "time-sensitive." F. Alexander and French (1946) were interested in finding shortcuts to the psychoanalytic method. Rather than Freud's focus on the abreaction of negative affect, they felt that a "corrective emotional experience" with the analyst provided the primary curative ingredient, thus highlighting the importance of the therapeutic relationship in the acceleration of treatment. These concerns represent the critique of the *brief therapist* across a range of brief therapy orientations (e.g., Budman & Gurman, 1988).

The Interpersonal and Family Therapist's Critique

Sullivan (1938, 1953) believed that all of psychopathology is best characterized by the recurrent forms of interaction that an individual has with significant others in his or her interpersonal environment rather than Freud's focus on the intrapsychic processes. This perspective had been further advanced by Yalom's (1995) work in the area of group psychotherapy, Klerman et al.'s (1984) work in interpersonal psychotherapy, and the early family therapists (e.g., Ackerman, 1958). It is the overemphasis of psychoanalysis on intrapsychic processes, to the neglect of the interpersonal sphere, which is the criticism of the interpersonal and family therapist alike.

Family therapists have strongly held that psychotherapy does not occur in an interpersonal vacuum, and that the members of the identified patient's primary social group are significantly affected by the patient's professional relationship with the therapist. Survey studies (e.g., Brody & Farber, 1989; Hatcher & Hatcher, 1983) of spouses, partners, and parents of patients who were receiving individual psychotherapy have shown that this treatment modality can, at times, have iatrogenic effects on the patient's significant others. It was found that these people were often affected by feelings of exclusion from the therapy, resentment over the intrusion of time and cost of the therapy, a feeling of being "talked about" in the therapy, feelings of inadequacy in their relationship with the patient, and a sense of "being blamed" for the patient's problems. This is nowhere more apparent than when a child is receiving individual psychotherapy without ongoing family consultation, and parents are left with their own worries about the quality of their parenting (E. F. Wachtel, 1992). Thus, whether or not they are physically present in the consulting room, the index patient's family is an integral part of what has been recognized as the *therapeutic triangle* (Doherty & Baird, 1983) in health care and psychotherapy that is discussed at greater length in chapter 9. In essence, the simplistic notion of the *dyadic* doctor–patient relationship has become increasingly regarded as a fallacy, in favor of the more accurate notion of the *triadic* doctor–patient–family relationship.

The Humanistic Psychotherapist's Critique

In Rogers's (1942, 1951) *client-centered* or *nondirective therapy* the therapist's stances of empathy, positive regard, and genuineness toward the patient were seen as the therapeutic conditions for change (Meador & Rogers, 1979). Client-centered therapy differed in this manner from the directive stances of several other approaches, including psychoanalytic interpretations, behavioral prescriptions for change, and problem-solving family therapy (e.g., J. Haley, 1976). Nevertheless, the therapeutic stance of interpersonal engagement by the client-centered therapist is also in marked contrast to the passivity or remoteness taken in the psychoanalytic practice of "technical neutrality." This is the focus of the *humanistic psychotherapist's* criticism of psychoanalytic technique. Similarly, *integrative psychotherapists* (e.g., P. L. Wachtel, 1977, 1987), drawing from both behavioral and psychoanalytic concepts, have noted that many patients require a more positively affirming stance by the therapist to their life circumstances than simple neutrality has to offer. P. L. Wachtel (1987) wryly offered the observation that "you can't go far in neutral."

The Behavior Therapist's Critique

With the more ambitious goal of personality reorganization supplanting Freud's earlier behavioral goal of symptom removal, psychoanalysts often focused on minute aspects of the patient's behavior during the course of a session that would shed light on changes in the patient's defensiveness or object relations toward the therapist as indications of improvement in the patient's emotional condition. The behavior therapists' criticisms focused on the psychoanalysts' inattention to the significance of the patient's "extrasession behavior change." They maintained that what happens to the patient in between therapy sessions with significant others behaviorally in their occupational and family environments is at least as important, and likely more important, than what happens within the session with the therapist.

BEHAVIORAL AND COGNITIVE–BEHAVIORAL THERAPY: TREATMENT BY PROTOCOL

Radical Behaviorism: The Nonmediational View

The movement toward behaviorism and ultimately behavior therapy was the first and most consequential backlash to psychoanalysis. It stemmed from the concerns of extended time and inattention to behavioral outcomes of the psychoanalytic approach, as well as what might be called the Freudian labyrinth of mediating variables and theoretical constructs. These include Freud's array of defense mechanisms and concept of the unconscious mind, which defied empirical assessment and testability. The early behavioral researchers thus relied on rigorous, step-by-step behavior therapy research protocols that offered the practicing clinician little in the way of addressing the internal or emotional life of his or her patients (Scaturo & McPeak, 1998). The behavioral research paradigm was generated from stimulus–response learning models with virtually no wish to examine what was contained in the theoretical "black box" (i.e., cognitive and affective variables) that might mediate the therapeutic stimulus and the outcome response to treatment.

The behavior therapy research protocols were the forerunners of what was later to become the manualization of therapy (e.g., Garfield, 1992b; Lambert & Bergin, 1992). The purpose of such manuals, most prominent in behavioral studies, was to enhance the integrity and uniformity of the therapy being investigated (Garfield, 1992b). The concern, however, over these psychoeducational manuals by more traditional and eclectic psychotherapists has been that the emphasis in such manuals may be more on education than on psychotherapy. Many therapists have great concerns over any approach that they might regard as entailing a preset agenda for treatment, as opposed to treatments that allow the agenda to gradually emerge from the patient. Most behavior therapists would likely argue that much of psychotherapy is indeed education (e.g., Bandura, 1961). They would further argue that the art of therapy is the ability to gently place the agenda of the patient into a form that is treatable by some empirically supported treatment protocol or template (e.g., DeRubeis & Crits-Christoph, 1998). However, when one speaks to experienced behavior therapists about case material, one is left with the impression that they (like Freud) allow themselves more latitude in the construction of the therapeutic agenda than the written protocols might suggest (e.g., P. L. Wachtel, 1982).

The Cognitive–Behavioral Movement: Mediational Factors Revisited

The need for more latitude in conducting treatment, particularly with respect to the patient's thoughts and feelings, led to what might be regarded as the backlash of the cognitive–behavioral movement in the 1970s to the prior use of behavior therapy alone (e.g., Mahoney, 1974; Meichenbaum, 1977). As the period of radical behaviorism came to a close, Bandura (1969) was ushering in the importance of cognitive mediation in the role of social learning theory and behavior change (Bandura, 1977b). In short, he was suggesting that the simple stimulus–response model in complex human learning was insufficient and that a stimulus–organism–response model was needed in which the individual's conscious processes served as the mediating organismic variable between the stimulus problem situation of the environment and the altering of a particular patient's response pattern. Accordingly, "cognitive factors partly determine which external events will be observed, how they will be perceived, whether they will have any lasting effects, what valence and efficacy they have, and how the information will be organized for future use" (Bandura, 1978, p. 345).

Mischel (1973) contributed to the confluence of thought in this area by reconceptualizing personality constructs as cognitive social learning person variables. These include factors such as one's subjective expectancies regarding various events, subjective values placed on various behavioral outcomes of events, modeling and vicarious learning, and the self-regulatory abilities of the human being. Although these constructs were regarded as *active* mediators of the interaction between a certain person and a given situation (Endler & Magnusson, 1976) rather than as *static* personality traits, the emphasis was on a return to intervening factors in behavior change, nonetheless.

With regard to psychotherapy, Bandura (1977a) postulated that psychological treatment procedures, whatever their theoretical orientation, affect the level and strength of a patient's *self-efficacy* (or perceived control and mastery) in a given problem situation as a transtheoretical construct. He hypothesized that one's expectations of personal efficacy in confronting a given situation determine whether coping responses will be engaged, to what degree, and for how long, in the face of adversity. It was Bandura's belief that effective psychotherapy promotes one's sense of mastery, enhances self-efficacy, and reduces maladaptive defensive functioning. The concept of self-efficacy is notably similar to Seligman's (1990) cognitive–behavioral construct of *learned optimism*, which has been predicated on his vast research in the 1970s on optimism's bipolar opposite construct of *learned helplessness* in mediating depressive behavior (Seligman, 1974, 1975).

At this same time, Meichenbaum (1977) was trying to bridge the gap between the earlier cognitive–semantic therapists, such as Frank (1961), Ellis (1962), Beck (1970), and Singer (1974), and straightforward behavior therapy. Meichenbaum and his colleagues (e.g., Meichenbaum & Cameron, 1974) addressed the clinical potential of altering inner speech and images through direct cognitive modification of self-instructional statements (i.e., self-talk) in which people engage during times of stress. He was able to show, for example, that test-anxious college students who made more productive and positive coping self-statements were able to enhance their academic performance in these situations (e.g., Meichenbaum, 1972). In contrast to earlier ideas of a generic, wishful positive thinking (Peale, 1952), or the more popularized, hollowly voiced notion of global self-affirmations (Smith, 1999), Meichenbaum's self-statements were specific instructions to oneself to better focus performance behaviors under stress. For example, a statement such as, "Relax; you're in control. Take a slow deep breath," is directed toward confronting and managing a stressor, whereas "Keep the focus on the present; what is it you have to do?" is intended to cope with the feeling of being overwhelmed (Meichenbaum, 1977, p. 155). That is, such subvocalizations become active mediators between the stressful stimulus and the problem-solving response. They potentiate a specific behavioral response that directly leads to improvements in outcome behaviors. Concurrent to Meichenbaum's work on cognitive–behavioral modification in the 1970s, P. L. Wachtel (1977) brought forth the seminal work on the integration of psychoanalytic and behavior therapy concepts and perspectives.

Insight and Behavior Change: The Structure of Beliefs

The Skinner–Rogers Debate

The debate over the utility of insight into one's behavior, and the therapeutic conditions that foster it in the psychodynamic psychotherapies and other insight-oriented approaches (e.g., client-centered therapy) versus the focus on behavior change in the behavioral treatment modalities, has been one of the most vehemently discussed issues in the fields of psychology and psychotherapy, until the more recent efforts at integrating these two realms of treatment (e.g., P. L. Wachtel, 1977). The debate that took place between Carl Rogers and B. F. Skinner at the American Psychological Association's annual meeting in 1956, and subsequent publication in *Science* (Rogers & Skinner, 1956), was perhaps the most well-known discussion of these issues that, even now, remain important to the field. Bandura (1969), too, had cogently articulated the ethical issues involved in these two viewpoints concerning the identification of specific objectives of treatment and the concern over behavioral control. In essence, humanistic psychotherapists typically depict behavior therapists as "antihumanistic, Machiavellian manipulators of human behavior" (Bandura, 1969, p. 81). Likewise, behavior therapists have criticized humanistic psychotherapy as nothing more than benevolent directionlessness (as the term *nondirective* therapy would imply) with nonspecific therapeutic goals such as *self-actualization*, which they typically view as "idealized pretensions" (Bandura, 1969, p. 81). It might be asked, however, what are the motivational forces at the heart of these heated polemics? Is it simply an intellectualized academic debate over who is more enlightened about the technical and ethical issues surrounding behavior change and the amelioration of human suffering? This seems unlikely or, at the very least, only a part of the picture.

Primitive and Higher Order Beliefs

Given the intensity of affect surrounding these two systems of treatment (i.e., behavioral vs. psychodynamic), it seems more likely that what is being debated here is a more basic, *primitive belief* (Bem, 1970; Rokeach, 1963) grounded in one's personal experience about how one copes and survives the stresses of one's environment, rather than a *higher order belief* obtained in the process of formal education and texts. Bem (1970, p. 7) cited as an example of a primitive belief by our founding forefathers "when they presumed to interpret reality for King George III: 'We hold these truths to be self-evident . . . '" So, one important question for each psychotherapist is, "Which truths are self-evident?"—the truths of a particularly well-conducted and elegant statistical meta-analysis of psychotherapy outcome studies, or the truths that Victor Frankl (1985) discovered about the importance of meaning in surviving a concentration camp? The question here is *not* which of these sources of data holds "the truth." Both hold truths. But, one highly relevant question is which truths are "self-evident" to a given psychotherapist and, in this particular instance, to Dr. Frankl? Similarly, all therapists have formative experiences regarding the survival skills of life, regardless of the severity of their respective life experiences. And, all therapists have formed primitive belief systems about how one best copes with life, in addition to the higher order beliefs formed by their formal education, which deeply influence the manner in which they work with their patients about similar concerns in their patients' lives. These belief systems are perhaps very similar to what the early personality theorists referred to as *Weltanschauung,* or *worldview* (Ivey & Simek-Downing, 1980). For each therapist, his or her view of the world, and how to grapple with it, profoundly affects his or her approach to the treatment of patients.

Given the somewhat pejorative implications of the word *eclecticism*, it is probably significant that, even since the advent of managed health care, one out of every three psychotherapists continues to identify him- or herself as eclectic in therapeutic approach (Norcross & Newman, 1992), refusing to align oneself with any single-theory approach. The notion of *theoretical purity*, it has been observed (Leahy, 2001), is a false dichotomy and tends to be more common among novices than among experienced clinicians. Although the term *integrative* has made the concept of eclecticism more academically acceptable, P. L. Wachtel (1991, p. 44) noted that "for most of us integration remains more a goal than a constant daily reality. Eclecticism in practice and integration in aspiration is an accurate description of what most of us in the integrative movement do much of the time." Nonetheless, P. L. Wachtel (1991, p. 53) also noted that "most efforts at integration have a 'flavor' that derives from the therapist's original orientation." So, whether or not a given therapist is fully aligned with either a psychodynamic or a cognitive–behavioral school of thought, or whether one is an integrationist maintaining an original flavor of either one or the other, what aspects of one's worldview are most relevant to such a choice?

Repression and Sensitization

Broadly speaking, the vast majority of psychotherapy patients are grappling with the emotional states of anxiety or depression. The thought content associated with the anxiety state is the threat of danger to one's domain, whereas the depressive state is of the perceived devaluation of one's domain (Beck, 1976). Thus, the characteristic way in which a given psychotherapist defends against threat to one's domain is likely to be an important part of his or her own worldview, thereby influencing the therapist's conception of how one's patients might best do the same. Byrne (1964, 1966) conducted a considerable amount of research on the concept of *repression versus sensitization* as a dimension of defensiveness in describing individual differences in response to threat. It is a rather small inferential leap to assume that therapists who have coped with their own particular life stressors by the avoidant means of denial and repression are likely to identify with a therapeutic approach that uses procedures such as thought-stopping and desensitization. Likewise, it seems reasonable to assume that those therapists who have coped with their life stresses by approach behaviors such as intellectualization and sensitization are likely to identify with a therapeutic approach that uses verbal-expressive methods that foster insight and self-reflection. It seems that such dearly held, primitive beliefs are more likely to be at the foundation of these longstanding heated debates between behaviorally oriented therapists and insight-oriented therapists. And, although the research dimension of repression–sensitization has undergone some criticism in its operationalization because of the influence by other variables relevant to the defensive avoidance of negative affect, such as one's degree of concern over social desirability (Asendorpf, Wallbott, & Scherer, 1983), this dimension has enormous heuristic value in conceptualizing an important aspect common to the worldviews of the patient, the therapist, and the process of psychotherapy itself (e.g., how best to cope with felt threat).

Accordingly, one of the significant observations of Byrne's (1964) work in this area was that neither overintellectualization of conflicts nor denial of them results in optimal psychological adjustment. Rather, Byrne (1966) noted that those individuals at either end of this dimension are less well adjusted than individuals falling within the middle range (i.e., a curvilinear relationship). This result may help to explain the adaptive value of many psychotherapists continuing to identify themselves as eclectic, despite the disincentive of lesser prestige or the lack of endorsement by managed care to do so. Implicit in this statement of identification is that, for most people, insight and behavior change are both necessary elements of adaptive functioning. As Norcross (1988) pointed out, behavior therapists do not own the concept of behavior change any more than psychoanalysts own unique genetic insights in treatment. Likewise, Keith et al. (1993) suggested that the insight–behavior dichotomy, like other dichotomies in clinical work such as mind–body, acute–chronic, and individual–family, exists largely as a conceptual problem. They noted that these concepts are thoroughly blended in the everyday experience of the clinician.

FAMILY THERAPY: ALL OR NOTHING?

Family Therapy: Birth and Adolescence

About the time that Wolpe (1958) was challenging the psychodynamic model of psychopathology with behavior therapy by reciprocal inhibition, the early family therapists (e.g., Ackerman, 1958; Bowen, 1959) began their work on the inclusion of the identified patient's primary social group (i.e., the family) to the conceptualization of both the problem and the treatment. Although family systems thinking was predated by Sullivan's (1938) earlier work on the relevancy of interpersonal processes to psychopathology, the early family theorists attempted to integrate some of the psychodynamic concepts (e.g., interlocking pathology and object relations), still then the dominant theoretical framework, into their therapeutic work with families. As the structural (Minuchin, 1974), problem-solving (J. Haley, 1976), and strategic (Madanes, 1981) models of family therapy began to evolve, and family therapy as a field looked more toward establishing a professional identity in the "adolescence" of its development, family therapists became increasingly adamant about the necessity of the family's presence in the *therapeutic system* in order for treatment to occur (e.g., J. Haley, 1970; Madanes, 1981). For example, Bowen (1965) undertook a research study that involved the hospitalization of whole families with a patient with schizophrenia, demonstrating the intense commitment to this conceptualization. However, the inflexibility of these positions entailed a dogmatism and elitism that alienated many mental health professionals trained in other, typically individual, approaches to treatment (Scaturo & McPeak, 1998). In addition, not unlike the radical behavioral approaches before them, these early systemic approaches simply failed to address many of the internal needs of individual family members.

The need to establish the independence of the family systems concept to demonstrate its viability as yet a separate theoretical force was understandable. Even in the past decade of psychotherapy integration (e.g., Feldman & Powell, 1992; Norcross & Goldfried, 1992), family systems treatment has tended to be confined to the integration of family therapy as a treatment modality, as opposed to family systems theory as a way of conceptualizing psychopathology and its amelioration. Nevertheless, as family therapy began to develop and evolve as a discipline in the mental health area, clinicians already solidly identified with the family systems approach (e.g., Nichols, 1987b) were beginning to recognize the importance of empirical contributions from other levels of theoretical abstraction. These levels of theoretical abstraction have included the psychodynamic–intrapsychic level of conceptualization (e.g., Strupp & Binder, 1984), the behavioral–symptomatic level (e.g., Barlow, 1988; Lewinsohn, 1974), and the cognitive level of intervention (e.g., Beck, 1976; Beck, Rush, Shaw, & Emery, 1979; Seligman, 1974, 1975). The recognition of these contributions by family therapists was termed a *rediscovery* of the self in the system (Nichols, 1987a, 1987b).

The Rediscovery of the Self in the Family System

Family systems theory genuinely offered clinicians a revolutionary way of viewing psychopathology and psychotherapy. Perhaps the single most important concept of this approach was the recognition that behavior is not simply a product of *self-determination*. Rather, a person's behavior is both a cause and effect of those with whom they interact most intimately on a day-to-day basis (i.e., their families). Although important with respect to etiology, what these theorists were saying was no less profound in the area of treatment. Both psychodynamic theory and cognitive–behavioral theory directly target the problem behavior, symptom, or internal conflict of the identified patient as the focus of intervention. The clinical contribution of recognizing the intricate interdependence of family members has been to, in addition, indirectly target the reactive behavior of those members that contributes to the maintenance of the index patient's presenting problems (Scaturo, Hayes, Sagula, & Walter, 2000). This is a powerful additive variable that affords the therapist increased therapeutic control, not only of the problematic behavior but also over the environment in which it thrives. Over time, however, family therapists experienced a growing awareness that ignoring the inner experiences and conflicts of individual family members was as limiting as ignoring the effect of family dysfunction on the individual (Nichols, 1987b). Object relations theory was able to provide an important conceptual bridge on which to discuss both the interactional and internal experiences of the patient and his or her family (e.g., Framo, 1970, 1976, 1992; D. E. Scharff & Scharff, 1987, 1991).

The Rediscovery of the Family System in Individual Psychotherapy

Finnegan Bell, the primary character played by actor Ethan Hawke in the 1998 cinematic remake of Charles Dickens's classic novel, *Great Expectations* (1861/1992), begins the narration of his life story with the kind of verisimilitude that is familiar to the psychotherapist's consulting room:

> There either is or is not a way things are: the color of the day, the way it felt to be a child, the feeling of salt water on your sunburned legs. Sometimes the color of the water is yellow, sometimes it's red, but the color that it may be in memory depends on the day. I am not going to tell the story the way it happened. I am going to tell it the way I remember it. (Linson & Cuaron, 1998)

Clinicians from a wide range of theoretical perspectives would largely agree that subjective distortions in family and interpersonal relationships are the stuff of psychotherapy, whether these are conceptualized as Freud's (1912/1958a) notion of transference, Sullivan's (1953) parataxic distortions, Bandura's (1978) cognitive mediation, Mischel's (1973) cognitive–social learning person variables, or the internalized object relations of childhood (Framo, 1970). However, both psychodynamic and behavioral clinicians seem to have had an insufficient appreciation of the significance of the reality of family relationships in their respective principles of treatment. Psychodynamic psychotherapists historically have worked with the transference of emotional conflicts in the therapeutic relationship, even though the original objects (i.e., other family members) that have formed these relational perceptions are frequently available for direct inclusion in clinical work (Bowen, 1976). Likewise, behavior therapists (e.g., Barlow & Waddell, 1985) have tended to view the spouse's involvement in behavior therapy protocols as *spouse-assisted behavior therapy* (Scaturo, 1994), using the spouse as a *support person* (e.g., J. O. Wilson, 1989) in, for example, carrying out the anxiety-provoking aspects of in vivo exposure therapy. Although the outcome and follow-up studies (e.g., Barlow, O'Brien, & Last, 1984; Cerny, Barlow, Craske, & Himadi, 1987) have shown superior therapeutic effects for the spouse-included groups over the nonspouse groups, the effects were mostly attributed to increasing behavioral compliance rather than addressing some of the possible *synergistic* effects (P. L. Wachtel, 1991) of including the spouse in treatment.

Individual therapists in both the behavioral and psychodynamic arenas began to speculate about the potential advantages of getting to know the families of their patients by way of periodic family consultations (Framo, 1976, 1992), if not ongoing family therapy. E. F. Wachtel and Wachtel (1986) outlined the rationale, clinical relevance, and guidelines for technique in "meeting the cast of characters" in the life of the individual psychotherapy patient. They have noted that we, in our society, have tended to view ourselves as autonomous individuals who "just happen" to be members of a family and of a larger social context. Furthermore, the medicalization of psychotherapy has made it easy for the psychotherapist to view his or her clinical responsibility to the identified patient, while almost completely disregarding the concomitant needs of those within the patient's primary social group (e.g., Doherty, 1995). Whatever we conclude from the evolution of psychotherapy over the past century, it should be acknowledged that psychotherapists of different theoretical persuasions share many of the same clinical dilemmas (e.g., Dryden, 1997; Scaturo, 2001; Scaturo & McPeak, 1998). The dominant schools of psychotherapy offer each other complementary clinical information that deserves to be integrated in the best interests of both the patient and his or her family.

IMPLICATIONS FOR PROFESSIONAL PRACTICE

The Manualization of Psychotherapy: Necessary, but Far From Sufficient

In many ways, the development of psychotherapy manuals represents a substantial advance for the professional practice of psychology. These manuals have helped us to focus on the salient and curative elements specific to certain treatment regimens (e.g., exposure therapy for phobic behavior) and those that are common among most regimens (e.g., self-efficacy as a general ingredient in almost all forms of professional helping behavior). These elements might be described as the necessary ingredients for a given type of psychotherapy with a given type of diagnosis or presenting problem. They have clearly advanced our knowledge by providing empirically supported treatments that offer demonstrated active ingredients and operative elements in various forms of psychotherapy (e.g., Cummings & Cummings, 2000). Outcome research helps to make each therapist mindful of the significant elements that need to be present to address particular types of clinical problems. Nevertheless, as Garfield (1992b, p. 336) noted, "It can be said, with at least some degree of confidence, that most therapists perform their own individual style with little conformity to some therapeutic manual."

The Ubiquitous Nonspecific Factors in Psychotherapy

Every form of psychotherapy incorporates interpersonal relationship factors to varying degrees, regardless of the particular theoretical underpinnings (Frank, 1971; Strupp & Hadley, 1979). Strupp (e.g., Strupp & Hadley, 1979) has termed these aspects of treatment *nonspecific factors* in psychotherapy. These include such components as (a) a confiding relationship, (b) a compassionate explanation of the patient's distress, (c) sychoeducational information regarding alternative ways of dealing with the patient's problem, (d) the arousal of hope and viability, (e) an enhancement of perceived mastery and interpersonal competence, and (f) an accompanying facilitation of emotional arousal and motivation for change. In the literature on psychotherapy integration (e.g., Arkowitz, 1992a, 1992b; Garfield, 1992a), these relationship variables, or nonspecific factors, have been termed *common factors*, in part because they are shared among the different forms of psychotherapy. This renaming has occurred, presumably, because there was a growing discomfort with the notion of nonspecificity (not unlike the discomfort associated with the concept of eclecticism and its revitalization with the term *integration*). Yalom (1980, p. 4), however, posed the following question regarding specificity: "Is it possible to define and teach such qualities as compassion, 'presence,' caring, extending oneself, touching the patient at a profound level, or—that most elusive one of all—wisdom?" (See also Karasu, 1992, and Scaturo & McPeak, 1998, for further discussion on the topic of "clinical wisdom.") Whether we as professionals like it or not, the inherently interpersonal nature of this profession is, not unlike our treatment manuals, also necessary, if not sufficient.

Quantitative statistical support for these qualitative clinical observations can be found in the literature on the therapeutic alliance. Reviews of studies examining the percentage of clinical outcome variance that is accounted for by the ratings of the quality of the therapeutic alliance have found an average of 30% or more of psychotherapy outcome variance to be attributable to the therapeutic relationship and other common factors (e.g., Lambert, 1992; Lambert & Barley, 2001). These data provide rather strong support for Strupp's (1981, p. 218) compelling observation that "psychotherapy is not a unitary 'treatment' that can be 'administered' or 'delivered' to an impersonal patient suffering from an impersonal 'condition' by an impersonal therapist." Only within the past decade have the notions of the therapeutic alliance and interpersonal processes begun to receive their due attention in the area of cognitive–behavioral therapy (e.g., Safran & Segal, 1996).

Efficacy and Effectiveness

In addition to the pervasiveness of nonspecific factors in psychotherapy, Seligman (1995) in his review of the well-known *Consumer Reports* study of mental health services ("Mental Health: Does Therapy Help?") has distinguished between the use of efficacy studies and effectiveness studies as complementing each other in the assessment of psychotherapeutic outcome. Noting that the more popular efficacy study contrasted some type of psychotherapy with a comparison group under reasonably well-controlled conditions, whereas the effectiveness study of *Consumer Reports* assessed how patients fared under the actual conditions of the open treatment setting, Seligman examined what the efficacy studies leave out. The advantageous properties of the effectiveness study include (a) the ability to study psychotherapy of an unfixed time duration; (b) the self-correcting nature of therapy in the field, which involves the debate on compliance with a manualized program versus the therapist's ability to adapt to the patient; (c) the factor of actively shopping for therapy by the patient versus the passive process of random assignment; (d) the increased ability to generalize using patients of complex, comorbid diagnoses in applied setting versus the well-screened single-diagnosis patients of the controlled study; and, finally, (e) the assessment of improvement in the general functioning of the patient versus the narrow focus on symptom relief. Seligman concluded that he no longer considers the efficacy study to be the "gold standard" in measuring treatment outcome, but rather a combined approach that incorporates the best features of both studies. As noted by a survey of the Clinical Diplomates of the American Board of Professional Psychology (ABPP; Plante, Andersen, & Boccaccini, 1999), ABPP clinicians largely believe that this practical level of empirical support, which addresses the complexities of the open treatment setting, may be ultimately necessary in order for practicing clinicians to embrace and integrate empirically supported treatment manuals into their actual practices.

Empirically Supported Treatments: Limitations in Practice

It is not reasonable to expect the duplication of an empirically tested protocol within an open treatment setting (Cummings & Cummings, 2000). Clinical uniqueness is, in part, attributable to the multiplicity of coexisting factors in the natural setting that provide additive effects that influence treatment outcome. Garfield (1996) noted that therapeutic success is multiply influenced and limited by the effectiveness of the empirically supported interventions, the quality and strength of the therapeutic alliance, as well as the sophistication of skills, competencies, and experience of the clinician administering the treatment program. Manualized treatments and psychotherapists alike need to be sufficiently flexible to allow for deviation from a given protocol when unexpected clinical events and patient crises arise (e.g., Garfield, 1996; Piper & Ogrodniczuk, 1999). Chambless (1996) noted that rigid adherence to manual protocols is likely to be less valuable than identifying the critical components of treatment (e.g., Cummings & Cummings, 2000) and understanding how and when to competently use them.

Some Critical Components of Effective Psychotherapy

Cummings and Cummings (2000) outlined six critical components of treatment in their cogent discussion of the art and essence of psychotherapy. They referred to these components as *key ingredients* of psychotherapy that have been identified by empirical research and amassed data from recurrent clinical experiences by master clinicians over time. First, they noted that effective psychotherapy has been repetitively shown to constitute what F. Alexander and French (1946) originally identified as a "corrective emotional experience" and empathic atmosphere conducive to change. The second ingredient they noted is to target realistic goals for human growth in treatment to expand the patient's behavioral repertoire in response to frustration and stress, rather than unrealistically attempting to eradicate archaic coping responses to traumas experienced during critical windows of early periods of development (Skinner, 1952). Third, another key ingredient of effective psychotherapy invokes a competent understanding of the concepts of transference and countertransference in the therapeutic relationship that attempts to bring about an intense and motivating therapist–patient relationship that, nevertheless, minimizes the patient's dependency. Fourth, a critical element of psychotherapy is the ability to address what Sullivan (1953) referred to as the patient's "parataxic distortions" in his or her relationships with others that result in attempts to respond to interpersonal situations in a skewed manner. Fifth, effective psychotherapy communicates an understanding of the patient's intrapsychic conflicts that surround problems with interpersonal closeness and intimacy resulting in approach–avoidance behaviors about significant developmental tasks in the life cycle. Finally, a sixth critical component of therapy identified by Cummings and Cummings (2000) includes the reasonable expectation by the psychotherapy patient that undergoing treatment would involve some reduction of symptoms, anxiety, depression, and emotional pain.

Intermittent Episodes of Psychotherapy

A significant contribution of Nicholas Cummings and his colleagues (e.g., Cummings, 1990; Cummings & Cummings, 2002) was the notion of utilizing episodes of *brief, intermittent psychotherapy* that take place for a patient over the course of that patient's life cycle and a given practitioner's professional lifetime. Whether or not these episodes consist of the highly brief forms of symptom-focused psychotherapy of six sessions or less that is common to managed behavioral health care (e.g., Bellak & Siegel, 1983), or the more moderately brief therapy of 12 to 15 sessions that was common to marital and couple treatment even before the age of managed care (e.g., Framo, 1980), or the more extended forms of short-term psychodynamically oriented psychotherapy that typically respond to a 20- to 24-session framework (e.g., Strupp & Binder, 1984), the practitioner who remains in a given locale for any substantial length of time and successfully treats a given patient is likely to see that patient again over the course of the patient's life cycle and its associated stressors. Although the psychoanalytic concept of a "cure" for a nonrecurring neurosis is predicated on a strict biomedical model of disease and treatment that may be tenuously transposable to the treatment of psychosocial problems, the concept of the returning patient in need of multiple and discontinuous episodes of therapy based on the general and family practice treatment approaches to medical care (e.g., Cummings & VandenBos, 1979) is particularly adaptable and exceedingly appropriate for the extended practice of psychotherapy within a life cycle model of care. Such an approach recognizes that multiple stressors and developmental impasses occur over the course of a given human being's life span for which he or she may be in need of professional assistance repeatedly and would prefer and benefit from follow-up care with the same practitioner who may have known and treated this patient previously and with whom there is a sense of familiarity, continuity, and comfort. That this should be recognized by patients, practitioners, and third-party payers should be not only understandable and obvious but also desirable in a field in which the repeated sharing of personal, intimate, and painful traumatic material to an unfamiliar practitioner may be difficult and a disincentive to seek needed treatment at critical points in time.

Clinical Training and Mentoring

Over 20 years ago, Strupp (1981) wrote a brief, but cogent article on what he called the *crisis of confidence* in clinical research and the practice of psychotherapy. At that time, Strupp believed that this so-called crisis of confidence by government, insurance companies, and society at large reflected, at least in part, a crisis in the professional training of psychotherapists. To illustrate the deficiencies in clinical training, he cited the lessons learned from the declining status of psychoanalysis at that time. Presently, some of these deficiencies have been well addressed in recent years by the attempts at manualization from a range of theoretical frameworks. Others have not. The attempts at manualization have fostered a healthier respect for empirical data than existed in the field two decades ago. However, a dogmatic adherence to any single theoretical model or technical approach, as well as an uncritical application of a unitary manualized approach to treatment, has the potential to replicate a number of the pitfalls of the doctrinaire psychoanalytic paradigm. At present, the almost unilateral advocacy of third-party payers for approaches that are cognitive–behavioral in nature, for example, may similarly discourage critical thinking in our students and inhibit a more sophisticated formulation of rival hypotheses based on a comprehensive understanding of the individual patient and his or her family history. As Strupp (1981, p. 218) noted two decades ago, unless we train thoroughly competent psychotherapists with a comprehensive knowledge base of technical skills, sophisticated interpersonal skills and compassion, and an ability to evaluate and self-monitor their clinical work on an ongoing basis, "it is predictable that governmental controls and bureaucratic rules will make a charade of professional work in this area." In the current millennium, these words are nothing less than prophetic.

As Keith et al. (1993) have discussed elsewhere in the area of medical education, more specific attention needs to be given to the role of the *mentor*, or preceptor, in the learning of psychotherapy, apart from the textbook knowledge and imparting of technical skills. Levinson, Darrow, Klein, Levinson, and McKee (1978) in their classic study of adult psychosocial development have noted that the mentor fosters the emotional development of the young adult in addition to providing a model of professional identity. He or she often provides mature advice, moral support, and encouragement at critical moments in the young adult's occupational socialization. Addressing the personal ramifications of inevitable clinical failures and how to maturely acknowledge and cope with them is only one of the many functions of the mentor, often approached by openly sharing similar clinical "war stories" of his or her own. The mentor helps to integrate clinical acumen into the broader context of the psychotherapist's functioning as a person. This process needs to occur early in clinical training, not just during internship, or in supervision–consultation with more experienced colleagues at one's first place of employment, as other authors have also noted (e.g., J. Haley, 1981). Clinical wisdom is always hard-earned knowledge gathered from an accrual of clinical experiences (e.g., Karasu, 1992; Keith et al., 1993; Scaturo & McPeak, 1998), and there is no substitute for the mentoring relationship in training competent professionals.

Professionalism and Behavioral Technology

Perhaps the gravest misgiving about the proliferation of manualized psychotherapy programs concerns the misinformation that they may, often by implication, provide to governmental sources, third-party payers, and the public at large. Of particular concern is the erroneous conclusion, potentially formed by poorly informed parties, that behavioral technicians can be adequately substituted for comprehensively trained professionals. Gurman, Kniskern, and Pinsof's (1986) review on process and outcome research in marital and family therapy, applicable to other forms of psychotherapy as well, concluded that a reasonable mastery of technical skills may be sufficient for preventing the exacerbation of, or maintaining pretreatment levels of, family functioning, but more refined psychotherapist relationship skills seem necessary to yield genuinely positive outcomes. In other words, experience, training, and professionalism all matter greatly in the treatment of emotional and behavioral disorders and are well worth the expenditure of time and training resources.

It may be particularly important as the field moves toward the practice of brief psychotherapy, in which the focus of intervention is narrowed, that the assessment and formulation of case material remain broadly based with increasing levels of clinical sophistication (Scaturo & McPeak, 1998). The psychotherapist must have an understanding of how psychodynamics, behavioral symptomatology, and family systems and history interact, and of how an intervention at one level necessarily affects all other levels. Nonspecific factors may be especially important in time-limited psychotherapies (Frank, 1971). Only a broad conceptualization of the patient's functioning can allow for rapid reassessments and shifts in therapeutic focus periodically needed in brief treatment that then can be integrated as part of a larger, comprehensive clinical picture.

Most professional psychologists are well aware that our understanding of behavioral technology is clearly not expendable. Our understanding of the parameters of demonstrated clinical techniques is most certainly a unique acquisition and contribution of a professional education in the behavioral sciences. Within the framework of the scientist–practitioner model, the scientist is largely concerned with how a specific treatment affects aggregate data (i.e., statistical significance). The practitioner, in contrast, is primarily concerned with the impact of the treatment on his or her individual patient (i.e., clinical significance). The well-informed practitioner logically attempts to generalize the application of an empirically validated treatment to the patients in his or her open treatment setting who most resemble the patients included in a given research sample (e.g., Barlow, Hayes, & Nelson, 1984). However, providing effective psychotherapeutic treatment and promoting meaningful behavior change remain complex clinical endeavors. It is critical that the elements of step-by-step treatment protocols be embedded in the professional practice of psychotherapy with a clinician who has been through extensive training and has been deemed through mentoring to possess a sufficient degree of psychosocial maturity, compassionate interpersonal skill, and sound clinical judgment. Otherwise, we will have surely lost our way as a profession.

CONCLUDING REMARKS

Many prudent practitioners are struggling with the question of whether the current "age of manualization" to which we have arrived in the evolution of psychotherapy constitutes an asset or a liability. Consistent with an integrative perspective on this topic, it is not possible to fully endorse either alternative of such a binary choice. The more specific behavior therapies have been demonstrated to have superior effects with specific symptom disorders such as anxiety and show the clearest superiority with phobic disorders (Lambert & Bergin, 1992). Overall, it appears that the more circumscribed the symptomatic presentation, the more likely a focused, step-by-step psychotherapy is to succeed. Thus, my inclination would be to rely more heavily on a manualized approach to the amelioration of circumscribed difficulties (e.g., simple focal anxiety) while using a more complex integrative clinical regimen in more generalized and complicated clinical pictures. Although the responsible clinician cannot abdicate his or her responsibility in helping the patient arrive at a therapeutic focus (e.g., Budman & Gurman, 1988), there are many human problems (e.g., complicated bereavement, complex posttraumatic stress) that present multilayered clinical pictures for which unidimensional solutions remain a fallacy.

Regarding the question of prescriptive treatments, is it possible to decide on a given approach with a given clinical problem based on empirically validated information? There are an increasing number of reviews of literature on the topic of empirically supported treatments for given problem presentations, and continued research will no doubt produce ongoing refinements. As examples, DeRubeis and Crits-Christoph (1998) have reviewed the empirical validity of various individual and group treatments for a number of adult emotional disorders, and Foa et al. (2000) have reviewed the efficacy of such treatments for clinical populations experiencing posttraumatic stress disorders. Yet, there are many patients whose clinical presentations show problems for which structured evidence-based treatment protocols may exist, but for whom the vast majority of experienced and adept clinicians would likely select from among the various validated treatment components and interventions. They would elect to individualize the treatment to the personhood of the patient and the character of the particular patient's family life. Manualized treatments are no substitute for comprehensive clinical competencies. If manualization becomes a way for professionally trained psychologists to better articulate precisely what they do through clinical intervention, then the efforts should be vigorously applauded. If, on the other hand, manualized treatments are misused by implying that the complex task of clinical work can be meaningfully distilled to a set of decision trees that can be applied by minimally trained behavioral technicians, such usage has the potential to do a grave disservice to our patients and our profession. The next chapter examines how the proponents of psychodynamic psychotherapy and other insight-oriented approaches to treatment have grappled with the problem of better articulating the broad psychoanalytic conceptualization of human functioning by more sharply defining the focus of therapy and enhancing the confrontational aspects of psychological treatment.

II

CLINICAL DILEMMAS AMONG DIVERSE APPROACHES TO TREATMENT

3

PSYCHODYNAMIC AND INSIGHT-ORIENTED PSYCHOTHERAPY: FOCUS AND COMPREHENSIVENESS, CONFRONTATION AND SUPPORT

At its heart, the process of psychotherapy is fundamentally concerned with the alleviation of human emotional suffering (e.g., Miller, 2004). Thus, over the years, many of the innovations in psychotherapy have been directed at providing treatment with increased degrees of brevity and efficacy. Psychotherapists working within psychodynamic and insight-oriented frameworks have faced a number of clinical dilemmas in attempting to accommodate the nature of such work to these demands in the modern health care milieu. Even before the advent of behavior therapy and the subsequent arrival of an array of brief therapies, psychotherapists within the psychoanalytic community itself were greatly concerned that psychoanalysis, as a treatment modality, was not "time-sensitive" (Scaturo, 2001). F. Alexander and French (1946)

This chapter is an adaptation of "Fundamental Dilemmas in Contemporary Psychodynamic and Insight-Oriented Psychotherapy," by D. J. Scaturo, 2002, *Journal of Contemporary Psychotherapy*, *32*, 143–163. Copyright 2002 by Kluwer Academic. Adapted with permission.

were among the first analysts interested in finding "short-cuts" to the psychoanalytic method. Their abbreviated method was punctuated by two principles of treatment: *flexibility* in the psychoanalytic technique and the concept of the *corrective emotional experience*.

Whereas Freud focused on the abreaction and discharge of negative affect predicated on a Helmholzian model of intrapsychic functioning and energy (e.g., Jones, 1955; Yalom, 1980), F. Alexander and French (1946) believed that a corrective emotional experience with the analyst provided the primary curative factor. Accordingly, the therapeutic task was to reexpose the patient under more favorable conditions to the emotional conflict that he or she has been unable to master. The importance of the therapeutic relationship in fostering the conditions under which treatment can be accelerated is paramount. Alexander and French illustrated the corrective emotional experience with the fictional character of Jean Valjean in Victor Hugo's (1862) novel, *Les Miserables*. In brief, Valjean was an exconvict whose view of his life and the world was radically altered by the overpowering and unforeseen kindness of a priest whom he had attempted to rob. In juxtaposition to this event of being treated better than he deserved, Valjean subsequently robs a helpless young boy and is confronted by a violent conflict that has thrown his emotional life into disequilibrium. He then faces a choice at which point he must reform his thinking or commit to it more fully.

In creating the conditions for a corrective emotional experience in psychotherapy, F. Alexander and French (1946) proposed a departure from the classical psychoanalytic principles in treatment (e.g., Langs, 1973), advocating for more flexibility in treatment. In this respect, they proposed variations in aspects of treatment such as the frequency of sessions, periodic interruptions and terminations in courses of treatment, returns for subsequent courses of therapy, and the consideration of therapeutic life experiences that occur outside the context of treatment. In this regard, they were strong *patient advocates*, asserting that the psychotherapist must flexibly adapt technique to the needs of the particular patient.

DILEMMAS IN BRIEF PSYCHODYNAMIC PSYCHOTHERAPY

The proponents of brief psychodynamic psychotherapy have relied on an increased use of *focus* and *confrontation* to abbreviate treatment. Specifically, establishing a more specific psychodynamic focus for treatment versus the more comprehensive goals of longer term treatment has been emphasized. In addition, the appropriate augmentation of confrontation of psychological defenses versus the amplified use of emotional support as in more nondirective psychotherapy has constituted a significant treatment dilemma for the brief psychodynamic psychotherapist.

The Psychodynamic Focus

A primary task in all brief psychotherapeutic treatments is to select a focus for treatment and, ultimately, to hold to it (Budman & Gurman, 1988). For the therapist, selecting the therapeutic focus, on the one hand, and holding to it, on the other, constitute somewhat separate, although related, challenges. The *dynamic focus* (e.g., Schacht et al., 1984; Sifneos, 1992) has been defined as the nucleus of the patient's problem that encompasses the cardinal symptom, a related intrapsychic conflict, a developmental impasse, a self-defeating belief about the self (i.e., self-schema; Horowitz & Zilberg, 1983), a persistent interpersonal dilemma, or a maladaptive coping pattern. In identifying the psychodynamic focus, it is important for the therapist to establish the *functional salience* of the patient's maladaptive coping pattern. That is, the focal therapeutic task is to relate the patient's maladaptive interpersonal coping behavior and presenting complaint connected to the emotional difficulty that the patient is trying to solve. The treatment of panic disorder provides an excellent example for psychodynamic focus. Panic attacks constitute the cardinal symptom that is frequently linked to a fear of abandonment from primary caregivers in the family of origin, that may be augmented during a developmentally vulnerable period such as the young adult leaving home for the first time, and that may extend into the object relations and an interpersonal pattern of excessive dependency on the spouse in the family of procreation (e.g., Friedman, 1985; Sable, 1994, 2000; Scaturo, 1994).

The psychodynamic focus is a facet of treatment that has appeared under a variety of terms over the years with an essentially similar conceptualization. Synonymous concepts related to the psychodynamic focus have been characterized by terms such as the residual trauma (Blos, 1941; Ekstein, 1956), the nuclear conflict (F. Alexander & French, 1946), the psychoanalytic sector (Deutch & Murphy, 1955a, 1955b), the core neurotic conflict (R. S. Wallerstein & Robbins, 1956), the central transference predisposition (Racker, 1968), focal psychotherapy (Balint, Ornstein, & Balint, 1972), the central issue (Mann, 1973; Mann & Goldman, 1982), the core conflictual relationship theme (Luborsky, 1977), the core psychodynamic conflict (McCullough-Vaillant, 1997), and the interpersonal–developmental–existential focus (Budman & Gurman, 1988).

The defining characteristics of a therapeutic focus involve a narrative from the patient that includes actions embedded within an interpersonal context with others that are generally organized around a cyclical psychodynamic pattern (Schacht et al., 1984; P. L. Wachtel & McKinney, 1992). They tend to provide a recurrent source of difficulties in living. When considering the range of foci in brief psychotherapy, Budman and Gurman (1988) humorously quoted the character of Inspector Louis Renault in the film, *Casablanca*, in which he instructs his police to "round up the usual suspects." These authors suggested that there are five "usual suspects" that form the basis of foci for brief therapy. These are (a) *losses* through death, divorce, separations, or relocations; (b) *developmental dysynchronies* that involve "the patient's sense that a significant aspect of what he or she had wished for at this point is not coming to pass, and that it may never come to pass" (p. 103); (c) *interpersonal conflicts* with friends, employees, or coworkers, as well as marital–partner conflicts with a spouse or significant other; (d) *symptomatic presentations* such as anxiety, dysthymia, or phobic responses; and (e) *severe personality disorders* in which the patient's characterological impediments and tendency to externalize interpersonal responsibility bring him or her to re-peated requests for therapy with recurrent complaints frequently centered on loneliness, isolation, and anger. Focus, by its nature, however, favors one area of examination while neglecting others (Scaturo, 2002c).

Thus, the dilemma regarding therapeutic focus concerns where the psy-chotherapist draws the line and sets the parameters of clinical exploration. How much does one incorporate as part of the clinical picture for treatment purposes? In attempting to answer this question, it may be more productive to provide a qualification. That is to say, how much should one incorporate as part of the clinical picture for this particular episode of treatment? An appropriate therapeutic focus may be more readily selected if psychotherapy is conceptualized as brief and intermittent courses of treatment that may occur for the patient throughout his or her life cycle (Cummings, 1990, 1991; Cummings & Cummings, 2000) rather than incorporating the notion of a psychodynamic "cure." In advancing this concept of intermittent episodes of treatment, Cummings and VandenBos (1979) originally envisioned a "gen-eral practice of psychology" somewhat analogous to the practice of the pri-mary care physician. In other words, a patient with the previously considered example of panic disorder may see a certain mental health practitioner at several critical points or developmental impasses, when the cardinal symp-toms reemerge, over the patient's life cycle and the practitioner's professional career. Thus, in utilizing this concept, it is advisable that every course of brief psychotherapy be terminated by posing to the patient the possibility of recurrences of the ongoing conflict in the patient's life (Gustafson, 1995). Such an approach to termination of a given course in treatment enables the patient to keep alert for, and thereby lessen the emotional disruption of, another exacerbation.

Confrontation Versus Support

Once having selected and established a psychodynamic focus for a given episode of treatment, then the task of *holding to the therapeutic focus* is the next item on the therapeutic agenda and generally more challenging and complex. Keeping "on task" requires that the patient and therapist have a strong *consensus* about what the nature of the therapeutic work entails, oth-erwise the patient is likely to view the therapist's efforts to keep on task as being primarily the therapist's concern and not his or her own. Even if a strong consensus and alliance exist, a persistent return to the therapeutic focus is likely to entail increased degrees of confrontation. Along with emotional support, silence, interpretation, and clarification, confrontation comprises one of the major interventions of psychodynamic psychotherapy (e.g., Langs, 1973). Confrontation generally involves *evocative questioning* intended to facilitate the process of interpretation, or the assignment of underlying meaning and causality to emotions and behavior, and is the sine qua non of insight-oriented psychodynamic therapy (Karasu, 1990). In addition, the hallmark of the psychodynamic approach to treatment involves a transferential relationship with the psychotherapist with whom the interpersonal manifestations of the patient's unconscious coping strategies can be explored (Karasu, 1990).

Scaturo and McPeak (1998) noted that one of the most prevalent, moment-to-moment dilemmas in the psychodynamic therapy session is how much to *confront versus support* a given patient at a given point in treatment. The essence of this dilemma seems to be this: Too much confrontation may overwhelm and diminish the patient's sense of self; too much support without any confrontation may yield no change or movement of the patient in therapy (Scaturo & McPeak, 1998). Metaphorically, if confrontation is the surgical incision in exploratory psychotherapy, then providing emotional support is surely the anesthesia. It is the psychotherapist's responsibility to decide how much confrontation a particular patient with a specific psychosocial history and a given diagnosis and defensive structure can tolerate at a particular point in time. Alternatively, how much emotional support is needed throughout this process? This decision is an ongoing one that occurs on a moment-to-moment basis as a result of therapy being a dynamic process in which the status of the above-noted variables is changing constantly.

The Anxiety-Provoking Psychotherapies

The brief psychodynamic psychotherapies (e.g., Davanloo, 1978; Malan, 1976; Sifneos, 1979) are predicated on an accelerated transference relationship through the use of evocative questions concerning the relationship between patient and therapist and interpretations of how this relates to the patient's interpersonal style and, ultimately, his or her interpersonal difficulties. Indeed, it is this confrontation of the patient's defensive structure at the outset of treatment that largely accounts for the abbreviation of therapy in these psychodynamic approaches (Scaturo & McPeak, 1998). However, intense challenging and interpretation of the transference relationship (i.e., the immediacy of the therapist–patient relationship as it plays out moment to moment in the consulting room) can be highly discomforting and emotionally inflammatory for the patient. For this reason, the short-term psychodynamic approaches to treatment have been referred to as an *anxiety-provoking* form of psychotherapy (Sifneos, 1992).

One of the primary intentions of psychodynamic psychotherapy is to allow the patient to experience his or her genuine emotions toward the therapist, and ultimately toward others, as they occur (Davanloo, 1990). The major obstacle to this is the defense mechanism of repression that is invoked by the patient because his or her true feelings are either too painful or unacceptable to him or her. Therefore, the confrontative techniques of brief dynamically oriented therapy are aimed at overcoming these *resistances*. Defensive behaviors in therapy may include such stances as vagueness in the narrative, emotional distancing from the therapist, silence, intellectualizations, and various obsessive and regressive defenses. Central to Davanloo's therapeutic technique is the intense challenge of the resistance and broad use of the transference in the dynamic interaction between the patient and the therapist. The intense focus on the emotional experience of the patient in the therapeutic relationship results in direct experience of socially discouraged emotions, such as anger, over their indirect expressions, such as defiance to and detachment from the therapist. Such hostility is reflected in the following therapist (TH) and patient (PT) transcript (Davanloo, 1990, p. 18):

> TH: So I question you, in that incident that you were talking about, that your father told you that you are a negative person, the question was that you were defying your father, in a sense not doing the way he wanted you to do? . . .

> TH: This is very important. Again you leave it in the state of limbo, "I think so."

> PT: Well I do think so! Goddamn it, I'm not a psychiatrist, I mean I . . .

The intensity of such confrontation has considerable potential for the patient to misconstrue the therapist's intentions. This is a very serious concern as the therapeutic alliance is the major, if not the sole, asset that the psychotherapist has in this, or any, form of treatment, and the risk of its rupture has even more potential within such confrontational approaches (e.g., Safran, 1993; Safran & Greenberg, 1993). For example, Davanloo (1990) introduced the word *crippling* to the patient for the purpose of describing to the patient how his or her defensive behaviors paralyze to some extent the patient's interpersonal functioning and satisfaction in life in an intense effort to overcome the resistance. However, a term such as *crippling* (or, its other forms, such as *being crippled* or *a cripple*) clearly has the potential to be construed by the patient as having a pejorative connotation. Although Davanloo appeared to take great pains to clarify to the patient that he was being critical of the patient's defensive behavior and not the patient as a person, it is highly questionable as to whether the subtleties of such a distinction are lost on most patients. Even the more passive, less confrontational, approach of weakening resistances by interpretation as in a more classical psychoanalytic technique has the considerable potential to be viewed by the patient as being accusatory in nature.

The Problem of Accusatory Language

Wile (1984) maintained that classical psychoanalytic theory, with its stress on the patient's gratification of infantile needs and developmental flaws, leads the psychotherapist to accusatory interpretations. In stating his case, Wile cited the published writings and case material of two well-known psychoanalysts, Otto Kernberg (1977) and Heinz Kohut (1979). Mr. Z. was a patient who was seen by Kohut in two separate analyses. During the first analysis, Kohut was practicing according to the principles of a more classical psychoanalytic approach. In the second analysis, Kohut had modified his approach considerably so as to include increased amounts of empathy and emotional support for the patient. When Mr. Z. was seen by Kohut in the first analytic style, Kohut observed to the patient that he had arrogant feelings of entitlement, had narcissistic demands of the therapist, and possessed deluded and grandiose expectations of others. Mr. Z. responded to the analyst with anger in response to feelings of criticism. Wile maintained that, in normal social discourse, the analyst's statements *were* indeed accusatory and critical. Mr. Z.'s defensiveness is a normative response to the perception of the analyst, as an important figure in his life, viewing him as "defensive and pathological—and having deviant and unacceptable feelings" (Wile, 1984, p. 354). His response to Kohut's statements and choice of language is similar to the defensive reactions of Davanloo's (1990) patient to his use of the word *crippling* in reference to the patient's coping behavior and style of interaction.

Much of what has been historically attributed by analysts to the patient's anger and resistance to the therapeutic process may in fact be an iatrogenic artifact of the therapist's use of pejorative and accusatory language (Wile, 1984). In one of the other cases examined, Kernberg (1977) was working with a woman attorney diagnosed with borderline personality organization. At one point in the therapy, Kernberg (1977, p. 97) interpreted the patient's regressive withdrawal and anger as "primitive defensive operations in the context of condensation of oedipal and preoedipal material centering around her masochistic search for a warm and giving, but also powerful and sadistic, father who would harm her in intercourse." In response to this interpretation, Wile (1984, p. 355) observed: "Although this may be everyday, commonsense talk to psychoanalysts, it has an accusatory, pejorative, and bizarre tone to many others." If such strong potential exists in classical psychoanalytic treatment without excessive consideration to time constraints, then how much more problematic is the use of language in *brief psychody-*

namic psychotherapy in which a specific focus is placed on confrontations of defense to more expediently work through the patient's resistance?

Other therapists share the perspective and concern over accusatory interpretations and observations in psychotherapy. P. L. Wachtel (1993) believed that there are "surplus meanings" inherent in the psychotherapist's remarks to his or her patient, observing that comments by the psychotherapist are rarely only an inquiry. Rather, the psychotherapist's questions and observations typically have a point to make to the patient. As a result, Wachtel advocated for the "art of gentle inquiry" by the therapist. By this, he meant

> the ability to inquire into aspects of the patient's experience and motivations that are troubling to him, into features of his sense of self or of his overall life structure about which he feels ashamed and which he tries to hide from himself and from others, and to do so in a way that is minimally accusatory or damaging to the patient's self-esteem. (P. L. Wachtel, 1993, p. 88)

Thus, the psychotherapist engages in cooperative and bilateral explorations with his or her patients, rather than unintended "interrogations."

To accomplish this, P. L. Wachtel (1993) recommended the use of various qualifying inquiries that reflect the multisided nature of interpersonal conflict and that articulate the ambiguities with which the patient is struggling. Consider, for example, the patient who frequently assumes the role of the "victim" in his or her interpersonal relationships. P. L. Wachtel (1993) posed the psychotherapist's dilemma as follows: On the one hand, to even contemplate, imply, or suggest to the patient that he or she may play some role in seeking out such scenarios and that he or she may obtain some paradoxical form of gratification and familiar comfort in assuming such a relational position has the potential to implicate the patient in a derogatory or demeaning fashion. On the other hand, if the unconscious, yet proactive selection, of such relationships is a genuine and substantial contributing factor in the patient's misery, this must be addressed in some way in the therapy in order for the patient to be helped. P. L. Wachtel (1993, pp. 80–81) suggested the use of the qualifier, "at least," as an entry phrase to gently lead the patient into an exploration of experiences that he or she usually keeps barricaded, easing the patient toward some increased degree of insight and self-acceptance: "I guess concentrating on how people mistreat you feels like the best deal you can get. If you can't have what you want, *at least* you can feel you are due the sympathy of someone who has been wronged." Careful consideration and the delicate weighing of one's words, which is often so necessary in psychotherapy (Scaturo & McPeak, 1998), may be out of necessity one of the more time-intensive aspects of treatment. Treating the patient in a briefer form of psychodynamic psychotherapy in a way that is less provoking entails a considerable amount of skill and elegance.

From Provocation to Regulation: A "Kinder, Gentler" Brief Dynamic Therapy

The modifications, which took place in Kohut's (1979) psychoanalytic technique between the first and second analyses of Mr. Z., that included substantially increased amounts of empathy and emotional support for the patient, constituted a "kinder, gentler"[1] form of psychoanalysis (P. L. Wachtel, 1993). Likewise, the developments that took place in the area of brief psychodynamic psychotherapy mirror the empathic direction of Kohut's metamorphosis. McCullough-Vaillant (1997) substantially modified the previous methods of short-term dynamic psychotherapy, discussed above, using a strongly empathic and collaborative therapeutic relationship to restructure defenses.

One important modification is that psychological defenses are more frequently *clarified* by the therapist, rather than confronted. As noted above, several problems exist with the highly confrontational approaches (McCullough-Vaillant, 1997). For one, intense confrontation can be perceived as an emotional assault. For another, confrontational approaches are both difficult to master and emotionally painful to use. Many skilled psychotherapists simply do not have the emotional constitution or therapeutic style to undertake such a confrontational approach in accordance with the long-held traditional principle of nonmaleficence in biomedical ethics (Beauchamp & Childress, 1994), to "first, do no harm" (Greenblatt & Levinson, 1967; Scaturo, 2002c). In this modified approach, there is a greater emphasis placed on the therapeutic "holding environment" (Winnicott, 1965) for the patient as the vehicle by which anxiety is modulated by the therapist. The difference between the two approaches is illustrated in the contrasting statements by the psychotherapist (McCullough-Vaillant, 1997, p. 13):

> Confrontation and challenge: You are avoiding my eyes right now as I ask about your feelings. And now you're drumming your fingers on the table. This silence erects a barrier between us. What will happen if you continue to evade these issues in treatment?
>
> Clarification and support: As I ask you about your feelings, you often look away and become silent. Are you aware that this is happening? Is this topic painful for you to look at? Is there some way that I can help you make it more bearable to face?

Another modification in this approach is that the anxiety felt by the patient is *regulated* rather than provoked by the therapist. Previous approaches to short-term dynamic therapy endeavored to provoke the patient's anxiety

---

[1]The term "kinder, gentler" was originally attributed to the quotation, "I want a kinder, gentler nation" by President George Bush in his acceptance speech at the Republican National Convention in New Orleans, Louisiana, August 18, 1988, *New York Times* (August 19, 1988). (From the Columbia World of Quotations, Columbia University Press, 1996; http://www.bartleby.com/66/89/9389.html)

without the use of support to break through strong psychological defenses. By contrast, the anxiety-regulating approach is intended to assist the highly defensive patient in confronting painful experiences in bearable doses so as to not be overwhelming to the patient. A safe therapeutic environment is deliberately fostered by design throughout the course of treatment as illustrated in the following excerpt (McCullough-Vaillant, 1997, p. 14):

Therapist: What is so frightening to you about exploring your sad feelings here with me?

Patient: I don't know. . . . My mother was depressed her whole life. I guess, if I look at my feelings, I might get depressed like my mother was [*pausing*]. But come to think of it, if my mother *hadn't* examined her feelings, she would have been even *more* depressed.

In sum, the developments that took place within the anxiety-regulating dynamic psychotherapy model offer the patient a "healing connection" (McCullough-Vaillant, 1997) with the psychotherapist rather than a "head-on collision" (Davanloo, 1980). Anxiety-regulating therapy provides a corrective emotional experience (F. Alexander & French, 1946) with the therapist confronting painful emotions in a continuous, graded fashion. It is interesting that this description from a psychodynamic framework is conceptually similar to the graduated exposure therapy rationale for the *systematic desensitization* of anxiety in the behavioral paradigm, although with quite different theoretical assumptions about human functioning and change.

Summary: An Amnesic History

The study of psychological trauma, one of the cornerstones of the psychotherapy professions, has had a "forgotten history" (Herman, 1992). That is to say, the manner in which it has appeared, disappeared, and periodically reappeared from prominence is reminiscent of episodic amnesia by the profession. Herman postulated that these periods of forgetfulness are not attributable to normal cycles concerning what is fashionable in this field of study, but rather that this subject area requires that the clinician come face to face with the worst of human tragedy and the vulnerability that affects us all. As such, the periodic amnesia holds some functional value for the clinician in serving to ward off the devastation of traumatic experience in his or her patients.

In like manner, the fundamental aspects of the therapeutic alliance as a holding environment and the importance of nonspecific factors, such as trust and the instillation of hope, in psychotherapy have had an amnesic history in the field as well, although perhaps for somewhat different reasons. In present-day Western culture, it is popular to highlight the active ingredients of psychotherapy that are consistent with the proactive, "can do" values of our society. Thus, the emphasis on active *technical interventions* over the more passive curative factors embedded in the therapeutic relationship likewise holds some functional value for the clinician wishing to keep pace with his or her contemporaries. Brief psychotherapies are highly valued in the current milieu, as is any ingredient that is viewed as actively shortening the therapeutic process. Taken to its logical extreme, if single-session therapy (e.g., Talmon, 1990) and a "quick fix" are possible, so much the better. As a result, the more understated, and perhaps more time-intensive, qualities of the psychotherapeutic relationship, such as empathy, genuineness, and positive regard, which most therapists regard as being a fundamental prerequisite to the effectiveness of all therapies, have likewise taken a back seat in this contemporaneous milieu. Thus, psychotherapists have periodically required a "rediscovery" of the importance of the facilitative therapeutic factors, originally identified by Rogers (1951).

DILEMMAS IN OTHER FORMS OF INSIGHT-ORIENTED PSYCHOTHERAPY

Other forms of insight-oriented psychotherapies, predicated on other assumptions about the ameliorative factors in psychotherapy, have been influenced by this trend toward briefer treatments as well. Historically, insight-oriented therapies have consisted of a number of psychological treatment approaches that share the assumption that behavior is disturbed in some way because of a lack of awareness of one's motivations (Davison & Neale, 1998). These approaches to treatment include the humanistic *client-centered psychotherapy* with its focus on conditions in the therapeutic relationship; *existential psychotherapy* with its focus on death anxiety and questions of freedom, isolation, and meaning in life; and the revitalization of *interpersonal psychotherapy* from its original Sullivanian conception to its current intersection with models of brief therapy and the rediscovery of the saliency of the therapeutic alliance. Numerous clinical dilemmas have emerged from the limitations of time and restricted therapeutic focus placed on each of these methods of treatment.

Client-Centered Psychotherapy[2]

In the evolution of psychotherapy (Scaturo, 2001), the psychoanalytic approach to treatment with its focus on the intrapsychic processes of the

---

[2]Consistent with the current trend toward the "medicalization" of psychotherapy by managed mental health care's requirement of "medically necessary psychotherapy" for reimbursement purposes, the term used throughout this article is the term *patient*, in line with the doctor–patient role relationship in the practice of medicine. However, to avoid confusion for the reader, the term, *client* rather than *patient* has been retained exclusively in this subsection of the chapter that discusses the topic of Rogers's "client-centered psychotherapy" and the "client–therapist" role relationship in the practice of counseling psychology.

patient was followed by the backlash of behaviorism (e.g. Dollard & Miller, 1950; Watson, 1913, 1925) and behavior therapy that focused exclusively on the overt behavior of the patient and his or her symptomatology. In turn, a "third force" in ideological conceptualization known as humanistic psychology and psychotherapy followed the behavioral movement (Bugental, 1964). Humanistic psychology was fundamentally concerned with concepts that seemed to have no firm place in either psychoanalytic or behavioral theory. These notions encompassed aspects of human potential such as love, growth, warmth, autonomy, meaning, and psychological health in marked contrast to a focus on psychopathology. At the heart of the psychotherapeutic arm of the humanistic movement was Rogers's (1951) client-centered psychotherapy or nondirective therapy. The client-centered interview was regarded as non-directive, because it was believed that human growth was best able to emerge from an atmosphere in which the psychotherapist imposed him- or herself as little as possible in the client's self-exploration.

The psychotherapeutic focus of client-centered therapy was placed squarely on the qualities of the therapeutic relationship, including the psychotherapist's genuineness, empathy, and positive regard. Rogers (1957) held so strongly to these treatment principles that he regarded them as both the necessary *and* sufficient factors in therapeutic change. Although most clinicians regard these therapeutic qualities as a necessary element or prerequisite to positive changes in psychotherapy, their sufficiency for change has been the subject of intense debate and challenge (e.g., Rogers & Skinner, 1956). Existing views of effective psychotherapy necessitate a sufficiency of attention to both the therapeutic relationship and technical skills on the part of the therapist (Scaturo, 2002d).

The principal method of client-centered psychotherapy is the *reflective* mode of therapeutic communication with the client (Carkhuff & Berenson, 1967). That is, the therapist attempts to accurately reflect or mirror what the client has said with perhaps some slight alteration of the response to simultaneously validate the client's perception, as well as offer a slightly modified perspective for the client to consider. The reflective method of communication dominates the client-centered therapeutic process and is the means by which the therapist communicates his or her empathic understanding and *validation* of the client's perception, worldview, struggle, and emotional suffering (Truax & Carkhuff, 1967a).

The dilemma of support versus confrontation in client-centered psychotherapy takes on its own particular dimension. On the one hand, accurate reflection of the client's expressed emotion has been regarded as predominantly a supportive mode of therapy. By the same token, the reflective process is markedly deceptive in terms of its confrontational quality. Thus, it is remarkably easy to undercredit the degree to which an accurate reflection of a client's struggle or dilemma, in slightly modified terms, can provide a substantial amount of confrontation in the client's worldview and perspective on the client's difficulties.[3] This observation may be particularly true of clients in the contemplative stage of change in which clients are most open to interventions such as observations, confrontations, and interpretations (Prochaska & DiClemente, 1992a).

Consider, for example, the massive confrontational impact of a simple reflective question in the following therapeutic interaction with a then 34-year-old combat veteran of the Vietnam war. The following excerpt was taken from the early phase of his very first course in psychotherapy, at the time, approximately 15 years after his involvement in the war as he was just beginning to contemplate the ramifications of his military experience and activities. His job in the service was that of a door gunner, and he is speaking of his reflections on shooting the Vietnamese people from the helicopter:

> *Client:* [appearing emotionally numb, staring past the therapist] When they ran, they looked just like jackrabbits. It was like shooting jackrabbits.
>
> *Therapist:* [attempting to quietly catch the client's eye] You felt as though you were shooting jackrabbits?
>
> (After a long pause . . .)
>
> *Client:* [tearful, staring directly into the eyes of the therapist, appearing somewhat shaken] They weren't jackrabbits. Were they?

Existential Psychotherapy

The theoretical underpinnings of existential psychotherapy (Yalom, 1980) are predicated on the existential philosophy of writers such as Heidegger (1962), Jaspers (1994), Kierkegaard (1957), and Sartre (1956). All of these writers have pondered the questions surrounding the issues of man's existence or nonexistence, and the emotional implications for life to confront death as the "impossibility of further possibility" (Heidegger, 1962, p. 294). Kierkegaard (1957) was the first existentialist to associate the concept of *dread* (or a pervasive generalized anxiety) to an underlying fear of death and nonexistence. It is sociologically significant that the burgeoning of existential thought and philosophy was an outgrowth of the "lost generation" (Hemingway, 1964) following the First World War, and the search for meaning as a societal response to the devastation, loss, and destruction of the Second World War (Frankl, 1985; Hall, Lindzey, & Campbell, 1997; Scaturo & Hayman, 1992). Maddi (1967) proposed the concept of an "existential neurosis" as a psychiatric disorder, although the diagnosis was never formally adopted in the *Diagnostic and Statistical Manual of Mental Disorders* (American Psychiatric Association, 1994) nomenclature. In addition to anxiety and

---

[3] I am indebted to Neal S. Smalley for this initial observation.

dread, Maddi saw the differential diagnoses between existential neurosis and depression to be even more complicated, owing to the characteristic features of blandness and boredom punctuated by periods of depressed affect common to both.

Establishing a specific therapeutic focus in existentially oriented treatment can be difficult, because of its necessarily broad implications. At its most comprehensive level, existential therapy is fundamentally concerned with the emotional issues surrounding existence and nonexistence (i.e., death). An existential approach is, however, inextricably intertwined with life span development and the stages of the adult life cycle (e.g., Levinson et al., 1978). Death anxiety underlies all developmental impasses, but most noticeably during the midlife transition (e.g., Jacques, 1965). One is confronted by the phase-specific developmental tasks of each subsequent stage as one passes through the eras of early, middle, and late adulthood (e.g., Levinson et al., 1978; Vaillant & Milofsky, 1980). The three phases of adulthood (see Erikson, 1950), signified by the bipolar resolutions of their respective developmental tasks, are intimacy versus isolation in relationship formation (early adulthood), generativity versus stagnation of meaningful work (middle adulthood), and integrity versus despair in one's advanced years (late adulthood). A developmental impasse may arise over the ability or inability to confront not only the age-appropriate task but also the vague awareness that to address each task is to pass on through each stage of life to one's ultimate demise.

In the midlife transition, one confronts the disquieting realization that "more years now lie behind than ahead" (Levinson et al., 1978, p. 215). The psychotherapist's job is to assist the patient to confront such truths about his or her life. Yalom (1980, p. 160) referred to the haunting of Charles Dickens's literary character of Ebenezer Scrooge by the Ghost of Christmas Yet to Come (i.e., confronting his own death) as "existential shock therapy" and being instrumental in the transformation of his nature. The existential psychotherapist's dilemma is to help the patient productively examine the question of balance between death's stark reminder that life cannot be postponed while offering the support and optimism that there is still time left for living. In this respect, the existential psychotherapist's task in confronting a patient's death anxiety is not unlike the well-documented, classic social psychological study of using fear appeals to effect attitude change (e.g., Oskamp, 1991), for example, the use of fear about death to change attitudes and behavior about smoking cigarettes. In this area of research, a curvilinear, or inverted U-shape, relationship has been proposed between the degree of fear confronted and the amount of attitude change, with the greatest change occurring at moderate levels of fear (McGuire, 1968). At low levels of fear, the patient's motivation for life change would be expected to be somewhat low. At higher levels of fear, the patient's interest and receptivity will be good and likely to yield some change. However, at very high levels of fear, both receptivity and yielding to change are likely to be diminished because of the patient's defensive avoidance and emotionally shutting down. Thus, therapeutic judgment requires the clinician to strike an optimal balance between the two in any given clinical encounter.

Yalom (1980, p. 207) proposed the following useful equation for clinical work: "death anxiety is inversely proportional to life satisfaction." Thus, if death anxiety is gently confronted with an appropriate degree of reality and support, there is the potential to promote a new and altered perspective on living the remainder of one's life. Furthermore, the question of meaning in life cannot be productively answered by armchair speculation and deep introspection. Rather, the concerns about the meaningfulness of one's life are better answered by the process of interpersonal engagement, that is, to "immerse oneself in the river of life and let the question [of meaning] drift away" (Yalom, 1980, p. 483). It may be significant that Yalom (1980), one of the foremost writers on existential psychotherapy, is also one of the foremost writers on group psychotherapy (Yalom, 1995), as well as being theoretically grounded in Sullivan's (1938, 1953) interpersonal theory of psychiatry. This backdrop may largely account for his proposition that social and interpersonal engagement are the antidote to questions and fears of meaninglessness in one's existence.

Interpersonal Psychotherapy

Running as a common thread throughout all of the insight-oriented approaches to treatment has been the revitalization of interpersonal psychotherapy from its original Sullivanian conception to its current intersection with models of brief therapy and the rediscovery of the saliency of the therapeutic alliance. Sullivan (1938, 1953) believed that psychopathology can be best characterized by the recurrent patterns of interaction that the individual has with others in his or her interpersonal sphere. The initial research on interpersonally oriented psychotherapy emerged from the New Haven–Boston Collaborative Depression Research Project by Klerman et al. (1984). What evolved from this and subsequent projects was a manual-based and empirically supported form of treatment for depression (e.g., Scaturo, 2001). The psychotherapeutic goal of interpersonally oriented treatment is to modify disrupted relationships in the patient's interpersonal sphere and alter expectations about those relationships (Stuart, 2002; Stuart & Robertson, 2003), thereby bringing about symptom relief.

Interpersonal psychotherapy is based on *attachment theory* (Bowlby, 1988) and the primacy of intimate emotional bonds. Accordingly, a person develops intimate emotional bonds with specific individuals as an instinctual mechanism that serves as a protective function in survival from birth through the entire life cycle. As a result, intense anxiety is associated with losing, or becoming separated from, an intimate other. The converse is also true: Emotional security is promoted by the physical and emotional availability of protective figures in early life. On the basis of this early learning, three patterns of attachment have been identified (Ainsworth, 1985a, 1985b). First, there is the pattern of *secure attachment* in which the person has considerable confidence that his or her parental figure will be available and responsive in times of threat or adversity. A person raised in such an environment generally feels able to transfer such confidence to other situations in exploring the world and the other relationships around him or her. Second, there is the pattern of *anxious–resistant attachment* in which the person has been raised by a parent being available and responsive on some occasions but not on others. Such a person feels uncertain and prone to separation anxiety and is generally insecure about exploring the world and other relationships. Finally, there is the pattern of *anxious–avoidant attachment* in which the person has no confidence at all that his or her need for comfort or cries for help will be responded to and instead expects rejection. In later life, such an individual attempts to be emotionally self-sufficient and to live without attachment to others in a somewhat self-absorbed or narcissistic existence. Each of these patterns of approaching others results in a certain style of interpersonal coping behaviors in the *attachment history* requiring the careful attention of and assessment by the interpersonal psychotherapist as he or she attempts to repair intimacy lost or gone awry (Siegel, 1992). In general, those patients who have grown up with more anxious, less secure attachments are more vulnerable to emotional symptomatology. However, even those with secure attachments may become symptomatic in response to the disruption of attachments related to normative losses that occur within the life cycle. Emotionally mediated communication, learned initially in infancy with the mother, is a key feature of intimate relationships through one's life. Correspondingly, emotionally mediated behavior becomes a key focus of attention in interpersonal psychotherapy.

The focus for interpersonal psychotherapy is based on the assumption that emotional symptoms (anxiety and depression) are the consequences of losses or disruption in the interpersonal support network of the patient. The primary foci of treatment have been distilled into four thematic problem areas for the purposes of interpersonal psychotherapy (e.g., Karasu, 1990; Stuart, 2002; Stuart & Robertson, 2003; Weissman & Markowitz, 1998) that are partially common to other forms of brief therapy (e.g., Budman & Gurman, 1988). These problem areas involve (a) *interpersonal losses*, (b) *interpersonal disputes*, (c) *role transitions*, and (d) *interpersonal skill deficits and sensitivity*. Interpersonal losses almost always involve both a grief reaction to the loss of a figure who has provided a sense of safety and security in the world (e.g., Weiss, 1974) and an existential loss involving a "shattered assumption" (Janoff-Bulman, 1992) that revises one's view about the relative degree of safety in the world. Interpersonal disputes are most likely to involve some form of marital or family conflict but may also focus on family of origin and discord with members of one's extended family (e.g., Framo, 1977) as well as discordant relationships with close friends or reference groups (e.g., coworkers, etc.). The notion of role transitions is closely linked with the difficulties in transitioning from phase to phase in the life cycle, but also the experience of "developmental dysynchrony" (Budman & Gurman, 1988) noted earlier in which there is a sense that an important aspect of what one had wished for or expected at a given point in time has not come to pass and may never. And, finally, the notion of interpersonal skill deficits and sensitivity to others involves deficiencies that the patient might have in requisite social skills, such as assertiveness or responsiveness to the affective life of others that serve to create and maintain supportive social relationships.

Once a designated problem area for treatment has been selected, the interpersonal psychotherapist maintains a consistent here-and-now focus on current life events in the patient's interpersonal sphere throughout the course of treatment. However, although the interpersonal approach is relationship-based, it does not use the interpretation of the transference relationship as a primary focus of treatment as do the brief psychodynamic approaches to treatment (Klerman et al., 1984). Rather, the actual relationship problems in the patient's everyday life are the target for problem-focused interpersonal intervention. Herein lies the first psychotherapeutic dilemma for the interpersonal psychotherapist. Achieving this focus on the patient's interpersonal sphere without discussing how this presents itself in the transferential relationship is, however, considerably easier in conceptualization than it may be in actual clinical practice. The presence of transference is ever-present from the outset in almost any professional helping relationship, so invariably there are exceptions to this stance regarding the therapeutic relationship. Thus, the therapist may shift the attention to the therapeutic relationship when the patient's reaction to the therapist becomes an interference to the selected focus of treatment (Karasu, 1990). For example, a grief-stricken patient may respond to the therapist in a way that parallels the patient's relationship with the deceased loved one or the way in which the patient responds to other situations of perceived abandonment. At what point the interpersonal psychotherapist focuses on the therapeutic relationship versus the relationships within the patient's external interpersonal sphere ultimately becomes a matter of clinical judgment. In general, however, the intent of the time-limited format of interpersonal psychotherapy is to complete treatment and "get out" before transference becomes a powerful and focal issue as in longer term treatment (Stuart, 2002).

Whereas the *exploratory* aspects of the patient's interpersonal life bring the treatment at times close to an examination of the therapeutic relationship as in brief psychodynamic psychotherapy, the *prescriptive* aspects of interpersonal therapy at times bring it close to the directive nature of behavior therapy as well. For example, when social skill deficits are identified, this element of treatment can take the form of social learning therapy, such as assertion training to enhance social contacts, with direct modeling by the therapist, and prescriptive instructions for and encouragement of behavioral homework. Herein lies a second psychotherapeutic dilemma for the interpersonal therapist. The periodic directive stance taken by the interpersonal psychotherapist creates the same fundamental dilemma frequently experienced by cognitive–behavioral therapists. Scaturo (2002d) discussed this dilemma in terms of the perceived role conflict that cognitive–behavioral therapists frequently experience in balancing the use of clinical techniques and attention given to the nonspecific factors of the therapeutic relationship. Thus, in either cognitive–behavioral or interpersonal psychotherapy, when behavior homework is assigned, the therapist necessarily adopts the role of the "educator" in treatment. Although psychoeducation is clearly an important component of most current psychotherapies, at times it falls short of what many mental health professionals and consumers of mental health services consider to be the role of the psychotherapist. These broader role expectations typically involve many of the concerns of traditional insight-oriented psychotherapists that include such aspects as the holding environment (Winnicott, 1965); the facilitative conditions of genuineness, empathy, and positive regard (Rogers, 1951); and the therapeutic alliance (Safran, 1993). These elements of treatment constitute "protracted role functions" (Scaturo, 2002d) for cognitive–behavioral, interpersonal, and insight-oriented therapists alike. In interpersonal psychotherapy, these nonspecific factors may be especially important when the psychotherapist gets beyond the "acute phase" of what is generally regarded as 16 weeks of treatment (Weissman & Markowitz, 1998) into providing the important and well-documented "maintenance phase" of monthly interpersonal psychotherapy sessions for preventing relapse (Spanier & Frank, 1993).

CONCLUDING REMARKS: DILEMMA MANAGEMENT IN INSIGHT-ORIENTED PSYCHOTHERAPY

An examination of the issues involved in identifying a therapeutic focus and approaching the various degrees of confrontation versus support in any given therapeutic interaction reveals that these are far from one-dimensional decisions, but rather display a complexity that requires the consideration and management of multivariate concerns. The psychotherapeutic process of dilemma management (Scaturo & McPeak, 1998) is a procedure that is characterized by three qualities. First, the management of dilemmas in therapy is a *dynamic process* in which moment-to-moment decisions transpire with a reasonable degree of spontaneity in the course of an ongoing and constantly changing therapeutic dialogue between the patient and therapist. Second, dilemma management is a *dialectical process* in which the patient and therapist work toward an integration or synthesis of the conflict by means of a thorough examination of each arm of the dialectic. The specific resolution of the conflict, in many instances, may be less important than the fully considered exploration of alternatives that are examined by the patient. The Socratic method of learning in therapy becomes an important analogue and tool for learning in life (e.g., Carey & Mullan, 2004; Overholser, 1988). And, finally, the management of dilemmas in psychotherapy is also an inherently *interpersonal process* in which the emotional and relational life of the patient is empathically considered. The dilemmas that are presented in the patient–therapist relationship, as well as those in the interpersonal sphere of the patient's daily life, have profound emotional implications and consequences that are a part of this particular dialectic. Examination of relational conflicts goes far beyond the cognitive and intellectual realm that was Socrates' primary domain.

Regardless of the specific theoretical approach taken (e.g., psychodynamic or cognitive–behavioral), what the psychotherapist says, as well as how he or she says it, is of critical importance to the patient and the healing process (Scaturo & McPeak, 1998). The following chapter looks at the processes involved in behavioral and cognitive–behavioral treatments in which the therapist is confronted with a dilemma similar to that of confrontation versus support, albeit from a different theoretical vantage point (i.e., directive vs. nondirective intervention). Thus, the dilemmas surrounding a given focus and the therapeutic task of adhering to it are a process that defines the nature of psychotherapy. The manner in which the therapist manages the variety of patients' concerns that arise in the consultation room ultimately mirrors and models for the patients an adaptive way of approaching the complexity of pervasive conflicts and dilemmas in their own lives.

4

COGNITIVE–BEHAVIORAL THERAPY: BALANCING DIRECTIVE AND NONDIRECTIVE ELEMENTS OF TREATMENT

Efforts to move toward an integrative form of psychotherapy have incorporated elements of both cognitive–behavioral and insight orientations in treatment (P. L. Wachtel, 1977). Increasingly, integrative therapists have aspired to approximate a more seamless form of psychotherapeutic integration (P. L. Wachtel, 1991). Students interested in psychotherapy integration often ask, "How do you shift from one modality to another?" or "Do you do both in the same session?" (P. L. Wachtel, 1991, pp. 43–44). Such inquiries reflect a more *eclectic*, or multi-interventional, perspective rather than an *integrative* perspective in which the separate elements of multiple orientations become synthesized. However, the difficulty in bringing about synthesis is linked not only to the differing assumptions and therapeutic tasks of behavioral and insight-oriented clinical work but also to the perceived con-

This chapter is an adaptation of "Technical Skill and the Therapeutic Relationship: A Fundamental Dilemma in Cognitive–Behavioral and Insight-Oriented Therapy," by D. J. Scaturo, 2002, *Family Therapy*, 29(1), 1–21. Copyright 2002 by Libra. Adapted with permission.

flict that behavioral and insight-oriented therapists experience in their respective professional role functions (e.g., Shaw & Costanzo, 1982).

Integrative psychotherapy is predicated on the attempt to reconcile two or more apparently conflicting views or foci of treatment (Norcross & Newman, 1992). It represents an effort to harvest the best therapeutic ingredients of each approach with the hope or intention of arriving at an amalgam or synergy between the two that offers an improvement over either approach utilized in isolation or in succession (P. L. Wachtel & McKinney, 1992). Synergism takes place when each form of two or more integrated approaches enhances the effectiveness of the other (Schacht, 1984). For the clinician, the process of psychotherapy integration often begins with a dilemma in the therapeutic situation involving two alternatives in treatment direction, each of which may be less than satisfactory. In every form of psychotherapy, including those that are highly structured by design, some form of "dilemma management" (Scaturo & McPeak, 1998) is incumbent on the therapist by virtue of the personal, sometimes idiosyncratic, configuration of the concerns that a particular patient brings to treatment. A major premise in this book is that clinical dilemmas are endemic to and inevitable in virtually all forms of psychotherapy. Furthermore, it is frequently impossible to anticipate or predict such dilemmas on an a priori basis, or to expect a predetermined content or process in therapy, no matter how detailed, thorough, or comprehensive the manual or approach to treatment that is being utilized (e.g., Dryden, 1997; Piper & Ogrodniczuk, 1999; Scaturo, 2002b; Scaturo & McPeak, 1998).

The topic of this chapter is the perceived role conflict that cognitive–behavioral therapists share, along with other directive psychotherapists, in attempting to address the functions of therapy that more often have been traditionally reserved for the more insight-oriented and nondirective therapies as noted in the previous chapter. Such clinical dilemmas are examined in light of cognitive–behavioral therapy. These dilemmas include (a) the necessary balance between technical interventions and maintenance of the therapeutic relationship; (b) the spontaneous, *moment-to-moment patient–therapist interactions* that constitute clinical judgment; (c) countertransference in cognitive–behavioral therapy; (d) the treatment of historical and developmental influences on behavior versus more contemporaneous influences; and (e) the manner in which cognitive–behavioral and directive aspects of therapy borrow on the nurturant function of the psychotherapist.

COGNITIVE–BEHAVIORAL THERAPY AND OTHER FORMS OF DIRECTIVE THERAPY

A fundamental dilemma for the integrative or eclectic psychotherapist in clinical practice today surrounds the *directive* aspects of cognitive–

behavioral therapy (Scaturo, 2002b; Scaturo & McPeak, 1998). Although it is, unquestionably, the most widely adopted form of directive treatment, cognitive–behavioral therapy is not the only approach to treatment that one could describe as directive in nature. For example, problem-solving or strategic family therapy has relied heavily on giving directives to a family in treatment (J. Haley, 1976; Madanes, 1981). J. Haley's (1976, p. 49) notion that "the main goal of therapy is to get people to behave differently" is thoroughly consistent with that of cognitive–behavioral therapy. Furthermore, some of the task assignments in the strategic approach are intended to solve problems as straightforwardly as traditional behavior therapy. For example, "a man who is afraid to apply for a job may be asked to go for a job interview at a place where he would not take the job if he got it, thereby practicing in a safe way" (J. Haley, 1976, p. 61), that is, to engage in *behavior rehearsal* (Lazarus, 1966) for courses of action and behavioral solutions that have been novel or unfamiliar to a given patient.

However, many strategic directives are intended to bring about other *indirect* results or changes in the family (Stanton, 1981), which are frequently couched in terms of either their *metaphorical* relevance to the family structure or their *paradoxical* intention (Frankl, 1960; Weeks & L'Abate, 1982). Much of this approach is predicated on Milton H. Erickson's techniques involving hypnotic induction (J. Haley, 1973). For example, in the presumed case of a family with an overinvolved mother, "a father and son are asked to do a minor thing that the mother would not approve of" (J. Haley, 1976, p. 60) in which event it would be difficult for the mother to orchestrate what they do when it is something that she, in fact, does not want. However, when using paradoxical interventions, it is important to ethically caution against the use of any directive technique—paradoxical or otherwise—which is undertaken in the absence of a thorough consideration and understanding of the patient's goals and patient–therapist relational dimensions (Mozdzierz, Macchitelli, & Lisecki, 1976). This perspective is consistent with the concerns related to the adequate maintenance of a constructive therapeutic alliance that are woven throughout the perspective presented in the following paragraphs.

PERCEIVED ROLE FUNCTIONS OF THE COGNITIVE–BEHAVIORAL THERAPIST

In contrast to the strategic therapies, directives in behavioral and cognitive–behavioral approaches to treatment tend to be rather straightforward tasks intended to bring about their stated intention. In behavior therapy, the directive versus nondirective dilemma is perhaps most typified by the assignment of *behavioral homework*. In essence, the behavior therapist has adopted the role of the *educator* in treatment (e.g., Authier, Gustafson, Guerney, &

Kasdorf, 1975; Bandura, 1961). Furthermore, the behaviorally oriented therapist is not uncomfortable with this role, as many of the behavioral techniques that focus on skill training for psychological–emotional problems (e.g., assertiveness training for the more passive or socially anxious patient) are predicated on learning theory and are therefore congruent with an educator or teacher's role behavior. Over the past number of years, a handful of learning-based behavioral techniques and procedures (e.g., systematic desensitization, implosion, token economies) have mushroomed into a behavioral armamentarium of well over 150 directive techniques that have been classified as having major, secondary, or minor breadth of application in behavioral treatment (Bellack & Hersen, 1985). In addition, a wide range of techniques relevant to the domain of cognitive interventions, broadly categorized into techniques for countering maladaptive belief systems and techniques for perceptual shifts, have also been catalogued (McMullin, 2000). Nevertheless, what distinguishes a psychoeducational approach from that which is merely educational? In its strictest sense, the role of the educator falls short of some of the more important expectations and role functions of what many mental health professionals and many consumers of mental health services (e.g., "Mental Health: Does Therapy Help?," 1995) consider being the role of the psychotherapist. These broader role expectations typically involve many of the concerns of the traditional insight-oriented therapist, which are equally relevant and important to the application of learning-based behavioral and cognitive–behavioral practice.

PERCEIVED ROLE FUNCTIONS OF THE INSIGHT-ORIENTED THERAPIST

Traditional Approaches to Insight-Oriented Psychotherapy

Many traditionally trained, insight-oriented therapists see their psychotherapist role as being inherently and fundamentally different from that of the educator. Historically, insight-oriented psychotherapy has consisted of any of several psychological treatment approaches (Davison & Neale, 1998), including *psychoanalytic* and psychodynamic psychotherapy, *humanistic psychotherapy*, existential psychotherapy (discussed in greater detail in chap. 3), as well as the more recent emphasis on *narrative therapy*. In brief, however, each of these approaches to treatment assumes a somewhat different curative element or primary ingredient for change and, thus, differing foci in treatment. Psychodynamic psychotherapy focuses on the resolution of core intrapsychic conflicts that are operative in a person's life and the abreaction of negative affect surrounding these experiences (Auld & Hyman, 1991). Humanistic psychotherapy emphasizes the curative qualities of the therapeutic relationship in which facilitative factors such as empathy, unconditional positive regard, and genuineness are seen as both necessary and sufficient conditions for psychological and behavior change (Rogers, 1951). Existential psychotherapy grapples with the more macroscopic enigmas of the patient's life, the more distal but nevertheless salient stressors, such as questions of interpersonal isolation, death anxiety, and the search for meaning of one's existence as the integrative factors in reducing emotional distress and psychopathology (Frankl, 1985; Yalom, 1980). Insight-oriented therapies share the fundamental assumption that behavior is disturbed in some way because of a lack of awareness of one's motivations (Davison & Neale, 1998) and that the essence of treatment involves an interpersonal method of bringing these motives into greater awareness. Since the movement toward the use of evidence-based treatments in which the cognitive–behavioral therapies have shown the clearest superiority (e.g., DeRubeis & Crits-Christoph, 1998), the insight-oriented approaches would appear to be declining in prominence in academic training programs and with the advent of managed behavioral health care. However, if one considers the recent plethora of insight-oriented therapy conducted under the rubric of "narrative therapy" that has emerged over the past decade, it becomes apparent that interest in insight-oriented treatment remains well sustained.

Narrative Psychotherapy: A Contemporary Insight-Oriented Approach

Narrative therapy is based on the notion that personal problems are constructed within the broader context of one's social and cultural milieu (M. White & Epston, 1990). Accordingly, people experience difficulties in their lives when the stories of their life, as they or significant others in their lives have constructed them, are discordant from their own life experience and the subjective meaning that they have derived from that experience. The goal of the narrative approach, achieved through the use of exploration and narrative construction, is to assist patients in excavating resources, skills, and abilities through a transformed reconstruction of self (Epston, Winslade, Crocket, & Monk, 1996).

Consider, for example, the well-accepted scenario in the treatment of psychological trauma in which the therapist helps the survivor of a traumatic life history (e.g., children of alcohol and abusive families) to move from a sense of *victimization* to a sense of *survivorship* in the personal narratives of his or her life (e.g., Scaturo, 2002d). In traumatic situations involving interpersonal or existential losses, the overall goal of treatment is regarded as assisting the patient in making this transformation (Budman & Gurman, 1988). To articulate further, Figley (1985) noted:

Victims and survivors are similar in that they both experienced a traumatic event. But while the victim has been immobilized and discouraged by the event, the survivor has overcome the traumatic memories and become mobile. The survivor draws on the experiences of coping with the catastrophe as a source of strength, while the victim remains immobilized.

What separates victims from survivors is a conception about life, an attitude about safety, joy and mastery of being a human being. Being a survivor, then, is making peace with the memories of the catastrophe and its wake. (p. 399)

Although a few authors have linked narrative therapy to cognitive and learning theory (e.g., Epston et al., 1996), more frequently it has been conceptually aligned in the literature with a range of insight-oriented approaches to treatment; these include psychoanalytic and psychodynamically oriented approaches (Giora, 1997; Roberts & Holmes, 1999; Schafer, 1992; Spence & Wallerstein, 1990), existential and humanistic psychotherapies (Hermans & Hermans-Jansen, 1995; McLeod, 1998), as well as brief and family therapies (Eron & Lund, 1998; Freeman, Epston, & Lobovits, 1997). Additionally, a substantial body of evidence on the effectiveness of narrative approaches to treatment has been compiled in the area of psychotherapy process research (Rennie & Toukmanian, 1992). In essence, there appears to be a substantial resurgence of interest in the psychotherapy patient's view of the value of psychotherapy as a verbal, insight-promoting medium (Furst, 1999).

Psychotherapeutic Processes

Along with the revitalization of interest in insight-oriented therapy is the resurgence of concerns about therapeutic processes that have traditionally been the domain of insight-oriented forms of treatment. These concerns affect the behaviorally oriented and cognitive–behaviorally oriented therapies, particularly when efforts at integration are made. Such traditional issues in psychological treatment include, but are not limited to, the following: (a) a recognition of the necessity of attention to multiple factors that have been historically associated with the therapeutic alliance, the relevance of which is now being more fully addressed in the cognitive and behavioral literature; (b) the moment-to-moment patient–therapist interactions in treatment requiring an ability to exercise clinical judgment and reasoning; (c) the role of countertransference in cognitive–behavioral therapy; (d) the cognitive–behavioral therapists' focus on the more contemporaneous (i.e., immediate) stressors, frequently to the exclusion of a historical analysis and assessment of the more distal determinants of behavior; (e) the manner in which cognitive–behavioral and directive aspects of therapy borrow on the *nurturant function* of the therapist; and (f) the relevance of these factors to the *protracted role functions* of the psychotherapist above and beyond that of "education" alone.

THE EMERGENCE OF TRADITIONAL PSYCHOTHERAPEUTIC DILEMMAS IN COGNITIVE–BEHAVIORAL TREATMENT

The Therapeutic Alliance: A Brief Review

Historically, the nature of the therapeutic relationship has been considered a critical factor in any form of well-conducted psychotherapy. Winnicott (1965) referred to the therapeutic relationship as a *holding environment*, metaphorically likening it to the safety and security of the holding that occurs in a healthy parental relationship. Alternatively referred to as a *facilitating environment*, it involves an atmosphere in which sufficient trust is present so that the child (in parenting) and the patient (in therapy) can facilitate emotional growth without distortions. In parenting, and more precisely in mothering, the holding environment need not be perfect for this to occur. Rather, it is only necessary that the child have a "good enough mother" (Winnicott, 1965) in whom he or she can experience being cared for and valued. In marital therapy, a variant of this term has been used to describe the essential goal for couples undergoing marital therapy, that is, to foster a "good enough marriage" between the husband and wife to function adequately in the developmental tasks basic to family life (Gottman, 1999). Likewise, in education, it might be said that the student is also in need of a "good enough teacher" to provide an atmosphere to learn properly (Rogers, 1969). Similarly, in psychotherapy, nurturance in the treatment environment also need not be perfect, only that the patient have a "good enough psychotherapist" in whom sufficient trust can be placed regarding the emotional vulnerabilities brought into treatment before the more directive aspects of the therapy take place. For most patients, it seems highly improbable that the directive aspects of therapy will succeed without a sufficiently nurturant and emotionally supportive therapeutic environment.

The next major emphasis on the therapeutic relationship came from the "third force" of the humanistic psychology movement and client-centered psychotherapy. Rogers (1951; Truax & Carkhuff, 1967b) focused on three facilitative conditions of the client–therapist relationship that he regarded as critical to the treatment process; these were the now classically observed factors of genuineness, empathy, and positive regard. *Genuineness*, the most basic condition (Rogers, 1959), involves the therapist's responses to the client as being congruent, or genuine, to his or her own honest reactions to the client. *Empathy* requires a true understanding of the client's phenomenological world and subjective reality, such that the psychotherapist not simply echoes the client's words but demonstrates an understanding of how the client subjectively experiences his or her life circumstances. And, finally, an uncompromising *positive regard* for the client is needed in which the therapist circumvents any verbal or nonverbal behavior implying judgment regarding the client's experience, and fully taking into account all of the subtleties of therapeutic communication (P. L. Wachtel, 1993). Perhaps the only unfortunate consequence of an adamant humanistic perspective was the implication that these three factors, critical though they may be, were regarded as both necessary and sufficient conditions to bring about positive psychotherapeutic outcome (Rogers, 1957). A number of behavioral critics, such as Skinner (Rogers & Skinner, 1956) and Bandura (1969), responded with criticism of the nondirective method, which suggested that the entirety of the approach was neither sufficient nor necessary. Neither seems to have fully considered the possibility that these therapeutic ingredients were indeed necessary but not sufficient to address a broad range of needs that the psychotherapy patient brings to treatment.

For many years, the interpersonal aspects of therapy, including concepts like the therapeutic relationship, resistance, transference, and countertransference, were absent from the behavior therapy literature and lexicon (P. L. Wachtel, 1982). A number of the early cognitive–behavioral therapists had suggested that behavior therapy extend beyond the bounds of rigidly defined behavior therapy protocols to encompass a more "personalistic psychotherapy" (Lazarus, 1971), incorporating the facilitative conditions of the therapeutic relationship, as well as *flexibility* and *versatility*. These notions were, no doubt, the forerunners of multimodal behavior therapy (Lazarus, 1976) and technical eclecticism (Arkowitz, 1992b; Lazarus, 1967).

Meichenbaum (1977), too, made similar observations when discussing the "educational (or conceptualization) phase" of cognitive–behavioral stress-inoculation protocols:

> The most important aspect of this phase is that the conceptual framework should be plausible to the client and its acceptance should naturally lead to the practice of specific, cognitive, and behavioral coping techniques. . . . It should be underscored that the scientific validity of a particular conceptualization is less crucial than its face validity or air of plausibility for the client. (pp. 150–151)

In other words, it is essential that the patient and the therapist arrive at a consensus about the likely etiology of the patient's difficulties and the approach by which they will grapple with it together. Furthermore, patient–therapist agreement on therapeutic tasks and goals is enhanced by explicit agenda setting and providing rationales for the methods used. Thus, cognitive–behavioral technical processes can be skillfully incorporated to enhance the patient–therapist bond and the therapeutic alliance (Beck, Freeman, & Associates, 1990).

Other cognitive–behavioral therapists (e.g., G. T. Wilson, 1984) have contended that training in cognitive–behavioral therapy always has maintained a focus on the "nonspecific factors" of the therapeutic relationship but that they simply spend less time discussing it in clinical supervision. If less time is spent on relationship factors in cognitive–behavioral supervision, why so? Such a stance on training would seem to imply that relational factors are somehow less important than the technical maneuvers or directives given in cognitive–behavioral intervention. If so, then this would be a perplexing position from the standpoint of psychotherapy outcome research, which has demonstrated that an average of 30% or more of the outcome variance can be attributed to the therapeutic alliance and other nonspecific relational factors (e.g., warmth, empathy, and the instillation of hope). In contrast, only about 15% of the variance can be attributed to specific technical interventions (Lambert, 1992; Lambert & Bergin, 1992). An excellent clinical illustration of these empirical observations is Blatt's (1995) subcategory of perfectionism in depressive disorders that does not appear to benefit from cognitive–behavioral technical interventions but does appear to be responsive to interpersonal psychotherapy primarily affected by a positive therapeutic relationship over time.

Safran and his colleagues (Safran, 1993, 1998; Safran & Greenberg, 1993, 1998; Safran & Muran, 1998; Safran & Segal, 1996) have written extensively on the *therapeutic alliance* in behavioral and cognitive–behavioral treatment. A critical consideration was the need to better articulate in systematic terms the relationship between specific technical factors of cognitive–behavioral interventions and the nonspecific factors of the therapeutic relationship (Safran & Segal, 1996). Embedding cognitive–behavioral therapy within the broader context of interpersonal theory and treatment has been a way to facilitate this interrelationship (Safran, 1998). Sullivan (1938, 1953), widely regarded as one of the most undercredited figures in the history of psychotherapy (Cushman, 1992; Havens & Frank, 1971), placed focal emphasis on the interpersonal interaction of psychotherapy in contrast to the psychoanalytic prominence on intrapsychic structures and conflict. The advantages of an interpersonal conceptualization and perspective have, only recently, begun to be appreciated and utilized in psychotherapy by clinicians working within a range of treatment areas; these include Klerman and his colleagues with the interpersonal treatment of depression (Klerman et al., 1984), brief psychotherapists (Budman & Gurman, 1988; Strupp & Binder, 1984), and more recently cognitive–behavioral therapists who have emphasized the importance of the therapeutic alliance in this approach (Safran, 1998). The application of interpersonal theory and concepts to cognitive–behavioral treatment has allowed the "in-session/in-context" behavior of the patient *in relation to the therapist* to be a focus of behavioral assessment and intervention, comprising data that previously have tended to be neglected or avoided by cognitive–behavioral therapists (Safran, 1998). This type of approach incorporates the affect associated with the immediate experience of the patient and the enhanced learning that takes place under these conditions (Safran & Greenberg, 1998). To be sure, effective cognitive–behavioral therapists have already conducted therapy in this manner for some time (Safran, 1998). Thus, one might extrapolate from Sullivan's dictum that "all people are simply human than otherwise" by concluding that "effective psychotherapists, regardless of their theoretical orientation, are more alike than unalike," utilizing elements of both action and insight (e.g., P. L. Wachtel, 1987).

Finally, the impact of increasing time limitations in the current trend toward brief psychotherapy on the therapeutic relationship and process has been a significant development bearing on these fundamental treatment issues (Safran & Muran, 1998). With the social and economic forces coalescing to bring the practice of brief therapy into the zeitgeist, and therapeutic rapport being predicated on increasingly fewer numbers of sessions, the fragility of the therapeutic alliance requires increasing attention by the prudent clinician (Safran & Muran, 1998; Scaturo & McPeak, 1998). The time pressures of brief therapy create additional clinical dilemmas for all psychotherapists. On the one hand, therapists who tend to approach the therapeutic alliance supportively and cautiously are likely to do so even more, so as not to risk rupture of a delicate therapeutic alliance (Safran, 1993; Safran & Greenberg, 1993) by premature and intrusive technical interventions. Such clinicians tend to sensitively monitor the readiness for change in a given patient with respect to active clinical interventions (Prochaska & DiClemente, 1992a). On the other hand, with less clinical time available to accomplish therapeutic change, more directive therapists are likely to feel a need to intervene quickly, and to utilize the interpersonal data of the patient–therapist interaction, both diagnostically and therapeutically. Thus, therapists' respective belief systems about what therapeutic behaviors will account for curative change are likely to influence the side of this dilemma on which different therapists prefer to err.

In summary, although adept cognitive–behavioral clinicians clearly have incorporated an understanding and knowledge of the therapeutic relationship into their professional functioning, the early literature often mentioned the concept "only in passing" (Lambert, 1983, p. 4). As a result, a systematic framework for integrating the concept of the therapeutic alliance and technical interventions did not appear to be outlined (P. L. Wachtel, 1982). Butler and Strupp (1986, p. 33) pointed out: "the complexity and subtlety of psychotherapeutic processes cannot be reduced to a set of disembodied techniques because techniques gain their meaning and, in turn, their effectiveness from the particular interaction of the individuals involved." Thus, a more realistic and comprehensive perspective would be to view technical interventions and the therapist administering them as "inseparable parts of an organic whole" (Safran & Segal, 1996, p. 35). In essence, the interpersonal context forms the catalyst for effective cognitive–behavioral interventions.

Moment-to-Moment Therapeutic Interactions

Another critical consideration in developing a systematic cognitive–behavioral approach to the therapeutic alliance is the further delineation needed in specifying the moment-by-moment, step-by-step clinical interaction between the therapist and patient in which the therapeutic relationship and the technical maneuvers of the therapeutic process are linked and catalyzed (Safran & Segal, 1996). In other words, what happens when the patient brings up something unexpected or that could not be anticipated or predicted by the therapist on an a priori basis? Consider the example of a hypothetical patient who is currently being treated by a behavioral protocol that appears indicated and is in agreement with the therapist with whom he or she appears to have a good rapport. What happens if or when this patient discusses something distressing that occurred earlier in the week that appears to be only tangentially related to the focal problem? Or, perhaps even more problematic, what happens if such a patient brings in a more disturbing, but distal, aspect of his or her history undisclosed by that patient in previous assessment? The adept therapist would most likely explore these thoughts or experiences and determine their potential relevance to the therapeutic task. However, this would, no doubt, be mediated differently by different therapists, predicated on the type of relationship and therapeutic contract that they have with that particular patient, as well as the therapist's ability to "think on his or her feet" in the clinical situation (i.e., clinical judgment). It is likely that these subtle interactional processes in therapy are as strongly related to positive and negative outcomes in therapy as are the therapist's technical skills (Foa & Emmelkamp, 1983). This question has led some researchers to propose the study of therapeutic behaviors of therapists who intrinsically form good therapeutic bonds with their patients (e.g., Sweet, 1984) to better understand the nature of this process.

These momentary decision-making processes challenge the therapist's ability to negotiate the clinical dilemmas that exist everywhere in psychotherapy, regardless of theoretical and technical orientation of a given therapist or treatment modality. The concept of the clinical dilemma in psychotherapy has been approached from a number of different perspectives (Dryden, 1997; Horowitz & Marmar, 1985; Ryle, 1979; Scaturo, 2002b; Scaturo & McPeak, 1998). For example, Ryle (1979) discussed various impasses to the psychotherapeutic process resulting from problematic ways in which different patients have in relating to their therapists, such as an "if/then" or "either/or" fashion, based on ways in which the patient has learned to relate to significant others in his or her interpersonal past. Horowitz and Marmar (1985) discussed recurrent dilemmas that emerge for patients as impediments to establishing a functional role relationship with their psychotherapist, as well as others in their past; for example, patients who are so terrified by their inner experience that they are unable to experience the therapeutic process as anything but intrusive. From each of these perspectives, the manner in which the therapist negotiates these interpersonal obstructions, by either maintaining the alliance or rupturing it, has integral impact on the technical success of the therapy.

Other Traditional Psychotherapeutic Concerns

Countertransference in Cognitive–Behavioral Therapy

Another important aspect of the psychotherapeutic relationship that has been receiving increased attention is the countertransference of the cognitive–behavioral therapist, that is, the therapist's emotional and behavioral reactions to the patient. The term countertransference, in juxtaposition to the term cognitive–behavioral therapy, almost carries with it a sense of awkwardness. The terms themselves, *transference* and *countertransference*, originate from psychoanalytic theory (Freud, 1912/1958a) and feel out of place in a cognitive–behavioral conceptualization. Nevertheless, "there is no reason to assume that cognitive therapists are any more immune to countertherapeutic reactions and feelings than their psychoanalytic counterparts" (Safran & Segal, 1996, p. 41). It seems probable that cognitive–behavioral therapists have both productive and unproductive emotional reactions to their patients, but they do not have the lexicon within the cognitive–behavioral framework to adequately address such experiences in clinical supervision. Cognitive–behavioral therapists are not alone in this difficulty. Marital and family therapists, particularly those from the structural and strategic schools of treatment, have also experienced this limitation (although there have been notable exceptions; e.g., J. S. Wallerstein, 1990). Such limitations impair not only the therapists' ability to deal with any countertherapeutic reactions that they might have toward the patient but also their ability to utilize observations of the ongoing therapeutic interaction as sources of data for productive clinical–cognitive intervention. Interpersonal theory and conceptualization provide a productive theoretical framework to enable cognitive–behavioral therapists to readily address clinical dilemmas relevant to the therapeutic relationship common to all clinical encounters (Safran, 1998; Scaturo & McPeak, 1998).

Historical Versus Contemporaneous Influences on Behavior

One of the concerns of insight-oriented therapists interested in incorporating behavioral techniques into their therapeutic approaches has been the impression that behavioral methods, historically, have given little attention to family history and factors surrounding psychosocial development. In the early forms of behavior therapy, the individual's "reinforcement history" has tended to be somewhat decorously addressed in the behavioral literature (Scaturo, 1987). Like other forms of brief therapy (e.g., Budman & Gurman, 1988; Pinsof, 1983), cognitive–behavioral treatment places an emphasis on the more immediate determinants of behavior as primary in the maintenance of a given behavioral problem and in relation to behavior change. Later versions of cognitive–behavioral treatment have incorporated more of an emphasis on the patient's longer term psychosocial history (Newman, 2000). Particularly relevant in this regard is Beck et al.'s (1990) work in adapting cognitive–behavioral therapy to the treatment of chronic and severe personality disorders in which the patient's historical data are prominent in the clinical picture. Integrative psychotherapists strongly note that both contemporaneous and historical factors are relevant to effective psychotherapy (e.g., Scaturo, 1994).

Directive Therapy and the Relational Bank Account: Borrowing on Nurturant Role Function of the Psychotherapist

There is a substantial body of research on the importance of *nurturance* in the psychotherapy setting. Psychotherapy patients expect a number of features in their therapists (Tinsley, Workman, & Kass, 1980). Among these are the facilitative conditions of treatment (i.e., genuineness, empathy, and positive regard), therapist expertise, and nurturance. In a study on the stages of change in psychotherapy (Prochaska & DiClemente, 1992a), the patient's expectations of the facilitative conditions, expertise, and nurturance in the psychotherapeutic environment have been significantly related to the contemplative and maintenance stages of change (Satterfield, Buelow, Lyddon, & Johnson, 1995). Furthermore, it has been shown that therapists and patients largely agree on these perceived role expectations of the psychotherapy setting (Martin, Moore, & Karwisch, 1977). Nurturance has also been found to be one of the major factors in how psychotherapy patients perceive and receive a sense of empathy from their psychotherapist (Bachelor, 1988). Nurturance has been found to be so critical to the psychotherapy setting that some authors (e.g., C. A. Carter, 1971) have considered this to be one advantage of being a woman therapist because women, in particular, traditionally have been allowed more freedom in the expression of nurturance and other emotionally relevant communications in their role functions.

Whether derived from perceptions of past parental figures, the therapist as an authority figure, the therapist as a caring figure, or the therapist as a protective figure, there is a demonstrated expectation by patients that one of the role functions of the psychotherapist is that of providing nurturance to people who have frequently experienced little of this in their lives. Many clinicians, too, regardless of theoretical orientation, believe that this is an important role function of the psychotherapist. Likely, also, a well-developed ability to provide nurturance to others tends to be an important motivation for entering the mental health related professions. Many, if not most, patients would not wish to see a clinician who does not appear intrinsically motivated to provide help, even if technically skilled. Most patients desire to see a clinician who is both compassionate and skillful.

Given the magnitude of this issue in treatment, it is reasonable to assume that every behavioral homework assignment or directive that is requested of the patient has the potential to be viewed as a demand from the therapist (Scaturo & McPeak, 1998). It not only creates the opportunity for resistance to the task but borrows on the therapeutic alliance as well. As a consequence, the cognitive–behavioral therapist needs to pose the following question to him- or herself prior to assigning a behavioral homework task to the patient: "How much therapeutic rapport do I now have in this patient's metaphorical 'bank account' to make a 'withdrawal' (i.e., request) at this point in time?" (Scaturo & McPeak, 1998, p. 3). It is incumbent on the therapist to gauge the strain of a given directive on the strength of the therapeutic alliance at any point in time to protect the quality and productiveness of the relationship and to avoid or minimize the potentiality of its rupture. According to Safran and Greenberg (1993), more directive treatment approaches, such as behavior therapy, are more likely to induce ruptures in the therapeutic alliance that stem from the patient's feeling of being controlled, "managed," or manipulated by the therapist. Thus, the question of directive versus nondirective intervention at a given point in time has direct bearing on one of the major patient expectancies in treatment and forms one of the critical dilemmas needing to be managed by the adept clinician.

CONCLUDING REMARKS: PROTRACTED ROLE FUNCTIONS IN COGNITIVE–BEHAVIORAL THERAPY

The age-old debate over action versus insight (P. L. Wachtel, 1987) in psychotherapy has constituted a professional role conflict (Shaw & Costanzo, 1982) or dilemma for clinicians over the use of directive versus nondirective aspects of treatment. There can be little argument that the technical facets of behavioral (Bellack & Hersen, 1985) and cognitive (McMullin, 2000) interventions are empirically supported active ingredients of change (DeRubeis & Crits-Christoph, 1998). They are a necessary and important part of a professional education in the behavioral sciences (Scaturo, 2001). Equally necessary, though, are the interpersonal skills that require further attention in graduate curriculum. It is insufficient to relegate and subsume this critical element of learning as something ancillary to be included or covered under the rubric of clinical supervision, as some have suggested (e.g., G. T. Wilson, 1984). An integral part of the graduate curriculum is to actively teach cognitive–behavioral skills in tandem with what we know to be their inherent interrelationship with the therapeutic alliance, and how cognitive–behavioral techniques are embedded and used in that context (e.g., Safran & Muran, 2001).

Contemporary cognitive psychotherapists have called for an enhanced creativity in the clinical training of cognitive therapists (Kuehlwein, 2000). The challenge for the current generation of cognitive–behavioral therapists is to draw on other psychotherapy models and frameworks creatively in the treatment context while retaining the essential cognitive character of these interventions in the therapy session. By using more integrative approaches to treatment, we will do a better job of teaching the protracted role functions of cognitive–behavioral therapists that actually exist in day-to-day clinical practice. In doing so, we will train clinicians who not only know empirically validated techniques but also know how and when to responsibly use them and when to responsibly do something else. Frequently, "something else" consists of the more nonspecific, nondirective aspects of the therapeutic relationship involving genuineness, accurate empathy, and positive regard.

When F. Alexander and French (1946) initially, and at the time radically, proposed a departure from classical psychoanalysis in psychoanalytic treatment, one of the principles that they discussed was that of flexibility in treatment. In this regard, they were referring to aspects such as the frequency of sessions, periodic interruptions and terminations in courses of treatment, and therapeutic life experiences that occur outside the context of treatment. In a parallel fashion, a "second-generation" of behavior therapists (e.g., Lazarus, 1971; Meichenbaum, 1977) gradually extended beyond the rigid systematic desensitization paradigm of reciprocal inhibition of the "first-generation" behavior therapists (e.g., Wolpe, 1958), identifying flexibility and versatility as key ingredients in effective therapist–patient interactions. Additionally, a "third-generation" of cognitive–behavioral therapists (e.g., Safran & Segal, 1996) have also noted a number of personal qualities of the therapist that have been empirically correlated with therapeutic effectiveness. These personal qualities include the *psychological health* of the therapist (Beutler, Crago, & Arrizmendi, 1986; Luborsky et al., 1986; Piper, Debbane, Bienvenu, & Garant, 1984; Ricks, 1974), which is reflective of psychosocial maturity. Other qualities include the presence of a genuine interest in helping the patient (Luborsky, McLellan, Woody, O'Brien, & Auerbach, 1985), which is akin to the concept of altruism. The therapist's competence, expertise, and technical skills are composed of an integration of these personal qualities and a knowledge of and adeptness with proven clinical techniques. Comprehensive clinical training needs to incorporate these multidimensional factors when considering the protracted role functions in cognitive and behavioral practice. Such multifaceted role functions become even further put to the test when the treatment system is broadened to include more than just the therapist and the individual patient. The following chapter explores the dilemmas that result from the inclusion of a spouse or significant other in the context of marital and couple therapy.

5

MARITAL AND COUPLE THERAPY: THE THERAPIST'S DILEMMAS WITH DYADS

Expanding the treatment system from that of the individual patient to that of the couple or family system carries with it unique challenges and fundamental dilemmas for the marital and family therapist. E. F. Wachtel (1979) outlined various dilemmas from the standpoint of the individually trained psychotherapist who may be attempting to incorporate a family systems perspective into his or her clinical practice. Likewise, the early pioneers in the field of family therapy recognized the problem of the inherent complexity in this protracted form of treatment (e.g., J. Haley, 1963; Napier & Whitaker, 1973). The intricacy of marital and family treatment has caused both research (e.g., J. F. Alexander, Holtzworth-Munroe, & Jameson, 1994) and clinical conceptualization (e.g., Budman & Gurman, 1988) to restrict itself to either one (e.g., marital–couple therapy; Gurman & Fraenkel, 2002) or the other (e.g., family therapy) of the two domains. The present discussion of clinical dilemmas in systemic therapy is restricted largely to those

This chapter is an adaptation of a paper presentation, *Clinical Dilemmas in Marital and Couple Therapy: Art, Science, and Wisdom*, by D. J. Scaturo, August 2002, at the 110th Annual Convention of the American Psychological Association, Chicago, Illinois. (ERIC Document Reproduction Service No. ED470724; http://ericir.syr.edu/Eric/adv_search.shtml)

conflicts posed to the clinician in marital–couple relationship therapy or what might be called *dyadic dilemmas*. Such dilemmas often focus on questions of balance in what has been termed the *central relationship dynamic* (Budman & Gurman, 1988) within the couple's relationship system.[1]

THE CENTRAL RELATIONSHIP DYNAMIC: THE THERAPEUTIC FOCUS IN MARITAL AND COUPLE THERAPY

The notion of a *therapeutic focus* is a universal concept in all forms of psychotherapy, and most significant in short-term and time-limited forms of intervention. The therapeutic focus is an attempt to narrow and define a given psychotherapeutic problem for a given episode of time-limited treatment. In brief psychodynamically oriented individual therapy, the concept of a *dynamic focus* (e.g., Schacht et al., 1984) is a well-documented clinical phenomenon. Furthermore, the concept of the psychodynamic focus appears in the literature under a wide array of synonyms, as noted in chapter 3. In each instance, though, the focus is seen as the nucleus of the individual's problem, encompassing the cardinal symptom, presenting problem, related intrapsychic conflict, interpersonal dilemma, and maladaptive coping pattern. The psychodynamic focus is also characterized by a functional salience in which the patient's presenting complaint and maladaptive interpersonal behavior pattern are integrally related to the emotional or interpersonal difficulty that the patient is trying to solve.

In assessing couples and families for treatment, there are dimensions that are common to both families and couples and dimensions that are specific to the couple's relationship (Budman & Gurman, 1988). With regard to the couple's dyadic relationship in particular, Budman and Gurman (1988) noted that the aspects of assessment for treatment should include (a) the marital relationship's history, (b) the specific nature of the marriage contract or understanding that the couple have with one another, (c) the couple's sexuality and sexual functioning, (d) the current level of commitment that each has in the marriage, and (e) the presence or absence of any substance or spouse abuse. Of the factors embedded in the couple's relationship history, the single most important aspect of marital assessment and the most useful in establishing a focus for treatment is the couple's central relationship dynamic (Budman & Gurman, 1988). This dynamic incorporates the recurring con-

---

[1]Some readers might legitimately observe that the discussion included in this chapter, and the one that follows, does not take into account the real possibility of individual psychopathology (e.g., schizophrenia) in one of the spouses or other family members, and how the family system deals with this issue. Such a discussion of mental illness in the family is far beyond the scope of these chapters. Suffice it to say that the present discussions are necessarily limited to the dilemmas that typically arise out of the family dynamics in the broad majority of families in which severe mental illness in a given family member is generally absent from the clinical picture.

flict and source of disharmony that has transpired for the couple over the development of their relationship. Like the concept of the psychodynamic focus in individually oriented treatment, the central relationship dynamic in systems-oriented treatment has been characterized by a variety of terms in the field with an essentially similar meaning. Aspects of the concept have been encompassed by various terms, including interlocking pathology (Ackerman, 1958), family homeostasis (Jackson, 1957), the marital quid pro quo (Jackson, 1965), the overadequate versus inadequate relationship (Bowen, 1960), the one-up/one-down relationship (J. Haley, 1963), complementarity (Bateson, 1935, 1972; Simon, Stierlin, & Wynne, 1985), and the concept of codependency (Scaturo, 2003a; Scaturo et al., 2000).

The dilemmas involved in maintaining an ongoing balance in a well-functioning, intimate relationship stems in part from the common clinical observation that "people choose spouses who have identical levels of immaturity but who have opposite defense mechanisms" (Goldenberg & Goldenberg, 1980, p. 98). Although individuals in the couple may be matched for their level of psychosocial maturity or level of differentiation from their families of origin (Bowen, 1985), partners also select one another on the basis of their opposite methods of coping with life. From an object relations theoretical perspective (e.g., D. E. Scharff & Scharff, 1991), this selection occurs in an adaptive effort to regain parts of one's self that were abandoned by the child in choosing a coping style early on in life. By choosing a spouse who has those traits one has "left behind," one has the marvelous ability, through the couple's relationship, to approximate a more whole sense of self and ability in managing the world.

For example, the husband with obsessive–compulsive tendencies who marries a somewhat histrionic wife is likely to have been initially attracted to her "fun-loving" ability in life—something that he may have largely abandoned a long time ago in his childhood. Ten years later, in the marital therapist's office, appreciation of her fun-loving nature may have been supplanted by a suspicion and distrust in her "overly flirtatious behavior" at parties. In like fashion, this histrionic wife may have been initially attracted to her obsessive–compulsive husband's "strength and ability for organization"—something that she may have given up years ago in her family of origin. Now, her perception of her husband's talent for organization and strength has been replaced by the critical descriptors of him as "overbearing, controlling, and stuffy." To further augment their difficulties, their mutual abilities to tolerate and respond to these criticisms have been curtailed by the growing feeling of insecurity that either spouse may no longer be as emotionally attached as he or she once was, as evidenced by the spouse no longer valuing the qualities he or she once did.

Such relational dynamics have important implications for the initial interview in marital therapy. The couple's presenting complaint is usually quite telling. Often, the presenting complaint that each spouse has of the other is of precisely those qualities that, at an earlier time in modified form, were those that attracted them to one another in the first place. It is for this reason that a critical question in marital assessment is: "What qualities did you first find attractive in your spouse?" This inquiry enables the couple in conflict to focus on something positive about their spouse while at the same time shedding light on the central relationship dynamic. In the black comedy film based on the novel, *The War of the Roses* (W. Adler, 1981), the actor Danny Devito plays a divorce attorney who is giving rather expensive "$450 per hour advice" to a man contemplating divorce. He tells the man of the horrific story of a couple, Oliver and Barbara Rose, who descend into hatred and cruelty of one another through a divorce proceeding that ultimately brings about their mutual demise. After relating this story to the young man, Devito's character offers him the following choice: to either prepare himself for the very worst because "a civilized divorce is a contradiction in terms" or "get up and go home and try to discover some shred of what you once loved about the sweetheart of your youth" (Brooks, Michlan, & Devito, 1989). For those who choose the latter, this is where couple therapy begins.

The sources of recurrent disharmony in an intimate relationship tend to be caused by only a relatively few major issues (Gurman, 1981). These are typically related to changes and alterations that take place in a previously comfortable central dynamic in the relationship as exemplified above. Most of a couple's dilemmas tend to be organized around this essential "marital bargain" or "quid pro quo" (Jackson, 1965), whether this exchange is conscious and verbalized, conscious but not verbalized, or mostly unconscious (Sager, 1981). Regardless of whether the dilemmas into which the couple draws the therapist appear to be about the substantive issues of power and money, sex and affection, responsibility and blame, divided loyalties between their respective families of origin, or simply the apportionment of the therapist's degrees of confrontation and support, these dilemmas and conflicts tend to be symbolically related to their central relationship dynamic. Given this backdrop, the following discussion outlines some of the more frequent and consequential dilemmas experienced by the therapist in marital and couple therapy.

CONFRONTATION AND SUPPORT: A TECHNICAL DILEMMA IN SYSTEMS-ORIENTED THERAPY

A common dilemma in therapeutic technique in all forms of psychotherapy involves the degree to which the therapist supports and validates a given side of a patient's personal conflict versus the degree to which the therapist challenges or confronts a given aspect of the patient's point of view. Verbal expressions of understanding and empathy tend to provide emotional support for the patient, whereas questioning the patient's perspective and inquiries for clarification tend to confront the patient's viewpoint and urge him or her to reexamine and reevaluate his or her thinking about a given issue. Metaphorically speaking, confrontation is the "surgical incision" in therapy, whereas the therapist's emotional support provides the "anesthetic" for any given intervention (Scaturo & McPeak, 1998). Confrontational intervention can take a number of forms, including the interpretations about a patient's or family's behavior within a psychodynamic approach to therapy (e.g., Scaturo, 2002c), psychoeducational interventions (e.g., teaching assertiveness skills) within a cognitive–behavioral framework (e.g., Scaturo, 2002d), or the assignment of directives or tasks as is done in a problem-solving or strategic family therapy approach to treatment (e.g., J. Haley, 1976; Madanes, 1981). Each of these more directive approaches borrows on the strength and quality of the therapeutic alliance that the therapist has with each and every patient or family member in treatment (e.g., Safran, 1993; Scaturo & McPeak, 1998). As a result, when confrontation takes the form of a homework assignment or directive that is given to a particular family in treatment, it is essential that the task given to the family equitably include an aspect for each and every family member so as to reasonably distribute the "request" (often seen by the family as a "demand") being made by the therapist.

Thus, in marital and couple therapy, the difficulty in balancing the confrontational and supportive aspects of psychotherapeutic technique is compounded by the need not only to decide when support versus confrontation is needed within a given individual, and in what degrees, but also to decide how and when to distribute degrees of support versus confrontation among each member of a couple, each of which may be in conflict with one another at any given point in time. Support of one spouse's position against the other's position forms what can be, at most, a temporary alliance with the supported member of the couple that can be tolerated by the other spouse for only a limited period of time without alienating him or her and appearing to form a more permanent coalition with one spouse against the other (Minuchin, 1974). As a result, the couple therapist may frequently feel as though he or she is constantly "robbing Peter to pay Paul" as he or she attempts to balance emotional support and the therapeutic alliance in the couple therapy session (Scaturo & McPeak, 1998). The couple therapist frequently finds him- or herself allying with the person who may be taking the more reasonable or more conciliatory stance at a given point in time, only to find his or her support shifting in the alliance a few minutes later as the rationality of the moment wavers or evaporates. Recognizing when one member of the couple is "extending an olive branch of peace" and capitalizing on the reinforcement of this is a particular skill of an adept systems-oriented therapist. The alternation of support and challenge of the systems therapist becomes part and parcel of the systemic interaction of the couple as a family unit.

The Family Hierarchy

To more fully appreciate the significance of these therapeutic maneuvers in couple therapy, this issue must be viewed in light of the hierarchy that exists in the family and in the therapy session. The notion of a hierarchy in family treatment outlines the power structure, role functions, and generational boundaries of the various subsystems within the family (Simon et al., 1985). Along generational lines, the parents hold more power and decision authority than do children in a functional family system. Role reversal and hierarchical inversion may result, for example, in the *parentification* of a child (e.g., J. Haley, 1976) that is a sign of pathological family functioning, which robs children of their childhood and deprives parents of their responsibility and authority within the family. When such hierarchical dislocations exist in a family in treatment, the family therapist generally works to put the parents back "in the driver's seat" (Minuchin, 1974). A clinical example of parentified behavior is that of an oldest daughter, age 10, of three siblings, who secures the house at night because her alcoholic parents are frequently too intoxicated to do so themselves. In addition to the treatment of the parents' alcoholism, a family therapist, in this instance, might directly assign the parents the task of locking up the house each evening in an effort to restore their adult roles and functionality within the family hierarchy. Just as the power distribution and clear role function definition in the family hierarchy between the generational subsystems are signs of healthy family functioning, recognition of the co-equal status of the partners within the couple subsystem is likewise a designation of relational health in the couple (Scaturo, 1994). Although the role functions of husband and wife may vary, the importance of equal value for these respective functions needs to be recognized by each member of the couple for this subsystem to thrive. For couples in conflict, however, truly valuing a partner's contribution to the family system can be easily lost in the heat of the moment.

The Treatment Hierarchy

For couples and families in therapy, superimposed on top of the couple and family hierarchical structure is the added feature of the *treatment hierarchy*. The marital and family therapist temporarily becomes a part of a given family's hierarchy with the children's generational subsystem on the bottom level, the couple's subsystem in the middle, and the therapist or co-therapist's subsystem occupying the upper level of the hierarchy. Recognition of the therapist's place within the treatment hierarchy is critical, because it serves to explain why a couple in conflict may vie for the therapist's support and approval in the same way that siblings within the children's subsystem vie for the approval of their parents in the next highest generational level in the family hierarchy. To gain the support and approval of someone at a higher status level in a given system is, therefore, to gain power in the conflict. When such power is obtained on an ongoing basis, a destructive coalition is formed. This is why, when a child "acts out" against or disrespects one of the parents in a family, it is frequently said that the child is able to do so because he or she "has friends in high places" (i.e., a coalition across generational lines with one of the parents against the other). The criticality of the balance of power within a couple's subsystem is also why the astute therapist will delicately balance and apportion his or her emotional support between the members of a couple. In doing co-therapy, especially when there is a bigender co-therapy team that is often used in training settings, it is crucial that the co-therapists work out a respectful and equal relationship with regard to intervening with the couple or family (Boszormeyi-Nagy & Framo, 1965). The modeling of equity within the couple subsystem is an important function of the co-therapy team and particularly significant in couple therapy.

One other point is relevant to the notion of the treatment hierarchy. For strategic therapists who are working within a *reflecting team model* (e.g., Andersen, 1987, 1991, 1992, 1993; Papp, 1980) behind a one-way observation mirror, it is significant to note that the reflecting team occupies the highest level within the treatment hierarchy, even above that of the therapists themselves. The clinical rationale for this model stemmed from the realization that a new system and hierarchy are created between the therapist and couple or family. The therapist, working directly with the family, may have periodic difficulty in maintaining an objective view of the treatment system of which he or she is a part (Simon et al., 1985). It is in part the increased objectivity of the reflecting team, as well as the mystique of the team fostered by their anonymity behind the one-way mirror, that allows them to occupy the highest level in the treatment hierarchy with the couple or family and lends power to their periodic interventions by telephone or intercom to the therapist(s). Although consideration of this approach extends the notion of the treatment hierarchy and adds to the richness of this issue, such a treatment model, like the notion of co-therapy itself, has been increasingly restricted to training settings because the availability of multiple therapists for a single clinical hour has become cost-prohibitive in an age of managed health care.

Perhaps a dissenting view of the hierarchy in treatment can be found in the more recent work of the *narrative family therapists* (e.g., Epston & White, 1992; M. White & Epston, 1990). Whereas traditional family therapists have historically given families directives for change (e.g., J. Haley, 1976), narrative family therapists primarily ask questions of their families in treatment. The treatment techniques in their clinical armamentarium include the use of questions to explore the exceptions to the family's problems and the significance of these variations, the raising of dilemmas to examine the possible aspects of a problem before those dimensions take place, and the use of letter writing to serve as a medium to continue the dialogue between the family and therapist between therapy sessions (Gladding, 2002). The narrative therapists' encouragement to take a collaborative listening position with the family and to ask questions that take a nonimposing approach with the family place them at variance with some of the previously noted observations of the therapist in the treatment hierarchy. Narrative therapists point to their use of questions rather than interpretations or directives as evidence of their co-collaborative, nonimpositional, and nonhierarchical stance in treatment. However, critics of this approach note that as much as the narrative family therapists wish to view themselves as nonmanipulative in their questions, they are indeed more directive than they claim to be. Nichols and Schwartz (1998) noted, "Regardless of how many questions they use, they are looking for a certain class of answers and, consequently, are leading clients to particular conclusions" (p. 417). Thus, the notion of hierarchy within the family in treatment, and the therapist's place within it, has saliency, whether or not one chooses to emphasize it within a given theoretical framework.

THE BALANCE OF POWER

According to strategic family therapists, "all couples struggle with the issue of sharing power and of organizing in a hierarchy where areas of control and responsibility are divided between the spouses" (Madanes, 1981, p. 29). Power in a relationship can take many forms and is a dynamic force that changes constantly over the life cycle in the couple's relationship predicated on a myriad of life factors that can affect the relative status of each spouse or partner at any given point in time. Thus, for a couple's relationship to function adaptively, the question of relational power is always a question of balance. More specifically, the term *power* frequently implies *decision power* over a given domain of family life. The various arenas for decision power can include housework versus employment, the emotional areas of life versus the intellectual side of life, and activities surrounding children and extended family versus social engagements with friends. Ultimately, it is incumbent on a couple to arrive at a mutually satisfactory arrangement regarding the division of power. Otherwise, the emotionally symptomatic behavior can develop as a coercive means of rebalancing or redistributing power that has been unjustly dominated by one or the other parties. In a minor form, one might consider the example of a spouse who develops a tension headache that exempts him or her from a social engagement with a certain group of friends that has not been properly negotiated and agreed on by the couple in the first place. More serious is the repetitive failure to negotiate equitable "say-so" in this area that results in chronic headaches on the part of one or the other spouse. In more linear terms, one might describe this as passive–aggressive behavior. From a systemic perspective, though, this is passive–

aggressive behavior on the part of *both* spouses, not only the symptomatic partner.

One of the more significant determinants of power and conflict in the couple's relationship is that of income-producing activity: Who earns the income? Who earns more of the income? What are the ramifications of this on the relationship? B. Carter and Peters (1996) believed that the old adage, "He who has the gold, makes the rules," is equally applicable to the establishment of power in an intimate relationship as it was for the business relationship to which the saying was originally applied, translating the original version to "Whoever controls the purse strings, controls the relationship" (B. Carter & Peters, 1996, p. 74). Also, the use of the pronoun, *he*, in the original adage is likewise applicable to the relational version, given the continued disparity between the higher incomes of men and the, most often, lower incomes of women, even in the current millennium. That money should be deemed so important is not particularly surprising from the standpoint of a hierarchy of motivational needs (e.g., Maslow, 1970). With physiological needs at the base of that hierarchy, and with the survival-related needs of air, water, food, sleep, and sex ordered within that foundational level, it is clearly understood that "money puts food on the table" and is a "bread and butter" concern. Given that lower needs must be satisfied before higher needs can be addressed by the individual, it is an undisputable position that income precedes subsequent needs for safety, love, and esteem. Thus, money and the need for it fall at a level of necessity for survival that lends power to one who is able to provide for it.

However, the need for *safety* occupies the very next rung of this conceptual ladder, even more basic than love and a sense of belongingness. Stability and constancy are necessities in a chaotic world. Although these needs are more psychological than physiological, the security of a home and the safety of a family clearly are co-requisites for maintaining stable income-producing activity for any sustained length of time. Familial bonds with significant others are as essential to the need for safety as they are to the need for love. Ultimately, the order of some safe living space and attending to the relatively mundane domestic tasks that provide this "base of operations" are shared by all human beings and have tremendous functional value. Most unattached individuals, particularly single parents, will comment freely on the Herculean effort that is required to accomplish both tasks alone (unless independently wealthy) in the complexity of today's world. The criticality of a partner who is able to equitably shoulder the "slings and arrows" of both the occupational and domestic worlds cannot be overstated. Findings from the Harvard University landmark longitudinal study of adult development across the life span have shown that the best predictor of good health and aging well is a secure marriage (Vaillant, 2002). Vaillant concluded from these data that marriage is not only important to a healthy aging process but also is a cornerstone of resilience in adulthood and late-life.

According to Bowlby (1988, p. 121), "although food and sex sometimes play important roles in attachment relationships, the relationship exists in its own right and has a key survival function of its own, namely, protection." Thus, Bowlby argued for what he called the "primacy of intimate emotional bonds." Given such primacy, a view that is shared herein, it seems that ultimately the *value* of that relationship, and what it provides in its own right, must be recognized by the couple regardless of whose activities earns the "lion's share" of the jointly deserved assets. Ultimately, B. Carter and Peters (1996) offered some guarded agreement on this point. Although they draw a distinction between what they consider to be financially *equal* arrangements and the term *equitable* for which they feel male therapists hold a particular penchant, noting that *equitable* means *fair*, they concede that equitable relationships (e.g., husband makes more money while wife does more child care) can indeed be functional. They qualify this by noting that such functionality is only possible if each member of the couple holds to the "personal belief that earning money and homemaking are equally important contributions of equal partners who share important decision making and have equal access to the money" (B. Carter & Peters, 1996, p. 82). It is particularly critical that the couple therapist advances such a belief, because there is almost always variation in income and corresponding variation in domestic responsibilities. The therapeutic task is for the clinician to help the couple in excavating what is truly functional and mutually comfortable for their own unique relationship.

In actual clinical practice, a frequent source of conflict brought in by couples, particularly couples in families with young children, is the question of devising an equitable division of family labor. In this instance, family labor means the total amount of man-hours (or person hours) that are required by a family to maintain their lives, both income producing and home upkeep (i.e., domestic tasks and child-care responsibilities). Families with young children are particularly vulnerable to this issue, because they must undergo a rather massive developmental adjustment from "an intimate game of two" (J. Haley, 1973, p. 53) to accommodating new entries and task demands into the family system that they had worked out previously. The addition of children into the equation increases the home-related labor enormously in myriad unanticipated ways. It is essential to recognize the need for an equitable division of the *collective* work hours. Thus, it is not sufficient for the primary income-producing party in the family to simply take the attitude or stance that "I worked today. I've done my job."—when four more "person hours" of domestic work and child care still exist at home even at the end of the work day. The noted social consciousness-raising saying is as applicable to family life and couple therapy as it is to societal functioning: "If you want peace, work for justice."

THE ATTRIBUTION OF RESPONSIBILITY AND BLAME

The upside to the question of who has responsibility in a relationship is having decision-making power and authority. The downside of personal responsibility concerns the question of blame for unfortunate decisions and courses of action. Some politicians are particularly adept at taking credit for the upside while evading blame for the downside. It should be noted that there are "politics of family life" (Framo, 1976, p. 209) as well. In reality, however, one cannot have it both ways. According to E. F. Wachtel (1979), the most significant psychotherapeutic dilemma from a family systems viewpoint concerns the question of "Who is to blame?" Within this framework, the responsibility for marital conflict is not seen as residing exclusively within any one individual, although the respective partners in a couple frequently enter treatment believing that this is the case. As a result, when a couple is in conflict, the question posed to the therapist by each partner tends to be some variant of "Is it me or my spouse?" who is to blame for the problem (Scaturo & McPeak, 1998). The clinician typically regards this as a question of internalization versus externalization of responsibility. With conflictual couples, both partners tend to present a fairly high degree of externalization at the outset of treatment. Each member of the couple is typically able to identify his or her spouse's faults with utter clarity and insight, while tending to minimize or overlook aspects of his or her own behavior that contribute to the problem.

Classic social psychological research (e.g., Heider, 1958; Oskamp, 1991) has distinguished between internal versus external attributions for interpersonal behavior and actions. An *internal attribution* is one in which a person concludes that the cause for a particular person's behavior (in this instance, his or her spouse) is due to some personal character trait, such as laziness or inconsiderateness. In contrast, an *external attribution* is one in which a person might conclude that the causes for a given person's behavior is due to some situational factor outside of the person's control, such as time pressures or a heavy workload. Interestingly, an important concept in this area of study has been the finding of *actor–observer biases* in making internal versus external attributions (e.g., Jones & Nisbett, 1971; Storms, 1973). An observer of someone else's behavior (e.g., his or her spouse's) is likely to attribute the reason for it to internal characteristics. For example, a spouse might conclude, "My spouse did not make it home in time for dinner with me, because he [or she] is basically an inconsiderate and thoughtless person." By contrast, however, an actor performing that same behavior frequently attributes its cause to any apparent situational pressure. By way of contrasting example, this same spouse might conclude, "I did not make it home in time for dinner with my spouse, because I was overwhelmingly busy at work." These social psychological observations have significant import for understanding and negotiating marital conflict.

Although such attributional behavior may be commonplace in interpersonal contexts, it becomes particularly toxic in an intimate relationship. According to Gottman (1994, 1996, 1999), "the four horsemen of the apocalypse" in marital demise are, first, the spouses' mutual and unrelenting *criticism* of one another, then the development of mutual *contempt* of one another, followed by mutual *defensiveness* in their behavior, and, finally, the *stonewalling* of any feedback or input from the spouse. The type of attribution that takes place in actor–observer biases is essentially the first horseman of the marital apocalypse. In this regard, it is important to note that *complaints* of one's spouse are not the same as *criticism*. Complaints are normative in marriage and address specific behaviors or actions. An example of a complaint might be, "Why didn't you clean up around the house?" By contrast, criticisms throw in blame and general character assassination of internal attributions by an observing spouse. A contrasting example of criticism might be, "Why didn't you clean up around the house? What's wrong with you, anyway? Why are you so lazy?"

As a result, in the beginning phase of marital therapy, it is often helpful to pose the following question to each member of the couple (Scaturo & McPeak, 1998, p. 4): "What do you think *you* could or should do to help alleviate some of the difficulty and improve your marital situation?" Such a question, which directs each member of the couple to look inwardly toward his or her own, contributing problematic behavior, is invariably helpful in a clinical context fraught with externalizations. It is an attempt to move the couple from the externalization of blame to the internalization of responsibility for what is essentially a co-owned problem. For the purpose of assessment, it is helpful to know whether a particular couple has the psychosocial maturity and the mutual ego strength to entertain such a question. For purpose of intervention, it serves to help the couple shift their viewpoint of their marital difficulties to a more systemic perspective, which may serve to reduce the tendency toward mutual blaming. Furthermore, if the couple is able to generate appropriate and reasonable responses to this intervention, then this may serve to point out some constructive avenues for therapeutic change.

BALANCING FAMILY LOYALTIES

Another topic that bears consideration when dealing with the question of blame is the therapeutic examination of the partners' respective families-of-origin contribution to the distress experienced by the couple. Framo (1993) estimated that as much as 80% of the variance in marital discord may be related to unresolved emotional conflicts within the respective families of origin. In therapy, it may be important for each member of the couple to understand that much of how they treat each other is derived from what each has learned about intimate relationships from his or her family of origin. The patient's dilemma surrounding perceived blame might be characterized by the question, "Is it my spouse or my parents?" who is/are to blame for the problem (Scaturo & McPeak, 1998). Articulated elegantly by Framo (1976):

> The price for robbing of self during the growing years exacts a toll and leaves a legacy, giving rise to the ambivalence that all people feel about their close relationships. Since old scores have to be settled and reservoirs of hatred cannot be contained, someone has to pay. Those someones are usually the current intimates—the mate and children; the demons of today are punished by the internal ghosts of yesteryear. (p. 208)

Assisting each member of the couple to see that the spouse is frequently a stand-in target for the anger and conflict often helps to alleviate some of the marital discord. A variation of this technique has been used frequently in individual psychotherapy to help lessen the self-blame that the patient may feel with an otherwise confrontational interpretation of a particular maladaptive or self-defeating behavior pattern that the patient is addressing in therapy (E. F. Wachtel, 1979). For example, a given therapist might say, "Of course, your behavior is an understandable response, given the family environment in which you were being raised" (Scaturo & McPeak, 1998). At other times, the mode of treatment that can best deal with this issue is the "family-of-origin consultation," used as an adjunct to ongoing individual or couples treatment (e.g., Framo, 1976, 1992; E. F. Wachtel & Wachtel, 1986). A family-of-origin therapeutic consultation is predicated on the assumption that working problems out directly, face to face, with the family of origin, rather than through a transferential relationship with a therapist, can have powerful curative effects (e.g., Boszormenyi-Nagy & Spark, 1973; Bowen, 1985; Framo, 1976; Whitaker, 1976). In this type of therapeutic approach, the patient would have the opportunity to discuss directly with the members of the original family group some of the historical concerns that have plagued him or her emotionally over the years. A central theme in this form of treatment is the aspect of forgiveness of the parents for their human failings, which helps to heal such wounds for both the parents and children (Enright & Fitzgibbons, 2000).

Most people are torn between confronting their families of origin, especially their parents, on their grievances from the past, on the one hand, and avoiding confrontation, on the other, fueled by powerful feelings of loyalty to those who have raised them. This dilemma becomes even more complex and augmented when the spouse has grievances (mostly, present-day concerns) with his or her in-laws, often about various forms of intrusiveness of a spouse's family of origin on the couple's life (e.g., how they spend their money, how they discipline their children). In these instances, the question of loyalty to one's parents versus allegiance to one's spouse forms the crux of this dilemma, which is not easily navigated. Once again, this can be a particular problem in the stage of the family life cycle for young couples who are recently married and raising young children. The life choices that the newly married couple make are generally entangled in some way with the alliances that each have (or do not have) with their respective parents. For example, if one set of parents (or both) continue to provide some type of financial support for the new family, then there is either an implicit or explicit expectation about how much "say-so" they have regarding various family matters, including aspects of how the grandchildren are to be raised (J. Haley, 1973). Couples must negotiate ways of having clear but semipermeable boundaries with each of their families. Couples who attempt to resolve this conflict by some type of complete emotional cutoff (Bowen, 1985) from their respective families of origin are generally not as successful as those who are able to achieve some independence while still remaining in emotional contact with their extended families. Marital therapists remain cognizant of Framo's (1980) axiom: "When you marry, you don't just marry a person; you marry a family."

CONCLUDING REMARKS: BALANCING ART, SCIENCE, AND WISDOM IN COUPLE THERAPY

Since its early beginnings, the art in the practice of psychotherapy has been inextricably intertwined with the science of its study. Freud saw psychoanalysis as a research method for studying various elements of mental functioning as much as he saw it as an approach to the treatment of mental disorders (e.g., Gay, 1998). After the Second World War the field of clinical psychology adopted a *scientist–practitioner model* for training that called for an equal emphasis on scientific research and clinical practice (Raimy, 1950). This marriage of science and practice has recently celebrated its 50th anniversary (Benjamin & Baker, 2000). Within the last 5 years, however, the integration of science and practice has been reconceptualized and predicated on the concept of the *local clinical scientist* (Peterson, Peterson, Abrams, & Stricker, 1997; Stricker & Trierweiler, 1995). In this conceptualization of training, it is no longer expected or required that the practicing clinician have the research skills necessary to contribute to the general body of scientific knowledge in the field of psychology. Rather, this approach expects competent clinicians to adopt a scientific attitude in their approach to clinical problems, an ability to apply available scientific knowledge to their work, and an empirical skepticism and hypothesis-testing attitude about practice that would typify that of a good scientist as well. Likewise in the field of marital and family therapy, there has been a movement toward the use of evidenced-based therapy in which the outcome of family systems theoretical and clinical approaches is scrutinized through the eyes of empirical testing (e.g., Gottman, 1999).

The art–science dialectic in the field of marital and family therapy is well illustrated in a scientific exchange concerning the outcome and follow-up studies comparing behavioral marital therapy (BMT) with that of insight-oriented marital therapy (IOMT; J. F. Alexander et al., 1994). In a study by Snyder and Wills (1989), although there were no differences in outcome between the BMT and IOMT conditions at either termination of treatment or the 6-month follow-up, a significant difference in relapse rate was found in which 38% of the 26 BMT couples had divorced whereas only 3% of the 29 IOMT couples had terminated their marriages at the time of a 4-year follow-up (Snyder, Wills, & Grady-Fletcher, 1991). In a flurry of responses, behaviorally oriented marital therapists and researchers (N. S. Jacobson, 1991a, 1991b, 1991c) argued that the treatment presented in the IOMT condition was representative of more recent "clinically sensitive" versions of BMT (i.e., "new wave BMT") versus the more "rigidly structured, outdated BMT" (J. F. Alexander et al., 1994, p. 604). In essence, the argument was that the IOMT was a mislabeling of "new, improved" BMT, comparing it then to a more traditional, highly structured version of BMT (N. S. Jacobson, 1991a). Assuming that the premise of this argument is valid, it is nevertheless interesting to reflect on the direction of change for the newer version of BMT, regardless of the label given. In this respect, it is important to consider just what is implied by the term *clinically sensitive* (indeed, one would be hard pressed to envision a couple that would wish to engage in a therapy that was *not* clinically sensitive). In essence, what appears to constitute the improvement in the IOMT condition over more traditional BMT, even from the behavioral marital therapists' point of view (e.g., N. S. Jacobson, 1991a; Markman, 1991), involves *less* rigidity and structure regardless of whether or not this treatment modification could be regarded as insight-promoting per se. Thus, it can be reasonably concluded that the components of empirically validated couple therapy must be artfully blended by the individual clinician to adapt the therapy to the needs of a given couple, rather than expecting the couple to adapt to the rigid structure of behavioral components for the purposes of scientific rigor. Such skillful blending becomes even more necessary as other members of the family (beyond only the couple), who are invested in maintaining the familiarity of the family's status quo by way of family homeostasis, are included in the treatment system, as the next chapter illustrates.

6

FAMILY THERAPY: DILEMMAS OF CODEPENDENCY AND FAMILY HOMEOSTASIS

Another source of the clinician's dilemmas in treating the family system is derived from a phenomenon that has been encompassed by the term *codependency*. Codependency is a concept that is reflective of a mutually dependent, but complementary role relationship among members of a family that is maintained by a homeostatic mechanism as a response to changes made or impacted on by a given member of the family. In its adaptive form, its function is to preserve the family from destructive influences and alterations and to prevent disintegration by keeping a dynamic balance within the family's system. In its maladaptive form, it rigidly prevents the family from making the necessary adaptations to normative changes that generally occur and need to occur across the family's life cycle. Because this central concept in family functioning focuses on maintaining an optimum balance

This chapter is an adaptation of "Codependency," by D. J. Scaturo, in J. J. Ponzetti Jr. (Ed.), *International Encyclopedia of Marriage and Family* (2nd ed., Vol. 1, pp. 310–315), copyright 2003 by Macmillan Reference USA; and "The Concept of Codependency and Its Context Within Family Systems Theory," by D. J. Scaturo, T. Hayes, D. Sagula, and T. Walter, 2000, *Family Therapy, 27*(2), 63–70, copyright 2000 by Libra. Adapted with permission.

within the family system, the notion of equilibrium itself suggests that the nature of family therapy is fraught with the dilemmas involved in avoiding either "too much" or "too little."

CODEPENDENCY AND THE ALCOHOLIC FAMILY SYSTEM: POPULAR DEFINITION AND USAGE

The concept of codependency in the family system had emerged originally from the study and treatment of alcoholism (Gorski & Miller, 1984). In the alcoholic family system, codependency may be defined as a particular family relationship pattern in which the alcoholic is married to a spouse who, despite being a nondrinker, serves as a helper or facilitator to the alcoholic's problem behavior (Scaturo, 2003a; Scaturo & McPeak, 1998). The spouse, therefore, plays a role in the ongoing chemically dependent behavior of the alcoholic. The spouse's behavior may, unintentionally, foster the maintenance of the drinking problem by *enabling* the drinking pattern to continue. For example, the codependent spouse may make "sick calls" to the alcoholic spouse's workplace following drinking episodes, thereby delaying the problem from coming to the foreground more quickly. Thus, the spouse is said to be a codependent of the alcoholic's chemically dependent behavior.

Although there are a variety of theoretical perspectives on alcohol abuse and its treatment (e.g., Scaturo, 1987), Bowen (1974) was one of the first family therapists to conceptualize alcoholism as a symptom of family dysfunction, encompassing the behavior of both the alcoholic and the codependent. Accordingly, the family is a system in which a change in the functioning of a given family member (e.g., the alcoholic) is followed by a compensatory change in another family member (e.g., the codependent). Furthermore, every family member is viewed as taking a part in the dysfunction of the dysfunctional member. Excessive drinking takes place when anxiety in the family is elevated. In family therapy, attention is first given to the overall degree of anxiety in the family, and anything that is able to interrupt the escalating anxiety is viewed as helpful. Thus, psychoeducational efforts to teach codependent spouses about family systems functioning can intervene and help control their reciprocal role in their spouses' drinking behavior. In this regard, Bowen (1974) contended that it is far easier to assist the overfunctioning spouse to reduce the overfunctioning than it is to help the dysfunctional family member increase his or her level of functioning. Clinical attention given to the enabling behavior of the codependent, therefore, has been a significant contribution of family systems theory to the field of addictions (Scaturo et al., 2000).

Beattie (1987) popularized the concept of codependency for the general public in the self-help literature (Starker, 1990). She defined codependency for the lay reader as follows: "A codependent person is one who has let another person's behavior affect him or her, and who is obsessed with controlling that person's behavior" (Beattie, 1987, p. 36). She noted that the expression has been used as "alcohol treatment center jargon" and "professional slang," and she acknowledged that the term, as it was used, had a "fuzzy definition."

The popularization of the term, codependency, has had both positive and negative consequences for the fields of psychotherapy and family therapy. On the positive side of the ledger, the self-help literature in general, and the popular usage of the term codependency in particular, have been helpful in raising public awareness of the complex interrelationships that take place within alcoholic families. It has provided, in relatively simple, straightforward, and understandable terms, an appreciation of the role that everyone assumes in a family where a severe psychological disorder such as alcoholism occurs. For example, a wife and children may "cover" for their alcoholic husband or father's inability to keep up with the everyday demands of the home and workplace because of his excessive drinking. No one in an alcoholic family is immune from the devastating effects that alcohol has on them, and others in the family may inadvertently contribute to the maintenance of an alcohol problem. Indeed, enhancing a general understanding of these complex family behaviors is an important contribution to the realm of public mental health education.

On the negative side, however, the widespread usage of the term, codependency, frequently has also resulted in misunderstanding and misuse of the expression by the general public, as well as some imprecision by professional mental health practitioners in clinic settings. With regard to the lay public, Fiese and Scaturo (1995) conducted group discussions with adult children of alcoholics (ACOAs) in an effort to understand the difficulties that they confront in parenting their own children, given the parents' prior problematic upbringings. In these group discussions, there was a frequent misuse of professional jargon by the ACOAs that often led to misunderstandings of the complex and painful life experiences that the group members were trying to convey to one another. The circuitous use of jargon seemed to prevent group members from communicating with one another in clear, commonly understood language. The use and misuse of such jargon also appeared to short-circuit group discussion by promoting a presumed commonality of family life experience that may or may not have been accurate. Group members prematurely resonated to the jargon used by others without waiting to discover whether actual life experiences were comparable between them. Overall, the use of professional jargon by the laypeople in these focus groups appeared to diminish the degree of coherence in their discussions. Even more problematic is that the widespread generality of the concept's usage has contributed to some degree of imprecision by practicing psychotherapists. The precise understanding of the concept of codependency by mental health care professionals has implications for how treatment of these family dynamics is conducted and how codependent patients and their families in treatment construe these concepts.

CODEPENDENCY AND FAMILY SYSTEMS THEORY: RELATED TERMS AND SYNONYMS

The notion of codependency is predicated on and encompasses earlier ideas about family functioning. These concepts have included the notions of interlocking family pathology, the overadequate–inadequate marital functioning, the one-up/one-down marital relationship, the marital quid pro quo, and marital complementarity. A somewhat separate but integrally related concept to the maintenance of the codependent family system is the notion of family homeostasis. A brief discussion of these concepts would be helpful in clarifying and understanding the nature and scope of codependency.

As discussed in the previous chapter, people tend to seek out marital partners whose neurotic needs and emotional issues "fit" with their own (Goldenberg & Goldenberg, 1980). This observation, which has also been termed the *interlocking pathology* (Ackerman, 1958) in family relationships, is based on a psychodynamic view of the family. This perspective highlights the interdependence and reciprocal effects of disturbed behavior among the various members of a family, rather than focusing on the emotional distress or internal conflicts of a single family member who is seen exclusively as "the patient." Ackerman (1958) asserted that an individual's personality should be assessed not in isolation, but within the social and emotional context of the entire family group.

A codependent marital relationship has been termed by various family therapists as *overadequate versus inadequate functioning* of each of the spouses (Bowen, 1960). This configuration has been described similarly with the terms of a *one-up versus one-down* marital relationship (J. Haley, 1963). "One-up" denotes a dominant position (i.e., the one who is "in charge") in the family hierarchy, whereas "one-down" denotes an inferior position (i.e., the one who is being "taken care of") in the power arrangements within the family (Simon et al., 1985). Importantly, Bowen (1960) pointed out that these functional positions are, in actuality, only family "facades" rather than representative of the actual abilities of each of the spouses, each one appearing to occupy reciprocal positions in the family in relation to the other. Thus, the *overadequate* spouse presents a picture of unrealistic facade of strength in the marriage. Likewise, the *inadequate* spouse presents a picture of unrealistic helplessness in relation to the other. In actuality, the emotional strength and maturity of spouses who have been married for any appreciable length of time is usually quite comparable (Goldenberg & Goldenberg, 1980). The codependent spouse, therefore, gives only the appearance of being overadequate in relation to the inadequate position of the alcoholic spouse.

The above-noted ideas about family systems, on which the popular concept of codependency is based, are clinical terms that have emerged from the field of family psychotherapy. As a result, codependency and its related concepts are a way of describing various kinds of *family dysfunction* or problem families in which there is some sort of mental health concern. However, degrees of psychopathology, or abnormal behavior, typically exist on some continuum from the "severely pathological" (e.g., psychotic behavior or suicidality in a given family member) on one end to relatively "normative social behavior" on the other, with various forms of human behavior falling somewhere in between these two poles. Thus, codependency as a dysfunctional form of family interaction is likely to fall on the pathological end of the continuum. However, this basic pattern of family behavior, in less extreme forms, can be seen in families at the normative end of the continuum as well.

Bowen (1960) believed that an individual's *emotional maturity* is synonymous with the degree of *differentiation of self* that has been established from the family of origin. He also believed that adults typically choose partners with a relatively equivalent degree of differentiation, or maturity, despite differences in outward appearances. As a result, when both members of a couple are poorly differentiated from their respective families of origin (as is typically the case in alcoholic families), there is an "emotional fusion" that takes place in the marital relationship. The fusion between marital partners is frequently a source of psychological distress, and the couple may use any of several strategies to alleviate their discomfort while remaining attached to one another in the relationship.

Scaturo et al. (2000) discussed three different strategies in emotionally fused relationships, although only one—complementarity—refers to the concept of codependency per se. One relational pattern, which may develop in an attempt to modulate the emotional distress caused by fusion in a marital relationship, is an *avoidance of conflict resolution* by periodically distancing from one another and then terminating the discussion prior to achieving resolution. Such a pattern allows for periodic emotional separation through sustained recurrent verbal conflict, which remains perpetual because of the inability to truly resolve a disagreement. The anorectic and psychosomatic families observed by Minuchin, Rosman, and Baker (1978) are illustrative of these kinds of enmeshed family relationships. A second family pattern used to modulate emotional fusion in a marital relationship is to incorporate another person into the couple's conflict. *Triangulation* refers to the expansion of a conflict-ridden dyadic relationship to include a third party, most often a child, to defuse the conflict (Simon et al., 1985), and is typically regarded as a pathological form of family communication (Minuchin, 1974). Finally, a third pattern used to modulate a fused dyadic relationship, *complementarity* (Bateson, 1935, 1972; Simon et al., 1985), is the relational pattern more commonly known as codependency (Scaturo et al., 2000).

Because codependency, then, is a pathological form of complementarity, it can be regarded as a specific form of overadequate–inadequate reciprocal functioning (Bowen, 1960). It is a relationship that is *asymmetrical* (Bateson, 1935, 1972) to the extent that the two marital partners, at least at an overt level of observation, do not hold co-equal positions of power and status within the family hierarchy, although they nevertheless interlock (Ackerman, 1958) or "fit together" in a dynamic equilibrium or active balance with one another. Examples of such complementarity include various dominant–submissive role relationships such as doctor–patient, parent–child, mentally or physically disabled–caretaker, and the alcoholic–codependent (Simon et al., 1985). Such rigid role definition in dysfunctional families serves to alleviate the discomfort and anxiety in families with members who are poorly differentiated from their families of origin (Bowen, 1960, 1974).

In addition, the notion of complementary needs among potential spouses has been cited as an important factor in selecting a mate (Winch, 1958). Likewise, Jackson (1965) applied the legal term *quid pro quo* in the sphere of marriage to describe the type of "bargain," or complementarity, to which couples typically arrive in an agreement to marry. Literally translated from Latin as "something for something," marital quid pro quo implies that arrangements in the marriage generally function best over the long run if a suitable agreement that is genuinely collaborative in nature can be reached by the spouses. For example, to run relatively smoothly, agreements typically need to be made in the "division of family labor," which takes into account the sum total of the labor (both income-producing and maintenance of home life) with sufficient fairness and acknowledgment of the contributions made by both. Only when this division of family functions becomes polarized and taken to the extreme (e.g., breadwinner vs. homemaker roles) does such a quid pro quo risk the possibility of rigidity, misunderstanding, and a proneness to family pathology. Codependency is one such form of polarized marital role behavior (e.g., the "helper" vs. the "sick" role) that signifies pathological complementarity and family dysfunction.

Codependency in Other Psychological and Family Problems

Codependent family dynamics have been observed in areas of psychological difficulty other than in families with chemical dependency. For example, Scaturo and his colleagues (Scaturo & Hardoby, 1988; Scaturo & Hayman, 1992) have observed codependent relationships, discussed in terms of *interlocking pathology* (Ackerman, 1958), in families of military veterans experiencing posttraumatic stress disorder (PTSD) following traumatic combat experiences in war. PTSD is a psychiatric disorder in which someone who has been exposed to a psychologically traumatic experience, such as military combat, experiences an array of disabling symptoms, including intrusive distressing recollections of the experience or recurrent traumatic nightmares, an avoidance of anything that might be associated with the trauma, a numbing of emotional responsiveness to significant others, and a hypervigilance or exaggerated startling in response to an overanticipation of danger (American Psychiatric Association, 1994). In marriages that took place prior to the wartime traumatization, the spouses of combat veterans seem to experience a genuine change in the character of the person that they knew before the war, and returning to an emotionally intimate relationship requires a substantial adjustment of mutual expectations. However, in relationships that began after the trauma, something much more like codependency, or interlocking pathology, becomes part of the couple's relationship. The posttraumatic disability is already a known quantity to both parties at the outset of their relationship. The helper versus sick roles are already established as a part of the mutual attraction to one another, and the codependency of the helper is an integral part of the relationship's development. The same observation would be applicable to forms of traumatic experience other than military trauma, for example, the survivors of rape.

Similarly, the psychiatric maladies of panic disorder and agoraphobia are another such example of where the helper versus sick roles play a part in coping with what ultimately becomes a family problem (Scaturo, 1994). Panic attacks are brief periods of intense fear without a clear precipitant (i.e., objective threat) with various psychophysiological symptoms of disabling severity, including heart palpitations, trembling, abdominal distress, and possible fears of dying (American Psychiatric Association, 1994). When the fear, or anxiety, is accompanied by fear of being outside one's home or being in a crowd or public place, and such situations are avoided and travel is restricted, then agoraphobia may be said to go along with the panic disorder. Again, if the syndrome of panic disorder is a known quantity at the outset of a marital relationship, a codependent situation with rather clearly defined helper versus sick roles may be easily established. Such a codependent marital dynamic may be one of the reasons that what has been termed *spouse-assisted behavior therapy* (Scaturo, 1994), in which the spouse is included in the anxiety patient's treatment, has been demonstrated to have superior effectiveness over the use of individual behavior therapy with the identified patient alone (Barlow, O'Brien, & Last, 1984; Cerny et al., 1987).

Family Homeostasis

Once the codependent family roles or positions have been established, then they tend to be held in place by a homeostatic mechanism within the family. *Family homeostasis* (Jackson, 1957) refers to the phenomenon of significant reactive changes in other family members that take place in response to the behavior changes or symptomatic improvements made by the identified patient undergoing some form of psychotherapy, either individual or family treatment. For example, the mother of a boy in therapy for low self-esteem may not be entirely pleased by his recent success in winning an achievement award (Jackson, 1957). In such an instance, the mother may rely on her son's low self-image and neediness to enhance her own feelings of usefulness and self-esteem, in which case the mother's subtle discouraging behavior may serve to maintain the boy's problem with poor self-esteem rather than to improve it. Family therapists, who anticipate the family's interdependent needs, are generally prepared for such an upset in the mother in response to such desired gains in treatment by the identified patient (in this instance, her son with low self-esteem). The family and its interaction patterns are thus seen as a homeostatic system that remains in a constant state of balance with respect to one another, often resisting change.

The System's Storm

McPeak (2003) referred to the family's homeostatic reactions to the therapeutic changes, or attempts at changes, made by the identified patient in a family as *the system's storm* to denote the intensity of other members' discomfort with alterations made in the family's pattern of relating to one another. Improvement in symptomatic behavior, such as the reduction of excessive drinking or the diminishment of a patient's panic attacks, also alters the level of neediness that the index patient has on his or her spouse and other family members. While at an overt level of analysis these changes that reflect an increased level of functionality in the index patient would appear to be welcome gains by those who care about them, often the changes result in an unwanted reaction by the codependent members of the family to the loss of their felt need or importance to the index patient. The patient may then experience this lack of receptivity to his or her newly learned behavioral effectiveness as a punishment from those who are important and significant in his or her life. In these instances, McPeak (2003) likened the role of the psychotherapist to that of a "wilderness guide" who is leading the patient into unfamiliar territory and climates. The guide would be wise to caution the patient–traveler with an appropriate "system's storm warning" of the risks and hazardous weather that may exist in breaking new relational ground with significant others. The "weather" of the family relationships can get cold rather quickly. The patient would be well advised to consider how the family might react to his or her newfound assertiveness, for example, and his or her recently acquired emotional freedom. It is the anticipation of such a system's storm that has led many seasoned behavior therapists conducting assertion training to invoke the important clinical caveat to avoid encouraging or recommending an assertive response in a patient that is likely to be severely punished in the natural environment.

Extinction Burst

From a behavioral or learning psychology standpoint, the codependent's strong, and often aversive, reactions to seemingly positive unilateral changes made in the family system by one of the family members, however functional they appear, resemble the phenomenon of *extinction burst* in operant conditioning (e.g., Cooper, Heron, & Heward, 1987). In conditioning experiments, when extinction is first initiated and reward stops, the rate of previously acquired behavioral responses actually increases before it decreases. So, for example, a young college student away from home for the first time may decide to be more assertive with his or her mother or father with regard to the student's likes or dislikes (which may be seen as differentiating from the family of origin) and may conclude in individual therapy while at college that he or she will no longer respond to (i.e., reinforce) the guilt-inducing reactions of an enmeshed parent. However, to the extent that the student's deferential, but stifled, behavior is either rewarding and provides some source of secondary gain to an authoritarian parent, or simply comforting by its familiarity to the codependent family member(s), the absence of his or her obsequiousness in the family interaction pattern places the codependents in the family on an extinction schedule of reinforcement. Thus, the likely immediate response by the parent(s) to this reduced reinforcement may be an increase in guilt-invoking "cold shoulder" reactions, which could be characterized by extinction burst. In other words, the student son or daughter may experience an increase or "burst" of his or her parents' guilt-producing emotional reactions rather than a diminishment of such reactions as he or she might have hoped. The student–patient needs to be well prepared for the likelihood of this reaction on the part of his or her parent, in other words, to be prepared for the system's storm. Often, this is the reason for utilizing family therapy with these types of difficulties rather than individual therapy, so that the systemic reaction of significant others can be taken into account and therapeutically addressed, if needed. This also may be one of the reasons why Barlow's (Barlow, O'Brien, & Last, 1984; Cerny et al., 1987) spouse-assisted behavior therapy program for panic disorder and agoraphobia may have been more successful than the individual behavior therapy program tested. Utilizing the spouse as an assistant retains his or her "helping role" with the loved one, but in a more adaptive fashion.

CLINICAL DILEMMAS IN THE TREATMENT OF CODEPENDENT FAMILY DYNAMICS

Confrontation of Codependent Behavior: A Dilemma in Therapeutic Technique

It is commonly regarded that the main therapeutic goal in alcohol treatment, regardless of the particular theoretical approach being utilized, is for the identified or index patient (i.e., the alcoholic) to stop drinking. One of the clinical contributions of the concept of codependency in the alcoholic family system has been to indirectly target the enabling behavior of the codependent that serves to maintain the alcoholism of the index patient in addition to directly targeting the drinking behavior of the alcoholic. And, by assisting the codependent in reducing the variety of activities, which he or she may do, that serves to maintain the alcoholic's drinking behavior, it is generally helpful and effective in reducing the drinking behavior on the part of the alcoholic as well. For example, the therapist might urge the codependent to stop calling in sick to work for his or her alcoholic spouse when the spouse is, in fact, intoxicated.

However, attenuating the enabling behavior of a codependent spouse is a delicate clinical matter in which the therapist is easily able to alienate the spouse unless one fully understands and appreciates the role, function, and intention of the codependent, and the complexities of the systemic behavior within the alcoholic family dynamics. Scaturo and McPeak (1998) noted that "targeting" the enabling behavior of a codependent spouse, although therapeutically well intended, places the clinician in the dilemma of potentially *blaming the victim* (Ryan, 1971) from the codependent's viewpoint. With regard to family homeostasis, this approach is not as simple as making a direct confrontation of the codependent's behavior, however obvious it may be to the outside observer that the behavior is indirectly supporting the alcoholic's consumption. Not only is such an approach unlikely to succeed, but it also is likely to engender the resentment and resistance of the codependent's spouse, as well as to potentially damage the therapeutic alliance. Rather, in a genuinely systems-oriented therapy, the codependent behavior of a spouse must be addressed in a way that concurrently (a) acknowledges and validates the well-intended nature of the codependent's responses and (b) assists the codependent spouse in finding new ways of being useful in the family in order to not deprive them of their helping role within the family (e.g., Scaturo & Hardoby, 1988; Scaturo & Hayman, 1992; Scaturo & McPeak, 1998).

Psychoeducational Intervention:
Codependency Versus Normative Nurturance

Another therapeutic consideration, this one in the realm of psychoeducational interventions, occurs when the patients present their own concerns and questions about their own self-observed "codependent behavior." In other words, these are instances in which the spouse overinterprets, overgeneralizes, and overattributes a wide range of family behaviors to a pathological "codependency." In these circumstances, it can be very helpful for the therapist to correct these misunderstandings, to clarify what the concept of codependency does and does not encompass, and to assist the family members in identifying their own life struggles and circumstances (often traumatic in nature) that have served to create this relatively disturbed, or undifferentiated, way of relating that has come to be called by them "codependency."

For example, at times patients mislabel nurturance as codependency. Periodically, in practice, clinicians may observe an ACOA mother engaging in inappropriate self-criticism for performing normal and necessary nurturing behaviors with her child that fall well within the normative range of parenting and pejoratively labeling these functions as unhealthy codependent behavior. In these instances, therapeutic clarification is indicated, and the therapist should point out to such a patient that not all care-taking behaviors are codependent in nature. Thus, it is essential that the therapist be attentive to how his or her patient is construing, or perhaps misconstruing, what is legitimately meant by the term codependency.

The Therapeutic Dilemma of Self-Labeling Versus Self-Exploration

Finally, the presumed commonality of life experiences that is often predicated on the use of self-help jargon and social labels (e.g., "codependency," "ACOA"), and the condensation of complex life experiences into labels that are derived from family role assignments (e.g., "I was the *people pleaser* in the family"), have important implications for clinical work with families (Fiese & Scaturo, 1995). Self-labeling may have some social utility in identifying with others in a support group, for example, but it imposes some rather profound limitations on the process of psychotherapy. Labeling one's self, or one's behavior, as codependent frequently becomes a way of describing intricate life experience in highly abbreviated form. This process of abbreviation often closes uncomfortable but useful avenues of self-exploration that are essential to the process of effective psychotherapy and behavior change (Fiese & Scaturo, 1995). In family therapy, the process of self-exploration is frequently needed to assist a patient in individuating from his or her family of origin (e.g., Bowen, 1960). Thus, the self-labeling that often occurs in both the self-help literature and in various support groups may, in fact, inhibit the process of emotional growth that it is presumably attempting to facilitate.

CONCLUDING REMARKS

Although the concept of codependency has not become a part of the formal psychiatric nomenclature of the fourth edition of the *Diagnostic and Statistical Manual of Mental Disorders* (i.e., American Psychiatric Association, 1994), the term is used frequently in psychiatric treatment settings and among the lay public and frequently, in both instances, with considerable imprecision. As increased accuracy and professionalism are required on the part of the clinician, particularly with the emphasis on briefer treatment modalities, articulating the relationship between codependency and other, more well-established concepts in the field of family systems theory becomes essential. More than simply a theoretical issue, the explication of the term codependency has practical implications for the manner in which treatment is understood and conducted by the clinician, how codependent family dynamics are managed and confronted, and how patients and their families in treatment construe these concepts.

The concepts of codependency and family homeostasis provide a wellspring of clinical dilemmas for the psychotherapist working with the systems that share a natural history created by blood ties, legal ties, affectional bonds, cohabitation, and life circumstance. By contrast, group psychotherapy is a system that is composed of individuals unrelated by family ties but that share a common bond nevertheless. Those bonds most frequently are the sharing of mutual, yet differing, interpersonal struggles in these individuals' respective lives, common symptomatic presentations, and a collective treatment history. Although family homeostatic mechanisms may not provide the point of origin for the dilemmas that arise in couple or family therapy, clinical dilemmas are not in short supply for the group psychotherapist either, as is discussed in the next chapter.

7

GROUP PSYCHOTHERAPY: MULTIPLE DILEMMAS WITH MULTIPLE PATIENTS

Clinical dilemmas are endemic to the process of psychotherapy in general and group psychotherapy in particular (e.g., Dryden, 1997; Ryle, 1979; Scaturo, 2002b, 2002c; Scaturo & McPeak, 1998; E. F. Wachtel, 1979). The global modern-day economic forces in the health care and behavioral health care arenas, across a variety of treatment settings and institutions, have profoundly influenced the traditional dilemmas in the practice of psychotherapy. In the United States, for example, the pressures of cost containment and managed care within health care systems are pervasive (Sekhri, 2000), whether in privately administered health maintenance organizations (HMOs) or in the government-administered Veterans Health Administration (VHA), the largest integrated health care system in the United States (Carey & Burgess, 2000). Similarly, in the United Kingdom, there is a similar concern for efficiency in the National Health System (NHS; e.g., Fox, 2002). In addition, comparisons have been made between the NHS in the United Kingdom and

This chapter is an adaptation of "Fundamental Clinical Dilemmas in Contemporary Group Psychotherapy," by D. J. Scaturo, 2004, *Group Analysis: The Journal of Group Analytic Psychotherapy, 37*, 201–218. Copyright 2004 by Sage Publications. Adapted with permission.

the Kaiser Permanente HMO system in the United States (e.g., Feachem, Sekhri, & White, 2002), citing shared concerns and constraints over cost and health care delivery.

These time-limited and problem-focused trends in mental health service delivery have had a direct effect on the clinical decision making that confronts the group psychotherapist on a daily basis. Myriad clinical dilemmas have arisen for clinicians, providing a range of traditionally valued mental health services, of both an ethical and a technical nature (e.g., LaPuma, 1998; Scaturo, 2002b). In this chapter, a brief *clinical taxonomy* is presented outlining five fundamental dilemmas in group treatment, the decisions of which vary along a number of bipolar continuums. The horns of these traditional clinical dilemmas that are discussed in light of the current group treatment milieu include the varying degrees of (a) homogeneity versus heterogeneity in patient selection for various types of groups, (b) the integration of psychoeducational methods with interpersonal process in group therapy, (c) the effects of time limitations on the collective therapeutic focus of the group, (d) the balance between support and confrontation in time-limited group treatment, and (e) the dilemmas surrounding the therapist's relative degree of transparency versus opaqueness in the group.

GROUP COMPOSITION: HOMOGENEITY, HETEROGENEITY, AND PATIENT SELECTION

Of the many consequences of cost containment in the mental health arena (e.g., Budman & Steenbarger, 1997; Chambliss, 1999), increased economic pressure for briefer and more problem-focused forms of psychotherapy has been one outcome (e.g., Budman & Gurman, 1988; Hoyt, 1995). Another consequence has been the favored use of the group modality over individual treatment modalities as a method for increasing clinical efficiency by providing services to an aggregate of patients in a single clinical hour (Fuhriman & Burlingame, 2001; Spitz, 1995). Yet a third consequence of cost containment in mental health care involves the intersection of the above two trends. That is, the use of time-limited, problem-focused psychotherapy groups has been a preferred mode of treatment by managed care companies, as well as government-administered clinics and hospitals, over the more generic form of interpersonal process group that traditionally has been a cornerstone of treatment (Yalom, 1995) and training (Fuhriman & Burlingame, 2001) since Moreno (1946) first advanced the use of group modalities. The result has been psychotherapy groups being offered among a range of the symptom or population areas such as anxiety or depression management, panic disorder and agoraphobia, alcohol abuse and chemical dependency, adult children of alcoholics, and military combat veterans (Scaturo & McPeak, 1998).

In the present-day behavioral health care environment, group composition and the selection of group members for therapy with varying purposes constitute an initial clinical dilemma in group treatment. When therapy groups are typically offered in a recognizable diagnostic or problem area, the relatively homogeneous group composition is predicated on the assumption that unity surrounding some degree of common experience will encourage an accelerated identification, trust, and cohesion among the members of the group (Fiese & Scaturo, 1995; Scaturo & Hardoby, 1988; Scaturo & McPeak, 1998). According to Yalom (1995, p. 255): "Homogeneous groups jell more quickly, become more cohesive, offer more immediate support to group members, are better attended, have less conflict, and provide more rapid relief of symptoms."

However, the greater the degree of homogeneity among the group members, the *less* the therapy group is able to become an accurate representation of a real-world "social microcosm" (Yalom, 1995), with all of its attendant opportunities for interpersonal learning. A certain degree of incongruity must exist between a given psychotherapy patient and the other members of the group in order for interpersonal learning to occur (Yalom, 1995). This notion is based on the social psychological assumption that interpersonal behavior change is preceded by a state of cognitive dissonance created by differing worldviews (or *Weltanschauung*) and different ways of coping with life's tempestuous stressors. Thus, the homogeneous therapy group has the increased likelihood of remaining at a relatively superficial level, or limited plateau, of therapeutic interaction. For example, in groups with adult children of alcoholics (Fiese & Scaturo, 1995), the level of self-disclosure (and, therefore, of truly knowing one another) may not get beyond mere identification with another's problems (e.g., "My parents were 'rageaholics' too"). If the goal of a particular group is limited to that of social and emotional support, then the identification that is developed by increased homogeneity over a given symptom or theme is likely to have clinical utility. However, if the goal of the group is to be psychotherapy, then a more extensive exploration of individual life experience that is enhanced by augmented heterogeneity in the group is indicated (Scaturo & McPeak, 1998).

In sum, even in groups highly homogeneous in obvious characteristics, facing the heterogeneity among the participants becomes an important therapeutic task for the group members and their psychotherapist. For example, in a relatively homogeneous outpatient psychotherapy group for traumatized combat veterans (Scaturo & Hardoby, 1988), each of the group members must grapple with the realization (despite the strongly developed "we-feeling" in the group) that, ultimately, "we are not all the same here." They must face with courage and equanimity that, at times, their gruesome experiences in combat have not been the same for all members of the group (S. A. Haley, 1974). Personal responsibility for one's own actions must be faced and worked through, both for what took place during the war and in dealing with significant others in their present environment since that time. If the current market trends toward brief and problem-focused therapy groups continue (Fuhriman & Burlingame, 2001), as it appears they will, it will be increasingly incumbent on the effective group therapist to extricate, to whatever degree possible, the heterogeneity from the homogeneously composed group (e.g., Fiese & Scaturo, 1995; Scaturo & Hardoby, 1988). To accomplish this, the therapist must utilize the group process that is available in all groups, including the highly structured psychoeducational group.

PSYCHOEDUCATIONAL GROUPS AND INTERPERSONAL PROCESS

In a survey of group psychotherapy training programs in the fields of psychiatry, psychology, and social work in the United States, it was found that increased market demands are expected for problem-focused, homogeneous groups in clinical settings, although training programs appear to place only a moderate degree of emphasis in this area (Fuhriman & Burlingame, 2001). Rather training programs continue to emphasize education in process-oriented, heterogeneous group treatment. Further still, psychiatry and psychology programs place little emphasis on training in support groups, although a majority of support groups have been shown to have some form of professional leadership (Goodman & Jacobs, 1994). Although seemingly contradictory, it is clear that the ability to work with interpersonal process in groups is largely regarded as a fundamental psychotherapy skill and prerequisite, regardless of the type, structure, or substantive focus of the group. Interpersonal process is omnipresent in groups, and the therapist working with those groups must be able to recognize and manage it, regardless of the degree of homogeneity over educational or substantive focus. Most therapists conducting psychoeducational groups find themselves in a dilemma in attempting to facilitate an optimal interpersonal learning environment, on the one hand, and trying to remain "on schedule" or "on task" with a given group therapy protocol, on the other.

On what bases does one distinguish a therapy group that has a more traditional interpersonal process orientation (e.g., Yalom, 1995) from a group that is oriented more toward a psychoeducational focus (e.g., Authier et al., 1975)? A hallmark of the psychoeducational approach to treatment is the focus on instructional learning that is acquired primarily from the direction of the therapist or group leader. Often, the learning that occurs takes place in a given, frequently narrower, predesignated subject area (e.g., assertiveness skills). In contrast, the interpersonal learning that occurs within an interactional group process is more spontaneously generated by the group, takes place along a broad spectrum of interpersonal behavior, and is acquired by contact with any or all of the group members.

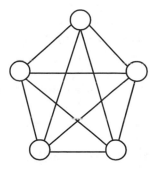 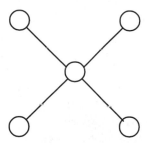

Completely Connected Pattern   **Wheel Pattern**

Interpersonal Process Group   *Psychoeducational Group*

Figure 7.1. Communication networks in psychotherapy groups. *Left:* completely connected pattern in interpersonal process groups; *right:* wheel pattern in psychoeducational groups. From "Communication Networks," by M. E. Shaw, 1964, in L. Berkowitz (Ed.), *Advances in Experimental Social Psychology* (Vol. 1, p. 113). Copyright 1964 by Academic Press. Adapted with permission.

Furthermore, there are constraints that are placed on group process by virtue of the pathways of interaction fostered by the group leader or leaders. Classic social psychological research on communication networks in small-group behavior tends to support the notion of these limitations (e.g., Shaw, 1964). The interpersonal process group is represented by a *completely connected pattern* of communication in which all channels of communication are open and multidirectional such that every group member can communicate directly with every other group member. Communication in the psychoeducational group, however, more resembles a *wheel pattern* in which the group therapist occupies a central and pivotal position and most, if not all, exchanges of ideas go through the leader. The two communication networks shown in Figure 7.1 illustrate the differences in patterns between the interactional process group and the psychoeducational group. These different pathways of interaction tend to build different types of group cultures. Psychoeducationally, the leader, rather than the group, is viewed by the members as "cornering the market" on "authoritative" information and looked to for the coordination of group activities. The time limits of brief group treatment, as well as a task-focused reason for convening, make the emergence of a leader-based communicational structure more likely in the psychoeducational group. Even groups that convene over more generic, process-amenable, "interpersonal problems" are typically more focused on specific problems such as assertiveness, panic, or anger. Such *demand characteristics* (Orne, 1962; Whitehouse, Orne, & Dinges, 2002) in the psychoeducational group make it more difficult for interactive group therapists who value the concept of group members learning from each other to develop this into a group norm and culture.

In attempting to bridge this instructional versus interactional gap, or arriving at some compromise or *détente* in technique, cognitive–behavioral group therapists (e.g., Fay & Lazarus, 1993; Rose, 1999; J. R. White & Freeman, 2000) have incorporated a skill-training component into most cognitive–behavioral group treatment protocols that generally involves some degree of in-group "behavior rehearsal" (Lazarus, 1966) with other group participants. *Structured learning therapy* (e.g., Goldstein, 1973, 1981; Sprafkin, Gershaw, & Goldstein, 1978; Sprafkin, Goldstein, & Gershaw, 1993) provides an excellent example of a behaviorally based, psychoeducational group treatment program that teaches a wide range of social skills to patients. Structured learning uses a standard format of four social learning group techniques that can be transposed from one type of problem-focused group to another to teach patients a wide range of social skills. These components include (a) the *modeling* of therapist(s) performing the specific behavior to be learned; (b) the *role-playing* or rehearsal by each of the group members of the specific behavior; (c) the *social reinforcement*, approval, and corrective feedback by the therapist(s) or model(s) and other group members; and (d) the facilitation of the *transfer of training* from the group room to the real-life situations in which the patient may encounter these problems. The social skills to which structured learning has been applied are of a broad range and highly specific. For example, conversational skills may be taught in groups that break down this general ability into the more specific skills of expressing a compliment, asking for help, expressing anger, or offering encouragement to others (e.g., Sprafkin et al., 1978). The theoretical foundation of using active involvement to provide the optimal arousal for learning in cognitive–behavioral groups is based on the classic Yerkes-Dodson law (Yerkes & Dodson, 1908). This principle holds that the efficiency of performance (in this instance, interpersonal learning) will increase, up to an optimal point, under conditions of arousal (in this instance, behavioral activity). In essence, it is this active method of *behavioral practice* in skill-training scenarios with other group members that cognitive–behavioral therapists would most likely see as the distinguishing feature between the instructional–lecture format that takes place in more didactic groups and the behavior therapy that takes place in psychoeducational groups.

By contrast, the therapeutic focus in the dynamically oriented psychotherapy group is on the *spontaneous emergence* of relationship concerns in the here-and-now discourse within the group, not on the a priori articulation of common difficulties in the outside lives of group members that led to the assignment to group treatment. The relational learning that takes place within group process is predicated on the natural development of unprompted interpersonal relationships over time and the examination of these relational behaviors in the group as they transpire. This constitutes a significant difference in the psychoeducational and interpersonal process forms of group treatment and a challenge for psychotherapy integration.

Nevertheless, both the psychoeducational group and interpersonal process group share the importance of creating a social–emotional atmosphere that is conducive to learning. Winnicott (1965) would have called this atmosphere the *facilitative environment*. It is the kind of atmosphere that Winnicott's "good enough mother" in families, or the "good enough teacher" in education, or the "good enough therapist" in the practice of psychotherapy, all, in turn, attempt to provide for their respective "learners." Likewise, behavioral and cognitive–behavioral approaches to group therapy have recognized, along with interpersonal process group therapists, that the nexus of interpersonal learning takes place within the behavioral interaction among group members. For the most part, these are the more time-intensive, yet essential, aspects of group therapy that remain a challenge to time-limited treatment.

TIME-LIMITED AND BRIEF GROUP PSYCHOTHERAPY

The brief and time-limited group psychotherapies share with their individual psychotherapy counterparts the greater need for a therapeutic focus than the longer term interpersonal process group therapy. Additionally, the brief therapy group has an increased need for a *collective therapeutic focus* than does the interpersonal process group. Historically, brief therapy has always posed a fundamental dilemma for the psychotherapist (e.g., Gustafson, 1995; Scaturo, 2002c). The therapeutic concern with brief treatment centers on the degree to which the depth and breadth of treatment and healing are sacrificed (Gustafson, 1995). The primary therapeutic task in perhaps all brief therapies seems to be the need for the patient and therapist to select a focus for treatment and hold to it (Budman & Gurman, 1988). In the time-limited psychodynamic psychotherapies, the term dynamic focus has been generally associated with the notion of the central problem in arriving at a time-efficient form of treatment (Schacht et al., 1984).

The therapeutic focus uniquely available in group psychotherapy is predicated on an interpersonal conceptualization of the patients' problems (e.g., Sullivan, 1938, 1953), the interpersonal interactions in which those problems can be demonstrated, and the interpersonal learning of alternative ways to approach those difficulties (Yalom, 1995). Current proponents of interpersonal psychotherapy (e.g., Klerman et al., 1984; Stuart & Robertson, 2003), delivered within an individual therapy format, have identified four primary foci for treatment and intervention, as discussed in greater detail earlier in chapter 3. In brief, these include (a) interpersonal conflicts that take place within marital, family, friendship, and workplace contexts involving misunderstandings, flawed communications, and unreasonable expectations of others; (b) role transitions involving developmental or life-cycle transitions (e.g., becoming a first-time parent) or job changes and alterations of job responsibilities; (c) interpersonal losses and grief associated with death, divorce, or relocation; and (d) interpersonal deficits and sensitivities when patients present with a paucity of supportive interpersonal relationships and an insufficiency of social and relationship skills needed to bring those relationships about. These problem foci are equally well suited for treatment delivered within a group format as well.

Thus, there is considerable overlap and consensus in the need for focus between the practices of brief individual psychotherapy and brief group therapy. The concepts of general systems theory (e.g., Berrien, 1968) and family systems theory (e.g., Minuchin, 1974), in many ways similar to the interpersonal focus (e.g., Stuart & Robertson, 2003), are useful in integrating combined individual and group psychotherapeutic goals in a brief therapy context (MacKenzie, 1993). The problem of a *common* therapeutic focus in group psychotherapy has clearly been addressed by the behavioral and cognitive–behavioral group therapies (e.g., structured learning therapy). However, the need for focused objectives and processes in time-limited group treatments is critical regardless of theoretical orientation or style of leadership (Burlingame & Fuhriman, 1990). *Focal group psychotherapy* highlights a number of factors that are common to most forms of brief group treatment (MacKay & Paleg, 1992). These factors include the use of structure in the group, targeting specific issues for the group to address, a strong goal orientation, behavioral homework assignments to capitalize on extra-session behavior change, psychoeducational–instructional learning methods, and proactive psychological modeling techniques by the group therapist.

Finally, the epitome of a heightened degree of focus in interactional group psychotherapy is exemplified by Yalom's (1983) single-session time frame for psychotherapy groups in an inpatient setting. Accordingly, the inpatient group psychotherapist cannot work within a longitudinal time frame because of the rapid turnover and brief durations of hospital stays. As a result, the life of the group is considered by Yalom to last only a single session. The nature of interpersonal focus in such groups, therefore, requires a higher level of activity than one might utilize or observe in a longer term outpatient psychotherapy group. Concurrent with this increased therapist activity is the need for increased structure of the group experience. Inpatient group therapists "must call on members; they must actively support members; they must interact personally with patients" (Yalom, 1983, pp. 106–107). In short, the inpatient setting is no place for the passive or inactive group therapist. This perspective of an active group therapist is thoroughly consistent with the viewpoint of the focal group psychotherapist (MacKay & Paleg, 1992). With the increased time constraints placed by cost containment measures on outpatient group settings, Yalom's admonishments to the inpatient group psychotherapist appear to have broader applicability to the vast majority of existing therapy groups in outpatient clinics as well.

DILEMMAS OF SELF-DISCLOSURE FOR THE PATIENT: SUPPORT VERSUS CONFRONTATION IN A GROUP SETTING

Group support, empathy, and compassion for the individual member's interpersonal suffering and life struggles are prerequisites for either an increased degree of self-disclosure by the group members or gradually increasing degrees of confrontation of one another. In brief and time-limited treatment, the provision of high levels of support in the group is likely to be the most important curative factor for members in such a group. This is enhanced by the notion of homogeneous problem focus that fosters a strong sense of identification among the respective group members. As the group presses on, however, a supportive group environment provides a sense of safety necessary for the risk-taking involved in increased self-disclosure by the members. As such, an individual member may gradually begin to offer information about oneself that is to some degree at variance with the nature of the information shared thus far by the current group members.

For example, in group therapy with combat veterans (e.g., Scaturo & Hardoby, 1988), group members may begin to explore the psychic trauma of their respective combat experiences by discussing the brutality that they observed in others on the battlefield, something with which the other group members may readily identify. With sufficient levels of trust, however, an individual member may begin to share information about not only the horrifying behavior observed in others but also the atrocious acts engaged in by him- or herself as well (e.g., S. A. Haley, 1974). With such self-disclosures, the identification from others may be less readily available, either because of the genuine differences between the group members in their actual behaviors in combat or because of the reluctance to admit to such guilt-laden acts. Only when the group members have gone beyond the mere identification and support of one another to the acknowledgment of critical differences between one another, and the availability of continued support and understanding of each other, with the group able to transcend to the psychotherapeutic function of group treatment (e.g., Fiese & Scaturo, 1995; Scaturo & Hardoby, 1988).

A similar observation can be made concerning the function of interpersonal confrontation among members in the group therapy setting. The hypothetical notion of uncompromising, unqualified social support, although critical to the process of group psychotherapy, would leave us with the question: "Why, then, is the patient seeking psychotherapy?" For one to seek or be recommended to group treatment, there is the implication of some social or interpersonal difficulty in one's life. Categorical acceptance of the patient's position in relation to others would imply that there is nothing to be learned from the other members of the group. It is necessary, then, to confront the patient on aspects of his or her interpersonal behavior that have, perhaps inadvertently, contributed to the relational difficulty or misery that has brought him or her into treatment in the first place. Yet, most group therapists struggle with the dilemma regarding the relative degree of group support versus interpersonal confrontation to provide the patient at any given point in time in the group's development.

For example, the highly defensive group therapy patient is likely to require substantial amounts of support to stave off anticipated feelings of rejection by the group—a degree of support that may take him or her only so far. If the defensive anxiety manifests itself in irritability and anger, inappropriately or excessively discharged at other members of the group, then some degree of confrontation of this member is likely to be required, either by the therapist or preferably by other members of the group (supported by the therapist), in an effort to curtail continued distortion that is likely to take place by the defensive member of the group. In doing so, the therapist further risks the potentially distorted perception of the confrontative interventions themselves. Every confrontational intervention by the therapist "borrows" on the prior investments made by the therapist in the therapeutic alliance and the previous degree of emotional support and nurturance experienced by the patient (Scaturo, 2002c; Scaturo & McPeak, 1998). Ultimately, effective group therapy consists of both the therapist and the group members being able to confront in a way that is experienced as empathic and emotionally supportive.

DILEMMAS OF SELF-DISCLOSURE FOR THE GROUP THERAPIST: THERAPEUTIC TRANSPARENCY VERSUS OPAQUENESS

If the risk of self-disclosure in group is a dilemma for the psychotherapy patient, it is no less a quandary for the group therapist. The degree of self-disclosure by the group psychotherapist has also been referred to as the therapist's *transparency versus opaqueness* (Yalom, 1995). In general, this dilemma appears to be as follows. On the one hand, the self-revealing group therapist is apt to be judged as more friendly, trusting, helpful, and facilitative by the group members (e.g., Dies, 1973). On the other, the self-disclosing group therapist is also seen as less relaxed, less strong, and less stable than the more remote group leader. In particular, the *brevity* of short-term or time-limited group treatment increases the impact of any misjudgment, regardless of the direction in which the group therapist chooses to humanly err. A therapist who, perhaps unwittingly, chooses to be excessively opaque or excessively self-disclosing in a particular group has less of an opportunity to modify his or her position on this dimension to realign him- or herself toward a greater degree of balance with respect to the group members.

How, then, is one to resolve this perplexing mix of positive and negative traits attached to essentially the same therapeutic behavior? Several factors are likely to be important in arriving at some resolution of or accommodation to this dilemma. The length of time that the therapist and patient have been in a group together is likely to be a crucial factor (Dies, 1973). The longer the patient has known the therapist in question, the more likely the patient will be to have a more complex picture of the therapist and is likely to have a broader repertoire of experience with the therapist against which to judge any given self-disclosure by the therapist. This poses a particular difficulty in an open-ended interpersonal process group in which different patients may have had different lengths of contact with the group therapist at any given point in time. In addition, the more favorable the opinion that a given patient has of a particular group leader, the more likely a given intervention—disclosing or not—is to be perceived by the patient as having a positive intention to help.

The guiding force behind any self-disclosure by the therapist should involve the good of the patient(s). Kahn (1997) cautioned therapists to scrupulously ask themselves whether what they are doing in any given therapeutic strategy is truly for the benefit of the patient or the therapist. This admonishment regarding therapeutic self-disclosure is intertwined with the question regarding countertransference in which the therapist is well advised to consider whether any given aspect of the therapy concerns "my life or my patient's life" (Scaturo & McPeak, 1998). In essence, it is critical that any self-disclosure by the group therapist take place in the service of the patient's treatment and not in the service of the therapist's countertransference. A group therapist's self-disclosure that is in the service of the patient rather than the therapist can be seen in the following clinical illustration from a psychotherapy group of combat veterans experiencing posttraumatic stress disorder. In this example, a distrustful new group member has just entered his first group session and confronts the therapist with the following defensive reaction:

> New group member: Why should I open up in front of you, doctor? What do you know of what it is like to be in combat? I imagine that you have had a pretty soft life, getting your education while I was tramping out there in the blood and mud.
>
> Group therapist: [after a long pause] Emotional pain can come from many things in this world . . . from the intrusive recollections and devastation of combat in some instances . . . and from the painful memories of things like severe and crippling childhood illness, for example, in other instances. You have experienced the former, and I have experienced the latter. In both instances, the emotional wound from your experience, like mine, is not readily visible to the outside observer as in the form of a physical scar [pointing to one member of the group], a missing arm or limb, or being confined to a wheelchair [gesturing to another group member]. However, I, and the group, are here to listen and to respond to some of your pain, if you are willing to share it.

The self-disclosure by the therapist in this example is very limited and, for the most part, nonspecific in its content, offering only so much information as to convey a sense of humanness and understanding. Yet, it offers the patient a possibility of emotional engagement with the therapist and the group without being a source of gratification for the group therapist's emotional needs for excessive self-disclosure.

One additional and critical point in this area concerns the degree of experience of a given clinician. Kahn (1997) suggested that the question of self-disclosure by the therapist can be placed somewhere along a conservative-to-radical continuum in the history of psychotherapy. On the conservative end is the classic psychoanalytic position in which nothing is shared with the patient other than interpretations (Rangell, 1969). On the radical end of the continuum is the encounter group movement of the 1960s and 1970s in which the therapist endeavored to reveal every possible feeling to the patient in the name of authenticity and in an effort to model such nondefensive self-disclosure to the patient (Schutz, 1967, 1973). Of the moderately conservative and well-respected psychotherapists (e.g., Gill, 1982; Kohut, 1971; Rogers, 1962) examined, "all moved to the left as their career progressed, coming more and more to trust their spontaneity and to express their human warmth" (Kahn, 1997, p. 148). However, this latitude is not for novice psychotherapists who, initially, are well served by their conservatism, discipline, and orthodoxy. Once these methods are well learned and deeply instilled, relaxing one's therapeutic stance can take place in ways that are cautious and safe for the patient and the therapist. Generally, it is easier and safer to relax well-learned rules than it is to rein in a therapeutic style that Freud (1910/1958d) once called "wild psychoanalysis."

CONCLUDING REMARKS: DILEMMA MANAGEMENT IN GROUP PSYCHOTHERAPY

Clinical skill in dilemma management in group psychotherapy encompasses a tolerance for ambiguity and an ability of the therapist to balance and integrate seemingly disparate points of view on an ongoing basis (Scaturo & McPeak, 1998). A number of problem areas discussed here provide examples in which this fundamental skill is exercised constantly by the group therapist. The question of balance for the group therapist begins with the selection of patients and anticipated composition for a planned therapy group. The question of homogeneity versus heterogeneity in group composition needs to be counterbalanced with the collective therapeutic focus of the particular group under consideration (e.g., interpersonal vs. symptom-focused), the predominant group methods intended (e.g., psychoeducational vs. process-oriented methods), and the temporal parameters of the proposed group (e.g., time-limited vs. open-ended).

The concept of an instructional–interactional continuum in the group is an ongoing dilemma for the therapist, regardless of the stated purpose of a given group. In a group defined as having an interactional focus, leadership requires the ongoing refinement of direction and overall interpersonal focus by the leader even though the group members exact a more enhanced participatory role in the group process. In a psychoeducational group with a predefined social–emotional problem or symptom focus (e.g., panic disorder), the group therapist must be able to interweave the individual contributions of the group members into the discussion and find relevance for the varied life examples and information, which validates each patient's membership and admission to the group. The balance and sway of the leader's degree of activity and intervention is only partly determined by the stated goal and purpose of the group at its outset, and is greatly modified by moment-to-moment clinical judgment directed toward augmenting the personal meaning of the group experience for each and every member.

Exacting an optimal degree of self-disclosure from a given group member at a given point in time in a given group composition with a particular focus is yet another intricate dilemma management skill for group therapists of any given theoretical persuasion. Whether one is attempting to elicit a personal example of passive behavior from an individual group member for the purposes of constructing a cognitive–behavioral skill-building exercise in assertive behavior, or whether one is confronting a group member on an aspect of his or her in-group behavior toward other group members as a part of an interpersonal process group, the degree of self-disclosure by the patient is a delicate therapeutic intervention. A careful assessment of the emotional fragility of each group member is necessary to know what degree of emotional support versus confrontation is the optimal balance at any given point in time. The relative degree of the therapist's self-disclosure in the group is a similar conundrum complicated by the differing meanings of the therapist's self-revelations (e.g., warmth vs. weakness) to particular members in the group at any given point in time.

Group therapy is a modality in which the concept of the clinical dilemma is no stranger. For example, it is a particular dilemma of the group therapist to be ever cognizant of the possible disparity between the clinical needs of the individual group member and the aggregate developmental needs of the group. Particular consideration must be given to the emotionally frail group member in assessing the speed and acceleration in the development of the group. Another such example concerns the ever-present question of whether group psychotherapy constitutes a primary or adjunctive treatment modality. There is no universal answer that exists for this question in all clinical circumstances. The question makes more sense in light of a particular patient's treatment program, whether the patient in question is likely to optimally utilize both individual and group modalities or whether he or she is likely to overutilize and underutilize one versus another. Group therapy is not a modality that frequently lends itself to cookbook answers to clinical questions, but rather challenges the therapist to think globally and integratively to provide sophisticated answers to complex interpersonal questions involved in the process of living. These time-held clinical questions take on new meaning for the group psychotherapist in the current world of behavioral health care. The limited economic treatment resources in the 21st century make it imperative for the group therapist to thoroughly reconsider the impact of time limitations, clinical efficiency, and therapeutic focus in light of the clinical needs of each and every group member.

Having examined the dilemmas that tend to arise in their own unique forms in a broad range of therapeutic modalities, the discussion that follows in the next part of the book turns toward the dilemmas that transpire in all treatment modalities because they are common to the interpersonal process inherent in all human treatment endeavors. The first such category of these dilemmas is determined by unconscious processes for the patient and therapist within the therapeutic context. These processes are typically subsumed under the psychoanalytic terms of transference, countertransference, and resistance.

III

CLINICAL DILEMMAS IN THE THERAPEUTIC PROCESS

8

TRANSFERENCE, COUNTERTRANSFERENCE, AND RESISTANCE: UNCONSCIOUS DETERMINANTS OF DILEMMAS

Transference, countertransference, and resistance are all psychological processes that affect the ongoing nature of psychotherapy, and all are presumed to be unconsciously determined (Auld & Hyman, 1991). *Transference* is an unconsciously influenced emotional reaction of the patient to the psychotherapist and (in a less technical sense) other health care providers that originates from the patient's earlier experiences related to significant others, especially caregivers, and that are inappropriate to the present context or way in which the therapist is currently dealing with the patient. *Countertransference* is the unconscious reactions of the psychotherapist (and other clinicians as well) that are stimulated by a given patient, the characteristics of a given patient, and, in particular, to the transferences of a given patient, that is, "countertransference proper" (Orr, 1954). If not consciously recognized by the therapist, these internal reactions are likely to be dealt with inappropriately by the clinician in his or her verbal or behavioral responses to the patient. Finally, *resistance* is an unconscious influence within the psychotherapy patient that acts against the therapeutic process, which results from the patient's wish to avoid the anxiety associated with his or her traumatic experiences, painful recollections, or personally unacceptable thoughts, wishes, or emotions that threaten to come into the patient's awareness.

Because all three of these important psychotherapeutic concepts are presumed to be unconscious mental processes, that is to say, processes operating outside the level of awareness, they are all predicated on a psychoanalytic or psychodynamic conceptualization of psychotherapy (e.g., Freud, 1912/1958a). In addition, most psychodynamically oriented psychotherapists would likely agree that the ambiguity that arises out of each of these processes tends to be a major source of clinical dilemmas, although perhaps seen as specific to the psychoanalytically oriented psychotherapist. For instance, there is substantial ambiguity surrounding what aspects of the session have been generated by the clinician and the current treatment context versus that which may be a carryover from the patient's past experiences, both with transference in the patient and countertransference in the clinician. Historically, all of these terms—transference, countertransference, and resistance—have felt somewhat out of place to psychotherapists working within a cognitive–behavioral or family systems framework (e.g., Scaturo, 2002c). Although the psychoanalytic terminology may feel awkward in other theoretical paradigms, the dilemmas that these processes generate have been viewed increasingly by those working in the area of psychotherapy integration as sources of conflict that are common to most treatment contexts with health care providers from diverse theoretical orientations and disciplines.

DILEMMAS OF TRANSFERENCE

Transference is a term that is formally reserved to refer to the unconscious relationship that a psychotherapy patient has with his or her psychotherapist, and more specifically a psychoanalyst. However, there has been increasing recognition that such a relationship exists not only in other forms of psychotherapy (e.g., cognitive–behavioral and family systems) but in other health care contexts as well. In essence, there is the potential for a variant of transference to exist whenever there is a relationship with a health care "provider" who is taking on some sort of caretaking role with the patient, reminiscent of the patient's relationships with earlier caregivers (e.g., parental) in his or her life. When applied to interpersonal relationships outside of the psychotherapeutic context, the transferential phenomenon is technically designated as *projective identification* in object relations terms (J. S. Scharff & Scharff, 2003). However, this phenomenon, as well as its pervasiveness outside the context of psychotherapy, has become most evident in the literature on the doctor–patient relationship with the family physician. Recognition of the importance of this relationship in all of its forms (i.e., conscious and unconscious) in part accounts for the proliferation of case consultation seminars, known as "Balint groups," in family practice residency training programs at medical schools across the country to grapple with the psychosocial aspects of the medical patient (Johnson, 2001; Johnson, Brock, Hamadeh, & Stock, 2001). The name of these case consultation groups is derived from the seminal work in this area in the 1950s and 1960s by Michael Balint (1957), a British psychoanalyst.

Balint's goal in conducting such case consultation seminars was to teach psychotherapeutic skills and recognition of the influence of the doctor–patient relationship to physicians in general medical practice (Keith et al., 1993). Because Balint's (1966) theoretical perspective was predicated on psychoanalysis, he tended to confine his attention to the patient's transferential and countertransferential relationship with the family doctor. That is to say, the patient's subjective distortions of the family doctor's relationship that emanate from the quality of the patient's past relationships with family, caregivers, and significant others, rather than from the objective current reactions of his or her family doctor, was of major concern to Balint. For the psychotherapist, these "parataxic" distortions (Sullivan, 1953) from the patient's past are most often considered to be the major foci of treatment. For the family physician, however, the patient's medical problems are the primary foci of treatment, rather than his or her emotional reactions or distortions in their relationship to his or her physician that are generally considered to be of secondary concern. Nevertheless, increasing the health care provider's recognition that such distortions by the patient (i.e., transference and transferential reactions affecting, in turn, the physician's countertransference to the patient) are ever present in the health care context is of enormous value in treatment and in clarifying doctor–patient communications about treatment.

In the Family Physician's Office

Consider, for example, a somewhat hostile young male patient in his early 20s in a visit to his primary care physician for a variety of symptoms of abdominal distress. A number of brief, one-word answers and hostile demeanor would appear to be unprovoked and seem to the physician as if to be "coming out of left field." In short, the patient's angry reactions appear to be excessive to the context and to be more than just the irritability associated with stomach distress. When emotional reactions are excessive to the context, the excess is likely an emotional overflow that comes from somewhere else, not simply "from out of left field" as is often the initial reaction, but usually from actual experiences in the patient's past. In this instance, a psychosocial history reveals that this patient was raised in a series of foster homes as a child with a series of caregivers who were minimally, or at least only temporarily, committed to this young man's physical and emotional well-being. A thorough history also reveals that some of these caregivers were variably physically, verbally, or psychologically abusive to this young man as a child. Although an understandable reaction from the primary care physician to the patient's apparent anger, especially a physician whose time constraints have been expanding exponentially in the current health care environment, might be a defensive reaction to the patient's cynicism or to simply ignore the evident hostility and provide a prescription, perhaps a more tempered response might engage the patient more so. A comment acknowledging the obvious and noting the history might provide a better doctor–patient connection:

> I can see that you are irritated, although I'm not sure what's causing it. I can see from your history that you have had a rather turbulent background, and I'm not sure if your previous contact with your doctors has seemed to you to be all that helpful, but here is what I think I can do to help . . .

Such a preamble to the medical aspects of the interview is direct and nondefensive, expresses understanding and empathy, and leaves the conversational door open for further discussion, if desired by the patient.

In the Psychotherapist's Office

To the therapist, this same patient would be likely to present not only as hostile but also guarded, avoidant of conversation, and cynical or sarcastic in interaction. The transferential issues with the authority figure of the psychotherapist are played out with a kind of verbal sparring to keep the therapist at some degree of emotional distance. However, for the psychotherapist, in contrast to the role function of the family physician, the patient's unprovoked hostility in his or her office in particular, and in the patient's interpersonal world in general, may be the primary focus of the patient's contact with a mental health specialist. The patient, understandably, may see his reason for being there from a more externalized perspective. That is to say, the patient's viewpoint may be more from the confusion that he experiences in wondering why so many people (e.g., boss or coworkers) whom he meets in life seem to be either hostile or uncaring. The task of the psychotherapist, however, is to help the patient to examine and modify his own contribution and to the creation (and possibly the selection) of such familiar relationships to assist this patient in considering what he may do about improving this scenario in his life through the modification of his own contribution. However, the difficulty as well as opportunity for interpersonal learning, and a "corrective emotional experience," arise when such unprovoked hostility becomes incorporated into the relationship that the therapist has with the patient, not simply the patient's relationships with others outside of the consulting room. However, because both the ambiguity and intensity of such interactions make navigation difficult, this is where the psychotherapist's skill and training come into play.

Two common emotion-laden areas of the patient's transference that have strong potential to stimulate a countertransferential reaction on the part of the therapist are that of the patient's *anger* and the patient's *seductiveness* toward the therapist. Take, for example, a patient with borderline pathology and a history of physical and verbal abuse followed by parental denial and invalidation of the abuse by his or her family. Such a patient may unjustly or inaccurately accuse the clinician of "not caring" about him or her after, for example, changing an appointment time. Following the patient's accusatory remarks, it is necessary for the clinician to respond to the patient, but how a given clinician might respond may vary, and such variations may have considerable impact on the therapeutic alliance. Ultimately, it will be important to point out the distortions that the patient is making in his or her perception of how the clinician has treated him or her by confronting the patient with real data (e.g., the therapist's history of very few canceled appointments with the patient), both now in the current situation and in the patient's treatment history with the therapist. However, it is critical that such confrontation not be a defensive reaction on the part of the clinician (such as a counteraccusation about the patient's missed or canceled appointments), but rather a matter-of-fact presentation that the patient's accusations do not conform to the reality of their clinical contact and history together. In doing this, though, the therapist runs the risk that the patient will perceive such confrontation as an invalidation of his or her experience, as was also a part of this particular patient's family history as noted above (e.g., "So you're telling me that it's all in my head!"). Such a misperception would likely be predicated on the *pseudomutuality* (Simon et al., 1985; Wynne, 1984; Wynne, Ryckoff, Day, & Hirsch, 1958) in his or her own family history in which there was the façade of harmony and an appearance of mutually respectful relationship with one another that is, in reality, undercut by the invalidating behaviors that follow. Clinically, then, it is incumbent on the therapist to point out to the patient that there is a substantial difference between what would be an "understandable distortion" by him or her given the family history and suggesting to the patient that "it never really happened."

The second emotion-charged area of the patient's transference that is likely to generate some sort of countertransferential response is that of an erotic transference to the therapist that is manifested through some form of seductive behavior by the patient. At a surface level of understanding, some type of gratification or flattery in the therapist might be obvious and expectable from the seductive behavior of a patient, especially one who might be acknowledged by the common culture as generically physically attractive. Fortunately, most adept therapists are able to monitor this reaction in them and respond with clinical appropriateness. What may be more problematic for the therapist, however, is the countertransferential reaction that is idiosyncratically evoked by an erotic transference from a patient (regardless of his or her actual physical attractiveness) that is reminiscent of the therapist's maternal or paternal figure from whom the therapist may have felt, for example, a paucity of gratification in his or her own family history. In such instances, these erotic transferences carry with them even more power to disorient the therapist and evoke an unconscious degree of personal gratification in the therapist that may make it increasingly difficult for the therapist to either monitor or make appropriate boundary management by the therapist more complicated. Transferences in such patients can evoke countertransferential reactions in psychotherapists that have the ability to start the therapist down a slippery slope of seemingly innocent responses that bring otherwise ethical therapists to tenuously skate the boundary of clinical ethics. Such responses are, in fact, ethical dilemmas that disguise themselves to the therapist as technical dilemmas, as noted previously in chapter 1. For example, the therapist may rationalize to him- or herself that this particular patient requires a greater degree of warmth from the therapist. At this point, such a quandary ceases to be a dilemma of psychotherapeutic technique and becomes primarily a dilemma of the therapist's countertransference. Indeed, many instances of sexual exploitation of patients in therapy might be avoided if the therapist were able to recognize the growing attraction and immediately seek consultation to either assist with the countertransference or make an appropriate referral of the case (e.g., Pope, 1994; Scaturo & McPeak, 1998).

DILEMMAS OF COUNTERTRANSFERENCE

The dilemma that every psychotherapist faces in grappling with strong countertransferential reactions is the question as to whether his or her reactions to the patient are stemming from, to paraphrase Framo (1968), "my life or my patient's life." In other words, the therapist must ask him- or herself, "whose agenda is being addressed in a given therapy session with a given patient or family, and why?" (Scaturo & McPeak, 1998, p. 6). A strong identification with a particular patient's life situation or defensive structure is not, by definition, a sign of poorly conducted psychotherapy. Rather, it is a marker of some increased intensity and complexity in the clinical context. In moments of greater candor, almost all psychotherapists will admit that they do not feel the same sense of rapport, identification, or closeness with each and every patient. In this respect, it is impossible to guarantee a uniform level of service to all patients as most managed care companies would like to claim. The psychotherapist, were he or she to have met certain patients prior to and outside of the clinical context, might easily imagine being friends with certain patients and definitively not with certain others. The patients with whom the therapist closely identifies, because of the therapist's almost instinctive understanding of their difficulties, stand to receive one of two things: either the very best or the very worst that such a clinician has to offer. If the clinician has sufficiently worked through the particular emotional issue that runs parallel to the issue in the life of the patient and is able to thereby maintain adequate objectivity in therapy, then the patient stands to gain much from the hard-earned intuitive understanding, which that clinician has by virtue of his or her own life experience. However, if the therapist overidentifies with the patient's conflicts and loses proper clinical perspective, then a grave disservice is being rendered to such a patient.

A powerful example of the intensity of these countertransferential feelings is portrayed in the dialogue of the play, *Equus* (Shaffer, 1973). The drama depicts a disturbed adolescent stable boy, named Alan Strang, in England who is undergoing court-mandated treatment after blinding six horses with a spike. The horses provided the boy with his first sexual experience. He would ride them naked in the evening until he reached the point of orgasm. The blinding incident occurred after his first sexual experience with a young woman that occurred in the stable with the horses present, leaving the boy feeling that he had betrayed them. The middle-aged psychiatrist, Dr. Martin Dysart, who is treating the boy is struggling with his own conflictual feelings surrounding the powerful yet destructive passion that his patient feels, a passion that has been long since absent in the therapist's own life and marriage. The following is an excerpt of a conversation that Dr. Dysart is having one evening with his friend, Hester Solomon, the magistrate who referred the boy for treatment (Shaffer, 1973, pp. 81–82)[1]:

Dysart:	He lives *one hour* every three weeks—howling in a mist. And after the service kneels to a slave who stands over him obviously and unthrowably his master. With my body I thee worship! . . . Many men are less vital with their wives.
	[*Pause*]
Hester:	All the same, they don't usually blind their wives, do they?
Dysart:	Oh, come on!
Hester:	Well, do they?
Dysart:	[*sarcastically*]: You mean he's dangerous? A violent, dangerous madman who's going to run around the country doing it again and again?
Hester:	I mean he's in pain, Martin. He's been in pain for most of his life. That much, at least you *know*.
Dysart:	Possibly.

---

[1]Reprinted with the permission of The Lantz Office and Scribner, an imprint of Simon & Schuster Adult Publishing Group, from *Equus and Shrivings* by Peter Shaffer. Copyright © 1973, 1974 by Peter Shaffer; copyright renewed © 2001, 2002 by Peter Shaffer.

Hester:	*Possibly?!* . . . That cut-off little finger you just described must have been in pain for years.
Dysart:	[*doggedly*]: Possibly.
Hester:	And you can take it away.
Dysart:	Still—possibly.
Hester:	Then that's enough. That simply has to be enough for you, surely?
Dysart:	No!
Hester:	Why not?
Dysart:	Because it is his.
Hester:	I don't understand.
Dysart:	His pain. His own. He made it.
	[*Pause*]
	[*Earnestly.*] Look . . . to go through life and call it yours—*your* life—you first have to get your own pain. Pain that is unique to you. You can't just dip into the common bin and say 'That's enough!'. . . He's done that. Alright, he's sick. He's full of misery and fear. He was dangerous, and could be again, though I doubt it. But that boy has known a passion more ferocious that I have felt in any second of my life. And let me tell you something I envy it.
Hester:	You can't.
Dysart:	[*vehemently*]: Don't you see? That the Accusation! That's what his stare has been saying to me all this time. '*At least I galloped! When did you?*'. . . [*Simply.*] I'm jealous. Hester. Jealous of Alan Strang.
Hester:	That's absurd.

Hester Solomon's reaction is not surprising. When one is not personally involved in the throes of a countertransference reaction of his or her own, then the intense countertransferences experienced by others can be easily perceived as "absurd." However, Dr. Dysart finds himself in the midst of a difficult dilemma. On the one hand, he has the unique ability to help his patient by virtue of possessing remarkable clinical talent and a personal understanding of the patient's problem. On the other hand, he is at risk for not being able to control his own feelings of envy of the patient and of losing adequate objectivity to properly conduct treatment.

In this particular example, the possibility of maintaining objectivity seems unlikely given the above dialogue. As a result, Dr. Dysart faces a second dilemma surrounding his countertransference concerning this patient:

Does the therapist *keep* or *refer* such a patient (Scaturo & McPeak, 1998)? Although it seems prudent in the above example to strongly consider referral given the intensity, an alternative might be for the therapist to obtain formal consultation, initially, to decide whether or not keeping or referring the case would be most beneficial to the patient. However, even a straightforward referral may have substantial and varied meanings and impact for the patient within the context of transference (Gill, 1984). One patient-oriented reason as to why the decision to refer a given case should never be taken lightly concerns the potential for patients to view a referral out to another professional as a rejection by the therapist, even if the reasons are valid. Carrying the case with ongoing consultation may be an option, but only if the countertransferential reactions of the therapist are openly acknowledged and well articulated with the consultant with a view toward providing the patient the best possible treatment.

Although discussions of countertransference traditionally have been relegated to therapists utilizing a psychoanalytic or psychodynamic method of treatment, there has been an increasing acknowledgment of the universality of this concept in cognitive–behavioral (e.g., Safran, 1998) and family systems treatment modalities (e.g., Framo, 1968). In a now-classic article frequently assigned in clinical training settings, Framo (1968) candidly, eloquently, and sometimes poignantly illustrates the range of the therapist's reactions to the patient in light of the resonance in the therapist's own life and family history, ranging from the benign internal response or reflection to the clearly problematic, inappropriate, and countertransferential response to the patient that has the potential for negative impact on the patient. Consider the following rather moving example of a statement made by the therapist during a family therapy session, followed by an internal reflection of the therapist in parentheses:

> Me to son: "While your mother was crying I noticed you looked very upset. It's hard for you to deal with her unhappiness, isn't it? You feel you have to do something, don't you?" (Only if parents are happy can children be. Me to mom at age of five: "Mom, don't cry . . . I love you; you still have me. When I grow up I'm going to buy you a washing machine, so you won't have to work so hard.") (Framo, 1968, p. 19)

Now, alternatively, consider the following intense, overdetermined statement made to the parents by the therapist stemming from a strong countertransferential overidentification with the parentified children, followed by the countertransferential recognition by the therapist in parentheses:

> Me to parents: "You exploit, make parents out of, and psychologically murder your children." (How much of my anger rides on the back of old angers? With which of my undigested introjects was I dealing? Who was I trying to rescue? On whom, really, was I wreaking revenge?) (Framo, 1968, p. 20)

The potential for all therapists, regardless of their own family history, to react with strong countertransference to emotion-laden patient scenarios is well exemplified by J. S. Wallerstein's (1990) work on the range of countertransferential responses associated with conducting therapy with family members who are undergoing divorce. Wallerstein's observations concerning therapists' countertransferences over grappling with this family crisis are predicated on her longitudinal outcome study of the long-term effects of the children of divorce at 10-year (J. S. Wallerstein & Blakeslee, 1989) and 25-year (J. S. Wallerstein, Lewis, & Blakeslee, 2000) follow-up periods. The outcome of these studies has, in particular, challenged two of what Wallerstein referred to as our society's "cherished myths" about divorce. The first myth holds that if parents are happier, even if the price of their happiness entails the dissolution of the marriage and family, then the children will be inevitably happier as well. On the contrary, the results of Wallerstein's landmark study show that the children, on the whole, do not look emotionally happier and more well adjusted even if one or both parents are happier. These children have shown more aggressiveness in school, increased difficulties in learning, more depression, more likelihood of being referred for psychological services, earlier onset of sexual activity, more children born out of wedlock, less marriages, and more divorces than peers from intact families. According to J. S. Wallerstein et al. (2000, p. xxix): "Indeed, many adults who were trapped in very unhappy marriages would be surprised to learn that their children are relatively content. They don't care if Mom or Dad sleep in different beds as long as the family is together."

The second cherished myth about divorce in our society is the belief that divorce is merely a temporary crisis that wields its most harmful effect at the actual time of the breakup. In other words, it is believed that if the parents do not fight, particularly not in front of the children, and are "rational" about the disbanding of the family, that the short-term crisis will resolve itself rather quickly. Rather, the reports from the children of divorce reveal that, unless there was domestic violence in the family, it is the many years of living in a divorced or remarried family that matter the most. What is of more importance to the children of divorce is the sense of loss, abandonment, and betrayal of childhood and the acute anxiety experienced when one reaches adulthood. These children enter adulthood with myriad unsettled questions regarding commitment, trust, and allegiance in intimate relationships. In essence, the life stories reported by Wallerstein and her colleagues (J. S. Wallerstein & Blakeslee, 1989; J. S. Wallerstein et al., 2000) belie the myths about divorce that our society has come to embrace.

Given the fervor with which these collective myths have been created and maintained in our society, it is no surprise that psychotherapists are not immune from intense countertransferential emotions when confronted by the often-denied reality of a dissolving family in the clinical context. Powerful countertransferences may occur not only as "countertransference proper" (i.e., reactions to the divorcing patient's rageful and seductive transferences to the therapist) but also as a normative response to marital breakdown and the diminished parenting of the children (J. S. Wallerstein, 1990). The collapse of the once-loved partner into the now-hated adversary can be frightening for a clinician to witness at close range. Such clinical experiences inevitably evoke anxiety in the psychotherapist and ultimately obscure objectivity and therapeutic neutrality. The divorcing individual brings to the psychotherapist the dilemmas that confront both clinician and nonclinician in his or her daily life: issues of love and hate, dependence and independence, and the myriad of bipolar problems of living in relationships with men and women. The psychotherapist is brought "up close" to not only the frequent impermanence of marital partnerships but also the enactment by a parent of the threat to abandon his or her children. The potential for the clinician to become lost in ambiguity is, perhaps, best exemplified by the unsettling perception that "There but for the grace of God go I" (J. S. Wallerstein, 1990, p. 339). Thus, it seems that regardless of the therapist's own family background, the possibility of a simply "neutral" response to such primitive emotions seems unlikely. That is to say, whether the psychotherapist originates from a family in which the parents loved one another for a lifetime, terminated their marriage in a bitter divorce, or stayed together in a lifeless marriage "for the sake of the children," the countertransferential reactions of the therapist are likely to be substantial. Furthermore, the dilemmas of countertransference are likely to occur whether the psychotherapist is carrying out divorce therapy and mediation with the couple and family, providing cognitive–behavioral coping strategies, or conducting psychodynamically oriented object relations reconstructive therapy on an individual basis with one or the other of the marital partners. As Gill (1984, p. 213) observed, "a transference relationship develops in every therapy, whatever the approach." Thus, the previous illustrations serve to point out the ubiquity of transference and countertransference in the psychotherapeutic context.

DILEMMAS OF RESISTANCE

A similar permeation exists for the phenomenon of resistance in the psychotherapeutic environment. To consider why this is, it is first important to consider exactly what the process of resistance is and what it is not. According to Auld and Hyman (1991, p. 114),

> [Resistance] is a force within the patient that acts against the therapeutic process, against the task of uncovering and dissolving the neurotic conflict. It is a force that works to maintain repression even at the cost of perpetuation, or even the expansion, of neurotic symptoms. . . . Resistance results from the patient's attempt to avoid the anxiety evoked in

the therapy when repressed feelings, wishes, thoughts, and experiences threaten to return to awareness.

The clinical dilemmas of resistance arise from the ambiguity of the patient wanting symptom relief and behavioral changes in his or her life, on the one hand, while feeling the safety of familiarity with the status quo, on the other. This ambivalence in the patient about psychotherapy and behavior change has given rise to several misconceptions about the nature of the patient's resistance. Auld and Hyman (1991) attempted to rectify some of these misconceptions by clarifying what resistance is not: Resistance is not an acting out of anger, resentment, or hostility against the psychotherapist. Resistance is not a refusal or oppositionality of the patient to accept the psychotherapist's ideas or suggestions. And, finally, resistance is not an attempt on the part of the patient to make his or her interactions with the therapist to be perplexing.

These clarifications point out an important distinction between the psychodynamic conceptualization of resistance and the behavior therapy models of resistance as noncompliance to therapeutic instructions (Leahy, 2001). Twenty years ago, P. L. Wachtel (1982, p. xiv) observed the following:

> In the behavioral literature, references to resistance are scant. If one only *reads* about behavior therapy, one is likely to conclude either that behavior therapists do not understand or do not notice resistance or that their methods overcome resistance or make it irrelevant.

According to the behavioral model, the failure of a patient to comply with therapeutic recommendations may be attributed to the therapist's selecting reinforcements that are not salient to the patient (e.g., teacher's praise for an oppositional adolescent) or noncontingent, or perceived as noncontingent, on the outcomes desired (Leahy, 2001). Accordingly, it becomes the therapist's job to construct ways in which to get the patient to comply with the treatment objectives (e.g., Lazarus & Fay, 1982). In this way, the behavior therapist's approach to the patient is strongly allied with the role of a teacher, instructor, or scientist.

For therapists who view the process of psychotherapy as being embedded within the broader context of an interpersonal relationship, the inherent ambiguity of resistance is more readily acknowledged and more broadly understood. In contrast to the behavioral approach, the role functions of the psychotherapist are viewed as that of the compassionate listener and the empathic observer (Blatt & Erlich, 1982). The perceived differences in professional role functions have corresponding effects on how the patient's resistances are viewed. Thus, Blatt and Erlich, for example, believed alternatively that the psychotherapist's job is to assist the patient in recognizing his or her resistance when it occurs and assess its various possible meanings for the patient, particularly with respect to the patient's fear or apprehension about the anticipation of change.

Rather than viewing the patient's resistances in potentially critical or pejorative terms, as many patients themselves are prone to do, it may be important to assist patients in discovering the positive function of their resistance to change and the maintenance of their symptomatology (e.g., avoiding overwhelming anxiety or panic). K. Adler (1972) offered the metaphor of the "symptom as a friend" to the patient. In other words, the symptom behaves as a good friend might to prevent the patient from making a premature and disorganizing life decision that the patient might not yet be ready to undertake (e.g., an impending marriage, divorce, or job change; Mozdzierz et al., 1976). Thus, the continuance of the symptom, or resistance to change, serves the positive function of giving the patient more time to prepare and achieve a greater readiness for important life changes. The dilemma in therapy, of course, is how much of a "friend" is the symptom in its resistance to change, versus the deleterious effects (i.e., the emotional cost) of maintaining the status quo of the symptomatology? This view of resistance and symptomatology is predicated on Freud's (1926/1959a) concept of *signal anxiety*. Thus, the anxiety serves as a signal or warning to protect the patient against the disorganization of an even greater traumatic anxiety or move that might threaten danger and throw the patient into a state of disequilibrium. Recent examinations of the concept from the standpoints of cognitive psychology, learning theory, psychophysiology, and behavioral neuroscience, as well as psychoanalytic theory, have shown some convergence of thought on the function of resistance anxiety (Wong, 1999).

The cognitive–behavioral and psychoanalytic perspectives on resistance need not be, however, diametrically opposed for the integrative therapist who is willing to entertain the elements of both in treatment. Rhoads (1984), for example, considered multiple ways in which aspects of the two approaches can be integrated and enhance one another. He believed that a psychodynamically oriented understanding of resistance and approach to intervention can be exceedingly useful when encountering resistance in the form of noncompliance in behavior therapy. Although behavioral noncompliance is far from being the only form of resistance, certainly behavior therapy patients have innumerable reasons for not counting baseline behaviors, not constructing charts and graphs, and not completing behavioral homework assignments in general. Rhoads recommended that, in such instances, the behavior therapist may shift to a more exploratory therapy with the patient concerning his or her feelings about having been asked to undertake such assignments and, perhaps, relate this to any similar reactions to such requests in earlier times of the patient's life, especially involving others who might have served as the relational prototypes in dealing with authority figures and their various requests or demands (i.e., to interpret the patient's transference resistance to the behavior therapist) in an effort to increase compliance.

Rhoads (1984; Feather & Rhoads, 1972) also suggested that target behaviors for such behavioral approaches be predicated on a more comprehensive psychodynamic understanding of the patient's psychopathology. For example, it has been proposed that one of the early sources for panic disorder and agoraphobia is the very real experience of some form of abandonment in the developmental history of such a patient (e.g., Friedman, 1985; Sable 1994, 2000; Scaturo, 1994). Once a psychodynamic connection to panic has been established in the treatment of a given patient, then it may be possible to tailor behaviorally oriented exposure therapy through systematic desensitization (Wolpe, 1992) to address both loci of the patient's anxiety (i.e., the fear of panic attacks in the present and the abandonment fears of the past). That is to say, rather than constructing a single hierarchy pertaining to the patient's fear of panic in only current contexts (e.g., a restaurant, grocery store, or a shopping mall), it may be possible to construct two separate hierarchies, one related to the above-noted anxiety-associated contexts of the present and one as a hierarchy of fears leading up to certain historical abandonment experiences of the past (e.g., the loss of a parent at an early age). It may also be possible for the therapist to construct a combined, overlapping hierarchy with graduated steps from both of the separate hierarchies moving up the hierarchy in an alternating fashion jointly desensitizing the patient to both sets of psychologically related fears, thereby providing a truer integration of past and present within a single behavior therapy regimen.

In cognitive therapy, resistance has been defined as anything in the patient's thoughts, feelings, or behavior that interferes with the demand characteristics (Orne, 1962; Whitehouse et al., 2002) or subtle situational expectations of the cognitive therapy approach. These demand characteristics include

> emphasis on the here-and-now, structured sessions, continuity across sessions, problem-solving orientation, rational thinking, collaboration with the therapist, psychoeducation and information sharing, an active role for both patient and therapist, accountability as evidenced by identifying and measuring goals and attainment of goals, and compliance with self-help assignments. (Leahy, 2001, p. 11)

Yet, even within this highly structured approach, resistance is seen as multifaceted and multidetermined. Leahy (2001) outlined several dimensions of resistance within a cognitive therapy model. First, a patient with depression, for example, may require a sense of validation for his or her feelings or perspective such that he or she truly believes that the therapist can understand the perceived helplessness and demoralization felt by the patient before the patient entrusts the therapist with a belief in the therapist's ability to help. Second, the patient may be resistant to change because of a need for *self-consistency* and the belief that he or she has been steadily committing him- or herself to a given course of action and is, thereby, reluctant to consider an alternative course (i.e., the discomfort associated with cognitive dissonance; Festinger, 1957). A third source of resistance to change might be the patient's personal need to view his or her past behavior as consistent with the view of his or her own sense of self or identity, that is to say, the patient's *self-schema* (Horowitz, 1988). A fourth impediment to behavioral change may be a type of *moral resistance* in which the patient may feel an obligation to significant others in his or her life to maintain the status quo and not disrupt the equilibrium in the family. A fifth dimension of resistance might be the secondary gain or reinforcement that a given patient may receive from significant others or provide to him- or herself in assuming the social role offered by victimization. Sixth, the patient may feel unable to assume the *risk* and responsibility associated with making changes in one's life, providing for oneself, and the fear of losing what little one gets from a familiar coping strategy in life. And, finally, resistance may take the form of a *self-handicapping strategy* by the patient in which the "designated problem" by the patient is in fact a solution (i.e., an excuse) by which the patient is able to avoid making other, more substantial changes in his or her life.

By recognizing the multifaceted nature of resistance, Leahy (2001) proposed the use of an *integrative social-cognitive model of resistance*. Accordingly, an "integrated social-cognitive model of resistance recognizes that resistance is often the result of emotional dysregulation (or overregulation), early (and later) childhood experiences, and unconscious processes" (Leahy, 2001, p. 20). This multidimensional model of resistance borrows heavily from its psychoanalytic predecessors that emphasize the self-protective mechanisms of psychological defenses and unapologetically acknowledges that many of these processes may lie outside of the patient's conscious awareness at given points in time. Even the staunch adherents of a psychoanalytic framework might find little to argue with in such a multidimensional approach to resistance.

CONCLUDING REMARKS: FROM ORTHODOXY TO INTEGRATION IN THE NOVICE AND SEASONED CLINICIAN

The clinical dilemmas that arise from the interpersonal ambiguities of transference, countertransference, and resistance to change span the major theoretical perspectives on psychotherapy regardless of whether the clinician believes or assumes that some of these resistances may be operative at an unconscious level of psychological functioning. Although adherents to other approaches that do not consider unconscious processes to be operative may view their clinical work purely from a cognitive or behavioral theoretical level of explanation, Leahy (2001, p. 14) observed that the notion of "theoretical purity" tends to be more common among novice clinicians. The more experienced and seasoned clinician generally shows a greater willingness to borrow concepts and methods from other modalities in an effort to enhance therapeutic effectiveness. Even the admonishment by P. L. Wachtel (1982) noted earlier concerning the limited understanding of the concept of resistance in the early behavior therapy literature was tempered by his observation that this is an illusion that disappears rapidly when one speaks with experienced behavior therapists about case material. In this respect, the movement toward integrative psychotherapy may well be an outcome or product of the maturation that has taken place in the field of psychotherapy. Reciprocally, advances in psychotherapy integration may also serve as a *maturing force* within the profession. The next chapter addresses the more consciously determined dilemmas that occur in the psychotherapeutic process related to the difficulty involved in the interpersonal negotiation of the therapeutic boundary between the neutrality of the therapist, on the one hand, and therapeutic engagement (and the therapist's self-disclosure) with the patient, on the other.

9

THERAPEUTIC NEUTRALITY, SELF-DISCLOSURE, AND BOUNDARY MANAGEMENT: DILEMMAS OF THERAPEUTIC ENGAGEMENT

The ambiguities of the patient's transference and the therapist's counter-transference, as well as the self-protective uncertainties of the patient's resistances in the therapeutic process, have made the establishment of therapeutic neutrality and the respect and observance of the professional boundaries of the psychotherapeutic relationship important methods for infusing measures of certainty and definition into what is, at times, a highly equivocal interpersonal process. As discussed in chapter 2, Freud (1912/1958c, 1917/1963, 1937/1964a, 1940/1964b) made recommendations regarding various ground rules of psychoanalytic treatment that have had a long history in this field of study. Included among these ground rules are that the therapist remain relatively anonymous to the patient and neutral with respect to the patient's particular life problems, as well as maintaining the boundaries surrounding the confidentiality of the patient's treatment. Freud in later years acknowledged: "The 'Recommendations on Technique' that I wrote long ago were essentially of a negative nature. I considered the most important thing was to emphasize what one should *not* do, and to point out the temptations in directions contrary to analysis" (see Jones, 1955, p. 241). As also noted earlier, Freud himself, on numerous occasions varied substantially from these published recommendations (Lynn & Vaillant, 1998). But, what dilemmas make it so difficult to *uniformly* apply these seemingly reasonable and straightforward, black-and-white rules or recommendations to treatment in each and every case?

DILEMMAS OF THERAPEUTIC NEUTRALITY

Therapeutic neutrality, or what has also been termed *technical neutrality* of the psychotherapeutic method, means that the psychotherapist should not provide the patient with directives regarding major life choices, nor should the therapist assume the role of educator, mentor, or teacher (Freud, 1912/1958c, 1917/1963, 1937/1964a, 1940/1964b; Lynn & Vaillant, 1998). The purpose of this recommendation was to respect the patient's inherent right to self-determination with regard to the safeguarding of the patient's autonomy, historically as a basic principle of biomedical ethics (Beauchamp & Childress, 1994), which also finds more recent support theoretically (Deci & Ryan, 1985), empirically (Deci & Ryan, 2002), and clinically (Sheldon, Joiner, & Williams, 2003). In an effort to help protect the patient from making precipitous life decisions that might have irrevocable negative consequences for him or her, while at the same time trying to avoid telling the patient what to do or which decision to make over matters that are truly of his or her own domain or province, a useful injunction traditionally invoked by psychoanalysts has been to recommend to the patient that no major life decisions (e.g., marriage, divorce, career change) be made until the analysis is complete. For a treatment that is typically measured in years rather than months or weeks, such a recommendation is seemingly unreasonable. However, even during the early days of psychoanalysis, the intent of this recommendation was likely not literal (e.g., waiting 8 years to marry) but rather a figurative intention to impede the patient from making impulsive or abrupt decisions with potentially severe detrimental consequences. Thus, a modified version of this admonishment for the patient to "slow down" (i.e., a postponement technique; K. Adler, 1972; Mozdzierz et al., 1976) can be made in prevailing psychotherapeutic modalities without robbing the patient of his or her essential right to self-determination (even if that right includes a certain amount of unraveling of his or her present life structure by particular life choices).

In this and other ways, the concept of the psychotherapist's neutrality has been largely misunderstood (Scaturo & McPeak, 1998). The term *neutrality* should not be taken to imply that the psychotherapist relates in a cold, emotionally distant, or impersonal manner in his or her interactions with the patient. Likewise, the related term of *therapeutic disinterest* should not imply that the therapist is uncaring or unconcerned with respect to the patient's emotional pain. Rather, disinterest in this context is intended to imply objectivity, such that the psychotherapist does not use the power differential inherent in the therapeutic role relationship to gratify his or her own personal needs or self-interest. For example, if the therapist experiences some gratifications of his or her sense of personal power by not having to struggle with the particular issue that a given patient has brought into treatment (e.g., unassertiveness with authority figures), the therapist does not gratify this need for power over the patient by engaging in even a smug sense of self-righteousness and "one-upmanship" in therapy that becomes subtly communicated to the patient and adds to his or her emotional pain or conflict in this area. Although the essential equality of the patient and therapist as respective human beings may be an "inalienable right" that we hold to be "self-evident," the patient–therapist relationship as a power arrangement is nevertheless an asymmetrical relationship (P. L. Wachtel, 1987). As such, the respective roles of one *seeking* help and the other of *providing* it carry with them an inherent power differential that is not to be misused by the provider, even in unobvious ways. Similarly, an ethical and astute therapist does not indulge any unresolved sexual conflicts within him- or herself by a "voyeuristic" gratification through listening to the patient's sexual history without a therapeutic purpose foremost in mind. Such behavior on the part of the psychotherapist is nontherapeutic not only to the extent that it is not directed toward being helpful to the patient, but also to the extent that the patient senses this experience with the therapist is actively detrimental to the patient's emotional condition.

P. L. Wachtel (1987), in a chapter cleverly titled, "You Can't Go Far in Neutral," commented on the limitations, misunderstandings, and misrepresentations of the concept of neutrality in psychotherapy. First, he noted that complete neutrality is an impossibility and that it is preferable to think in terms of *relative neutrality*. In other words, any reaction of the psychotherapist, however slight, carries with it some concomitant meaning for the patient. Even silence, as well as the attempt to withhold a reaction, is a powerful form of communication to the patient. Although originally intended to provide the patient with an atmosphere of emotional safety in the psychotherapeutic context to fully and freely disclose his or her concerns and conflicts, Wachtel noted that a neutral stance on the part of the therapist may not be the best vehicle to foster this sense of safety in all circumstances. He pointed out that when the psychotherapist is consistently ambiguous and silent, the patient's inclinations to experience a sense of rejection by the therapist are given full reign. Thus, there is reason to believe that a psychotherapist's stance of ambiguity can even, at times, increase the patient's anxiety and its pervasiveness (P. L. Wachtel, 1987). The therapist's neutrality on various issues may be experienced by these patients as an invalidating response and contribute to a questioning of their own perceptions and doubting their sense of reality about their life experiences. Rather, many patients are in need of a more positively affirming stand to their life circumstances, perceptions, and emotional dilemmas (Scaturo & McPeak, 1998).

Herman (1992) addressed another problematic dimension of the concept of neutrality. She noted that a distinct difference exists between the notions of technical neutrality and *moral neutrality* that, she contended, is an untenable position for psychotherapists working with victimized populations in particular. According to Herman, a committed moral stance is required of the therapist and solidarity with the patient over the moral injustice done. Therapeutic neutrality in the face of a profoundly moral issue is simply too weak of a stance for the psychotherapist to assume. In other words, in clinical work with these populations, it is reasonable for the victim to expect that the therapist will share in his or her moral outrage and that it is, to some degree, visible to the patient in the session. It is essential for the psychotherapist to be able to demonstrate an implicit understanding of the injustice that is inherent in the traumatic situation.

By way of example, Herman (1992) cited the clinical work of Danieli (1984) with respect to treatment of Holocaust survivors and their families. When, for example, the survivors spoke of their relatives who "died" in the Holocaust, Danieli freely affirmed that the patient's relatives were, in fact, "murdered." Danieli's use of the less neutral word, *murder*, clearly pointed out the moral stance and perspective of the therapist, even if the patient was still defending against this conclusion. In essence, she deliberately used more "toxic," less neutral, language to denote the inherent moral toxicity of the traumatic experience. The therapist's moral alliance with the patient was seen as a necessary component of the psychotherapist's empathic attitude toward the patient.

The clinical dilemma for the psychotherapist is how to be sufficiently engaged with the patient, on the one hand, without losing one's sense of clinical objectivity and ability to be effective with the patient, on the other (i.e., therapeutic neutrality vs. therapeutic engagement; Scaturo & McPeak, 1998). As becomes increasingly apparent, therapeutic neutrality is not a simplistic, unidimensional answer to the complex question of boundary management in clinical practice. The absence of the therapist's "self" in the clinical interview through the concealment of one's reactions to what the patient brings to the session is hardly reassuring to most patients. Indeed, it is questionable as to whether the masking of the therapist's personal reactions is even possible, when one considers the subtle attitudinal metamessages intrinsic in almost all clinical interpretations (P. L. Wachtel, 1993). Alternatively, however, this does not imply that excessive self-disclosure on the part of the psychotherapist is a viable therapeutic stance either.

DILEMMAS OF THERAPEUTIC SELF-DISCLOSURE

How much self-disclosure on the part of the therapist is needed for successful therapeutic engagement of the patient in therapy? There is, of course, no uniform answer to this question. Clinical needs vary from patient to patient, each with different attachment histories. Perhaps a theatrical example will serve to illustrate. In the Academy Award winning film, *Good Will Hunting,* the character of Will Hunting is a troubled, highly defensive college-age mathematical genius working as a custodian for the Massachusetts Institute of Technology, whose underachievement is associated with a history of severe child abuse in a seemingly unending series of foster homes. Once Will's Einstein-like intelligence comes to the attention of a mathematics professor who wishes to exploit his problem-solving ability, he is referred for psychotherapy to Dr. Sean McGuire, a similarly brilliant counseling psychologist at a local community college, whose subtler underachievement is also associated with a traumatic past. Will's defensive sarcasm and verbal sparring with Sean characterize the outset of their doctor–patient relationship. There is a serious question as to whether Will's memories of abuse and neglect will sufficiently allow him to trust Sean, or any therapist for that matter, in order to establish a working therapeutic alliance. After an initially stormy first session in which Will pretentiously insults a painting made by Sean and hanging on the wall in his office, Sean counters Will's remark in a second session, during which it will ultimately be determined whether the two can create a working therapeutic alliance (Damon & Affleck, 1997, pp. 71–72)[1]:

SEAN

So, if I ask you about art you could give me the skinny on every art book ever written . . . Michelangelo?

(beat)

You know a lot about him I bet. Life's work, criticism, political aspirations. But you couldn't tell me what it smells like in the Sistine Chapel. You've never stood there and looked up at that beautiful ceiling. And if I asked you about women I'm sure that you could give me a syllabus of your personal favorites, and maybe you've been laid a few times, too. But you couldn't tell me how it feels to wake up next to a woman and be truly happy. If I asked you about war you could refer me to a bevy of fictional and nonfictional material, but you've never been in one. You've never held you best friend's head in your lap and watched him draw his last breath, looking to you for help. And if I asked you about love, I'd get a sonnet, but you've never looked at a woman and been truly vulnerable. Known that someone could kill you with a look. That someone could

---

[1]From *Good Will Hunting* (pp. 71–72), by B. Affleck and M. Damon, 1997, New York: Hyperion. Copyright 1997 by Hyperion. Reprinted with permission.

rescue you from your grief. That God had put an angel on earth just for you. And you wouldn't know how it felt to be her angel. To have the love to be there for her forever. Through anything, through cancer. You wouldn't know about sleeping sitting up in a hospital room for two months holding her hand and not leaving because the doctors could see in your eyes that the term *visiting hours* didn't apply to you. And you wouldn't know about real loss, because that only occurs when you lose something you love more than yourself, and you've never dared to love anything that much. I look at you and I don't see an intelligent, confident man; I don't even see a peer, and I don't see my equal. I see a boy. Nobody could possibly understand you, right, Will? Yet you presume to know so much about me because of a painting you saw. You must know everything about me. You're an orphan, right?

Will nods quietly.

SEAN

Do you think that I would presume to know the first thing about who you are because I read *Oliver Twist*? And I don't buy the argument that you don't want to be here, because I think you like all the attention your getting. Personally, I don't care. There's nothing you can tell me that I can't read somewhere else. Unless we talk about your life. But you won't do that. Maybe you're afraid of what you might say.

Sean stands,

SEAN

It's up to you.

More orthodox psychoanalytically oriented therapists might clearly feel that Sean has overstepped the professional boundary by making clear self-disclosing references to his own life. Less orthodox therapists from the humanistic school of thought might say that Sean has not gone far enough, making only oblique references to the resumé of his life experience and not relating these experiences in a more direct, genuine manner. Adherents to both schools of thought might agree that, even if the tactic were successful in engaging this otherwise resistant patient with a high risk of being lost to treatment at this point, the maneuver was still problematic and flawed as a boundary infraction because the intense manner in which it was delivered suggests that this dialogue is emanating more from the therapist's impulsive interpersonal need for self-disclosure (i.e., countertransference) than it was a planned and deliberate intervention directed at the patient's need to be engaged in treatment. Nevertheless, in this instance, Dr. McGuire's unorthodox risk at engaging the highly guarded patient by providing a glimpse of his own humanity, emotional pain, and life experience appears to have paid off. What if, however, the patient was still reluctant to engage in treatment? Would further pursuit of this patient by the therapist be advisable or inadvisable? It is important for psychotherapists to be mindful of the fact that, even though a patient lost to treatment is nevertheless a treatment failure by default, unless the patient can be engaged in treatment within the boundaries of professionalism, then the patient's level of readiness for treatment may not make the patient amenable to therapy at this particular point in time. Furthermore, that is not to say that such a patient may not be able to be reasonably engaged in treatment at some other point in time. Ultimately, effective therapists must be able to relate to their patients genuinely, while respecting the professional boundaries of the therapeutic relationship and their patients' inherent right to the self-determination of their own lives.

THE DILEMMAS OF BOUNDARY MANAGEMENT

Meaningful and effective clinical work requires a consistent and vigilant attention to, and management of, the therapeutic boundary in all sessions with patients and their families. Such vigilance entails a number of aspects. First, it necessitates professional and ethical competency on the part of the clinician, such that he or she has not only training and skill in therapeutic techniques but also a thorough familiarity with the professional standards and ethical guidelines of one's own profession. Beyond that, however, is the need for an awareness of the patient's emotional neediness, as well as his or her psychopathology, that is likely to present itself interpersonally during the course of the therapeutic relationship (transference). In addition, there must be a constant awareness of the therapist's own emotional and interpersonal neediness at any given point in his or her life cycle with its current life crises and stressors (countertransference). The therapist must be cognizant of how this interplay of personal needs may bilaterally affect the rationalizations and distortions that may occur in patient–therapist interactions. And, finally, the therapist must be observant of the multiple levels of communication (e.g., verbal and nonverbal) that can occur in any given therapeutic interaction. All of these facets require the therapist's mindful attention to effectively navigate and manage the boundaries of the therapeutic relationship.

An example from literature of the consequences of an inattention to such necessary boundary management can be found in the novel, *The Prince of Tides*, by author Pat Conroy (1986). The story involves a high school football coach from South Carolina named Tom Wingo who, in the midst of a marital crisis, spends his summer in New York City consulting with his sister's psychiatrist, Dr. Susan Lowenstein, following his sister's psychotic episode and hospitalization while in a catatonic state. During this time, Mr. Wingo and Dr. Lowenstein become involved in a personal and sexual relationship. Consider the following dialogue early in the book as Mr. Wingo and Dr. Lowenstein grapple with the definition of their professional versus personal relationship (Conroy, 1986, pp. 140–141)[2]:

---

[2]From *Prince of Tides* (pp. 140–141), by P. Conroy, 1986, New York: Houghton Mifflin. Copyright 1986 by Houghton Mifflin. Reprinted with permission.

"What's your first name, Doctor?" I asked, studying her. "I've been up here for almost three weeks and I don't even know your first name."

"That's not important. My patients don't call me by my first name."

"I'm not your patient. My sister is. I'm her Cro-Magnon brother and I'd like to call you by your first name . . . . You're calling me Tom and I'd like to call you by your given name."

"I'd prefer to keep our relationship professional," she answered. . . . "Even though you are not my patient, you have come here because you are trying to help me with one of my patients. I would like you to call me Doctor because I'm most comfortable with that form of address in these surroundings. And it scares me to let a man like you get too close, Tom. I want to keep it all professional."

"Fine, Doctor," I said, exasperated and bone-tired of it all. "I'll agree to do that. But I want you to quit calling me Tom. I want you to call me by my professional title."

"What is that?" she asked.

"I want you to call me Coach."

"My name is Susan," she said quietly.

"Thank you, Doctor," I almost gasped in my gratitude toward her. "I won't use your name. I just needed to know it."

I saw the softening around her eyes as we both began to voluntarily withdraw from the field of conflict.

Before this conversation is through, Mr. Wingo asks Dr. Lowenstein out to dinner, and she accepts the invitation. The violation of professional boundaries provided in this example is not that Dr. Lowenstein allows Mr. Wingo to call her by her first name but lies in the context in which this permission is given. In the course of this conversation, Dr. Lowenstein retreats from the wavering professional argument that she has already given Mr. Wingo, a family member of one of her patients, and has taken her first step down a slippery slope through which she allows a professional relationship to gradually disintegrate into an intimately personal relationship. Ultimately, and unfortunately, she accepts the patient's definition of the context and his punctuation of reality (i.e., that he himself is technically not her patient, although his sister is so). In point of fact, her familiarity with professional codes of ethics would clearly indicate that this argument and rationalization does not hold validity. For example, in the American Psychological Association's (2002) *Ethical Principles of Psychologists and Code of Ethical Conduct,* it is plainly stated in Ethical Standard 10.06 that "Psychologists do not engage in sexual intimacies with individuals they know to be close relatives, guardians, or significant others of current clients/patients" (p. 1073).

The patient, for a variety of motives, is not necessarily expected to correctly perceive the boundaries of the professional relationship without some possible distortions. It is, however, the psychotherapist's professional responsibility to perceive the parameters of the dyadic doctor–patient relationship and the triadic doctor–patient–family relationship (Doherty & Baird, 1983)

Index Patient

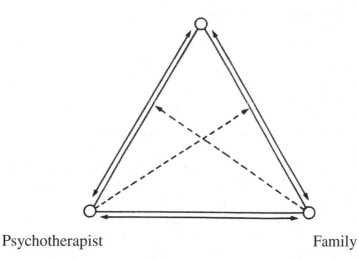

Psychotherapist   Family

Figure 9.1. The therapeutic triangle in psychotherapy. From *Family Therapy and Family Medicine: Toward the Primary Care of Families,* by W. J. Doherty and M. A. Baird, 1983, p. 13. Copyright 1983 by Guilford Press. Reprinted with permission.

and to act accordingly. The professional's punctuation of the relationship, thereby, assists the patient in reducing or minimizing any possible distortions that might occur. Yet another dimension of this dilemma contributing to the poorly defined nature of the professional relationship in this fictional example is the probable emotional agenda of Dr. Lowenstein, who allows the boundary to be violated when faced with her own emotional neediness rather than handling these inner conflicts through internal controls, professional consultation, or even referral of the case. Her failure to do so thus places the boundary violations exhibited by her squarely in the domain of ethical conflict (e.g., Bersoff, 2003).

The Therapeutic Triangle in Psychotherapy

In considering the broader scope of professional boundaries, it is helpful for the clinician to consider Doherty and Baird's (1983) notion of the therapeutic triangle that exists in clinical practice, as illustrated in Figure 9.1. Although Doherty and Baird referred specifically to the therapeutic triangle that exists for the family physician in medical practice, the clinical triangle to which they referred is also present in the practice of psychotherapy in general and perhaps most underrecognized in the practice of individual psychotherapy in particular. The fundamental point made by these authors is that the doctor–patient relationship is *multilateral* rather than *bilateral.* They asserted that the view of the health care provider's relationship with the patient as exclusively one-to-one is an "illusion of the dyad" in the doctor–patient medical model. Family members always influence and are involved in the patient's health care to one degree or another and always have certain expectations for appropriate care. Metaphorically speaking, the family is always considered to be the "ghost in the room" when the health care provider is interacting with a solitary patient. That is to say, the extended influences of the family on treatment take place even if the health care provider has not seen or interviewed the other family members. Thus, every health care provider who deals with patients—physician, psychotherapist, or other professional—is involved in a therapeutic triangle.

Hatcher and Hatcher (1983) conducted a survey of spouses and parents of psychotherapy patients involved in individually oriented treatment. These authors titled their study, "Set a Place for Elijah," originated from the tale of Elijah, the prophet, for whom a seat at the Passover table is reserved. According to the custom, it is expected that the mysterious guest will participate in the family gathering at some point during the meal. The results of these authors' research survey demonstrated that when a spouse or child sees an individual psychotherapist, the therapist's invisible presence joins the family, and while being primarily a help, it may also unwittingly distress the other members of the family. The presence of this metaphorical "family member" (i.e., the therapist) may have considerable influence on the relationship of the patient and his or her family. The spouses and parents of psychotherapy patients are affected not only by the realities of time, money, and a sense of intimacy that they must share with the unknown psychotherapist, but also by their fantasies, anxieties, and often fears about being blamed for the patient's difficulties. Nowhere is this perhaps more apparent than when a child is being treated in individual psychotherapy and the parents are excluded from the treatment process. The tendency for many parents to feel that they are to blame for whatever state of misery or discomfort their children are experiencing is far too often validated by their exclusion from therapy sessions and the treatment program. It is interesting that many managed care companies refuse to reimburse for child therapy not supplemented by family treatment that jointly targets problematic family interactions concurrent to the inner conflicts of the child as the index patient (e.g., E. F. Wachtel, 1992, 1994). Individual psychotherapy, by its nature, involves a kind of secret, special, and intimate relationship from which the spouse or parent may feel excluded. Themes of competition and rivalry with the psychotherapist for the affection of the patient are strongly felt by family members. "No matter how helpful the treatment may be, no matter what promise of happier life it may hold, therapy may drive a kind of wedge between the spouse or parent and the family member in treatment" (Hatcher & Hatcher, 1983, p. 75). This is, of course, an unintended side effect of treatment, but an effect that is best anticipated, planned for, and mitigated by the manner in which the psychotherapist deals with the family's metaphorical presence in the treatment context and the therapist's metaphorical presence in the family's life.

On the positive side, there is considerable clinical potential to be gained from this triangular perspective in treatment (Doherty & Baird, 1983). The therapist who, with the consent of the patient, has the availability of family members, even if limited, likewise has some access to the patient's key social support system. This advantage is particularly important with patients who are fragile or with patients in crisis, such as the depressed patient who temporarily has become a moderate, or somewhat uncertain, suicidal risk. In addition, the therapist's directives, for example, practicing relaxation techniques, obtaining behavioral baseline information, or working toward graduated behavioral goals in vivo, are better performed with the support of the family (i.e., increasing treatment compliance). Furthermore, the quality of primary dyadic relationships (e.g., husband–wife, parent–child) is enhanced by the support provided to these relationships by significant others outside of the immediate family system, such as a significant teacher, clergyman, family physician, or psychotherapist (Friesen, 1985), as illustrated by the dotted line originating from the psychotherapist in Figure 9.1. Likewise, the family of the patient is in a powerful position to either support or undermine the psychotherapist's relationship and clinical work with the patient, as suggested by the other dotted line originating from the family in Figure 9.1. When possible and appropriate, nurturing the patient–family relationship by the therapist is likely to result in the reciprocal nurturing of the patient–therapist relationship by the family as well.

Family Consultations in Individual Psychotherapy

The clinical decision to interview a psychotherapy patient's family need not be an either-or choice between individual or family therapy. E. F. Wachtel and Wachtel (1986) were among the first integrative psychotherapists to recognize the relevance of and rationale for "meeting the cast of characters" in the life of the individual psychotherapy patient. The purpose of conducting family consultations with patients in individual psychotherapy is clearly not to transform the individual treatment into couple or family therapy, but instead to enrich the clinical work with the identified patient. Thus, this treatment perspective rejects the view that individual and family therapies are necessarily competing or inconsistent models of treatment. The clinical information by the patient's significant others provides an additional perspective on developmental or historical events in the patient's life that affords a fuller construction of his or her reality. An interview with other members of the family can offer the therapist an opportunity to measure what he or she sees in the meeting against what has been reported to him or her clinically by the patient in earlier sessions. Perhaps a father's apparent "narcissism," for example, is not as self-centered or as unresponsive as was originally presented by the patient. In addition, the therapist can also obtain a sample of the patient's interactional style with the family. Thus, the therapist, as significant "other," can both validate and help modify the patient's perspective of the family in health-promoting ways. Such data can provide the therapist with an opportunity to make more informed decisions regarding therapeutic directions with the patient. For example, is there more potential for change in the family relationships than the patient might have believed, or is it more productive to therapeutically work toward an acceptance of the system's limitations with greater equanimity on the part of the patient? Such family consultations might serve to correct the tendency toward blaming that often occurs in families and might enable the individual therapy patient to view parents more realistically and in a more positive light (Framo, 1992).

E. F. Wachtel and Wachtel (1986) set forth a number of useful guidelines for techniques intended to offer the clinician some limited and purposeful consultation with their patients' families while preserving the integrity of the boundaries in individual treatment. As with other advocates of periodic consultations with the patient's family (e.g., Framo, 1976, 1992), E. F. Wachtel and Wachtel emphasized that preparation for such a meeting is of great importance to both the patient and the therapist. In general, thorough preparation and patient readiness to have family or significant others join in a consultative session are essential to providing adequate structure to ensure emotional safety in an interview (i.e., boundary preservation). In developing the patient's "agenda" for discussion in such a family consultation, it is important to familiarize the patient with the kinds of questions that are frequently asked in such sessions and to obtain prior approval regarding the limits of such a discussion (i.e., what the patient does and does not want addressed with the family). Thorough preparation involves an exploration of the concerns with matters that the patient wishes to avoid in the family session, and ultimately honoring the patient's request regarding these boundaries. The therapist must convey to the patient that the therapist will "take charge" and will avert any potentially destructive interactions. The predominant tone in these preparatory sessions is the sense of collaboration between the patient and therapist and respect for the patient's confidences.

E. F. Wachtel and Wachtel (1986) underscored the intense anticipatory anxiety that is typically felt by all when such consultative interviews are conducted. Patients seem to have an intuitive awareness as they experience anxiety over the potential emotional intensity present in session with a family unit in general and a family-of-origin unit (i.e., parents and siblings) in particular. Framo (1976, 1992) commented on the varied reactions of patients to the suggestion of bringing in their families of origin, ranging from disbelief (e.g., "you're kidding!") to affirmations that it is "out of the question." People are aware of unresolved feelings of anger, and they fear that the confrontation of it—to any degree—may result in parents having a heart attack or possible nervous breakdown. Framo (1976, p. 198) noted the reaction of one of his patients, "Ask me to climb Mount Everest, ask me to swim across the Atlantic Ocean, but please don't ask me to bring in my mother!" and observed that both individual and family therapists sensed the danger of hostilities of unrealistic proportions by bringing in the patient's parents. It is as if one senses that he or she is venturing into the "belly of the beast" as the source of original family conflicts. Conversely, though, such family consultations offer a unique opportunity to achieve some genuinely corrective emotional experiences with one's primary social group. And, even in these intense clinical encounters, the therapist most often has the ability and latitude to establish a viable and working boundary with the patient and his or her family.

CONCLUDING REMARKS:
THE SEMIPERMEABLE THERAPEUTIC BOUNDARY

In his classic text on family therapy, Minuchin (1974) conceptualized boundaries in family treatment as varying along a continuum involving degrees of *permeability*. In family therapy, when boundaries between family members are too diffuse or permeable, then there is not sufficient autonomy among the family's members and subsystems to properly perform their necessary role functions. For example, a parent may be too much of a "friend" to his or her adolescent child to make appropriate executive decisions when needed. When the boundaries are too rigid and not permeable enough, then there is not sufficient contact among the family's members and subsystems for them to provide support and protection of one another. Similarly, in a therapeutic system, boundaries between the therapist, the patient, and his or her family must be distinct enough so that the therapist can act in his or her professional role function with sufficient emotional distance, objectivity, and ethicality. Likewise, the therapist's boundaries should be permeable enough to engage with the patient or family and communicate the needed warmth and emotional support to the patient and his or her family as appropriate. Thus, the therapist's boundaries with the patient and his or her family are perhaps best viewed as *semipermeable*, whether the therapist actually meets the patient's family in some type of conjoint consultation or not. Generally speaking, in the present-day practice of psychotherapy, the therapist's boundary with the patient and with the patient's family system should be less permeable than the boundary that the patient and family have with each other, but more permeable than the rigid boundary offered in the classical psychoanalytically oriented framework.

It is most beneficial that the psychotherapist model for the patient a reasonable degree of balance with respect to boundary management. Ultimately, it is intended that a measured degree of reality and "sanity" will rule the day with regard to such issues. Whether pertaining to the family system and the various members and subsystems within it, or pertaining to the therapeutic system and the related role relationship positions with respect to the therapist, patient, or family within it, the boundaries of the system serve to define who participates in the functioning of that system and how. The purpose of boundaries in any human system—either family or therapeutic system—is to protect the respective role differentiation within that system. For the system to function effectively, the boundaries of the individuals within it must be clear. They must be defined well enough to allow the system's members to carry out their respective role functions (e.g., patient–therapist, parent–child) without impairment, yet they must be permeable enough to allow sufficient contact and closeness (i.e., "emotional glue") between the members.

Invariably, there are instances in which the boundary with the patient's family is necessarily impermeable. Usually, this occurs when a patient is being seen in individual therapy and is ambivalent about something that has direct bearing on the relationships with the spouse or family members (e.g., ambivalence about whether to stay in a marriage). Or, these times in treatment may involve the revelation of a life experience involving some degree of shame or guilt about which the patient feels unable to relate to the spouse or family safely but for which the patient is in some need of resolution, emotional release, and catharsis (Garfield, 1992a; Nichols, 1974), for example, the patient's need to discuss the existence of an extramarital affair. In these instances, it is generally best if the impermeability and sanctity of the therapeutic boundary be defined and agreed on at the outset of therapy or as soon as it becomes apparent that this is what is needed and required for this particular patient in this particular course in treatment. This is not to say that the addition of concurrent or subsequent marital or family therapy could not be added or conducted in tandem with the initial phase of individual treatment, if indicated. But, in such instances, it is likely that referral to a separate and independent marital–family therapist for the second-phase treatment goals likely will be recommendable.

In summary, having thus far examined in Part II the clinical dilemmas that occur within a variety and range of psychotherapeutic treatment modalities, and having examined in Part III those dilemmas that take place in treatment largely because psychotherapy is an interpersonal therapeutic process, Part IV of this book will consider the dilemmas involved in attempting to integrate these necessary, but at times disparate or conflicting aspects of treatment into a coherent theoretical perspective. Thus, a three-phase integrative model of psychotherapy is presented that is predicated on learning theory. The heuristic model attempts to organize, incorporate, and integrate the various aspects of treatment discussed historically in the psychotherapy literature as important elements of treatment into a coherent overall structure for understanding the treatment process. The three phases that will be addressed include the therapeutic alliance, technical interventions, and the relearning of coping strategies that takes place in the patient's natural environment. The relevance of various forms of learning, including associative, vicarious, and instrumental learning, to each of these phases of treatment is also discussed.

IV

CLINICAL DILEMMAS IN PSYCHOTHERAPY INTEGRATION: THEORY, PRACTICE, AND HISTORICAL CONTEXT

10

A THREE-PHASE LEARNING-BASED INTEGRATIVE MODEL OF PSYCHOTHERAPY: THERAPEUTIC ALLIANCE, TECHNICAL INTERVENTIONS, AND RELEARNING

In the movement toward the use of empirically validated psychological treatments, the more directive therapies, and specifically cognitive–behavioral therapy, rather than the more nondirective psychotherapies have tended to top the lists of treatments considered to be efficacious. However, recent reexaminations of the centrality of the therapeutic alliance have suggested that the interpersonal context of therapy, typically emphasized by the more nondirective approaches, forms the catalyst for effective technical interventions. In this chapter, a three-phase heuristic model that includes the major components for integrative psychotherapy is outlined. The three-phase model incorporates the seemingly separate contributions of the therapeutic alliance's foundation in therapy, the significance of proactive technical interventions in accelerating more adaptive behavioral changes, and the in vivo relearning that takes place in the patient's natural environment that have been identified in the psychotherapy literature over the past century or more (see Freedheim, 1992).

In addition, it is proposed that one of three forms of learning tends to be predominant in mediating each of these three phases of treatment. First, *associative learning* in the initial alliance-building phase allows the patient to gradually pair, or associate, in a less directive form of learning, a sense of safety and viability in the psychotherapeutic context with the prospect of behavior change. These therapeutic relationship factors in the treatment environment are conditions that many authors regard as necessary ingredients for the psychotherapy patient regardless of the specific nature of the problem(s) that the patient presents to the therapist. Second, *vicarious learning* in the technical interventions phase accelerates the learning of new behavioral alternatives through the more directive form of learning via psychological modeling and proactive psychoeducational instructions. Although some aspects of the technical interventions phase are more generic (e.g., Howard, Lueger, Maling, & Martinovich's [1993] concept of remediation) and equally applicable to the treatment of a broad range of psychiatric maladies, on the whole, the technique phase of therapy tends to be more problem related and symptom specific. Therefore, a range of psychotherapeutic techniques from this realm of directive interventions in cognitive–behavioral and family systems treatment are categorized and discussed as relating more specifically to the treatment of anxiety states than to the treatment of depression. Third, *instrumental learning* is largely involved in the relearning through the performance of new operant problem-solving behaviors tested by the patient in his or her natural environment. These new responses to previously problematic situations are able to yield different and more adaptive consequences in the patient's everyday life with the therapy sessions periodically available as a touchstone for the patient. Finally, although the sequential order of the treatment phases is seen as important and the form of learning subsumed under each is considered to be dominant for each phase, it should be noted that neither the phases of treatment nor the learning processes discussed herein are regarded to be mutually exclusive of one another. Further, it is assumed that there is overlap in the transitions, whether more gradual or more sudden, between the phases of treatment and the forms of learning generally subsumed under each phase.

The increased utilization of empirically supported treatments for psychological disorders has been a focus of a number of research reviews (e.g., DeRubeis & Crits-Christoph, 1998; Foa et al., 2000) as well as the subject of a psychotherapy task force report by the American Psychological Association (Chambless et al., 1998). Empirically supported treatments typically have been accompanied by the use of psychotherapy treatment manuals (Scaturo, 2001; Woody & Sanderson, 1998) that have served to enhance the uniformity and integrity of the technical interventions under study (Garfield, 1992b). For example, DeRubeis and Crits-Christoph (1998) studied both individual and group therapy modalities and examined treatments for a wide range of mental disorders, including depressive disorders, generalized anxiety, more specific phobic disorders, posttraumatic stress, schizophrenia, and chemical dependency. Of the treatments assessed by these authors, behavior and cognitive–behavioral therapies have tended to dominate the lists of treatments considered to be efficacious. Possible reasons for the dominance of behavioral and cognitive behavioral treatments have included, among other factors, the active or directive nature of cognitive–behavioral therapy's technical interventions. Although behavior therapy is not the only treatment approach considered to be directive (e.g., compared with problem-solving family therapy approaches; J. Haley, 1976), behavioral and cognitive–behavioral therapies are certainly the most widely used form of directive treatment. In addition, cognitive–behavioral therapy as a treatment modality has enjoyed the widespread support from managed mental health care organizations as well.

As discussed previously in chapter 4, one of the fundamental dilemmas for nonbehavioral, insight-oriented psychotherapists attempting to integrate cognitive and behavioral interventions into their clinical practices surrounds these directive aspects of the therapy (Scaturo, 2002d; Scaturo & McPeak, 1998). Directives in behavior therapy tend to be rather straightforward psychoeducational tasks prescribed by the therapists intending to bring about their stated intention and are perhaps most typified by the use of behavioral homework assignments in a "therapist as educator," psychoeducational fashion (e.g., Authier et al., 1975; Bandura, 1961). Over the years, a handful of early learning-based techniques and procedures (e.g., systematic desensitization, implosion, progressive relaxation) have been expanded into a massive clinical armamentarium of behavioral (Bellack & Hersen, 1985) and cognitive (McMullin, 1986, 2000) technical interventions. Furthermore, the use of directives may well be the most important single distinction between cognitive–behavioral therapy and more traditional insight-oriented and nondirective approaches that range from psychoanalytic therapy (Auld & Hyman, 1991), client-centered therapy (Rogers, 1951), existential psychotherapy (Yalom, 1980), to the more recent proliferation of narrative therapy approaches (e.g., Epston et al., 1996; M. White & Epston, 1990).

The use of directives and behavioral homework in cognitive–behavioral therapy potentiates the enactment of newly acquired behaviors in the patient's natural environment. As a result, the patient may engage in alternative operant behaviors in solving his or her problems. Engaging in these behaviors in the patient's own "life space" (Lewin, 1936) ultimately becomes instrumental in maintaining the newly acquired behaviors learned in the previous phase of treatment with the therapist in the clinical setting. Progressively successful attempts at problem solving, reality testing, and generating new behavioral alternatives for coping lessen the sense of helplessness to one's environment (Seligman, 1975) and conversely enhances one's ability to learn optimism (Seligman, 1990). The parallel concepts of self-efficacy (Bandura, 1977a, 1997) and the feminist therapy principle of empowerment (Kaschak, 1999) have been postulated as general factors in enhancing the patient's ability to cope with his or her environment and enhance mental health. In essence, the "technical" aspects of cognitive–behavioral therapy are designed to affect the patient's sense of self-efficacy and provide an increased sense of one's ability to manipulate his or her environment and the ability to experience instrumental behavior as effective in one's life.

Generally in treatment, directives, instructions, or behavioral assignments for the patient to do something *proactive* are frequently the most recent therapeutic steps (or phases) in therapy just prior to some behavioral change made by the patient in his or her everyday life. Thus, it is tempting to attribute the effectiveness of cognitive–behavioral therapy to the directive aspects of this regimen. However, the technical intervention stage of cognitive–behavioral therapy is only the most recent step (or phase) in the treatment process prior to the patient instrumentally testing new problem-solving behaviors in the patient's natural environment. The initial step (or phase) in the treatment process involves the development of a context in which safety and emotional security are enhanced (Bowlby, 1988; Winnicott, 1965), and fear and demoralization (Howard et al., 1993) are reduced. At the outset of therapy, it is essential to associate these elements with psychotherapeutic contact in advance of presenting of ideas concerning the newness of potential behavioral changes. Correspondingly, the patient is generally unlikely to test new and unfamiliar behaviors in an atmosphere of uncertainty without genuinely felt emotional support. Thus, the criticality of the need to associate the prospect of change within an atmosphere of safety has been instrumental, for example, to Safran and his colleagues (Safran, 1993; Safran & Greenberg, 1993, 1998; Safran & Muran, 1998; Safran & Segal, 1996) in emphasizing the significance of the therapeutic alliance in cognitive–behavioral therapy.

LEARNING IN THREE FORMS AND PHASES

In the present learning conceptualization, the three phases of psychotherapeutic treatment involve alliance-building, technical interventions, and relearning that incorporate three forms of learning as illustrated in Figure 10.1. In the first phase (Figure 10.1a), the factors relevant to the therapeutic alliance that are common to all forms of psychotherapy are regarded as the primary element in the initial phase of treatment. Furthermore, it is postulated that associative learning mediates this phase of treatment in which the patient learns to associate, or pair, expectancies for behavior change with aspects of safety and viability (i.e., hope). In the second phase (Figure 10.1b),

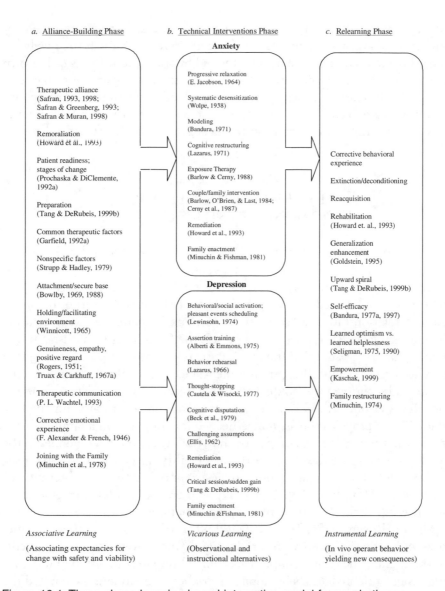

Anxiety

Progressive relaxation
(E. Jacobson, 1964)

Systematic desensitization
(Wolpe, 1938)

Modeling
(Bandura, 1971)

Cognitive restructuring
(Lazarus, 1971)

Exposure Therapy
(Barlow & Cerny, 1988)

Couple/family intervention
(Barlow, O'Brien, & Last, 1984;
Cerny et al., 1987)

Remediation
(Howard et al., 1993)

Family enactment
(Minuchin & Fishman, 1981)

Depression

Behavioral/social activation;
pleasant events scheduling
(Lewinsohn, 1974)

Assertion training
(Alberti & Emmons, 1975)

Behavior rehearsal
(Lazarus, 1966)

Thought-stopping
(Cautela & Wisocki, 1977)

Cognitive disputation
(Beck et al., 1979)

Challenging assumptions
(Ellis, 1962)

Remediation
(Howard et al., 1993)

Critical session/sudden gain
(Tang & DeRubeis, 1999b)

Family enactment
(Minuchin &Fishman, 1981)

Therapeutic alliance
(Safran, 1993, 1998;
Safran & Greenberg, 1993;
Safran & Muran, 1998)

Remoraliation
(Howard et al., 1993)

Patient readiness;
stages of change
(Prochaska & DiClemente,
1992a)

Preparation
(Tang & DeRubeis, 1999b)

Common therapeutic factors
(Garfield, 1992a)

Nonspecific factors
(Strupp & Hadley, 1979)

Attachment/secure base
(Bowlby, 1969, 1988)

Holding/facilitating
environment
(Winnicott, 1965)

Genuineness, empathy,
positive regard
(Rogers, 1951;
Truax & Carkhuff, 1967a)

Therapeutic communication
(P. L. Wachtel, 1993)

Corrective emotional
experience
(F. Alexander & French, 1946)

Joining with the Family
(Minuchin et al., 1978)

Corrective behavioral
experience

Extinction/deconditioning

Reacquisition

Rehabilitation
(Howard et. al., 1993)

Generalization
enhancement
(Goldstein, 1995)

Upward spiral
(Tang & DeRubeis, 1999b)

Self-efficacy
(Bandura, 1977a, 1997)

Learned optimism vs.
learned helplessness
(Seligman, 1975, 1990)

Empowerment
(Kaschak, 1999)

Family restructuring
(Minuchin, 1974)

Associative Learning

(Associating expectancies for
change with safety and viability)

Vicarious Learning

(Observational and
instructional alternatives)

Instrumental Learning

(In vivo operant behavior
yielding new consequences)

Figure 10.1. Three-phase learning-based integrative model for psychotherapy.

a number of well-documented cognitive–behavioral technical interventions are outlined for the treatment of both anxiety disorders and depressive disorders as the two fundamental emotional states for which the instructional aspects of cognitive–behavioral therapy have had demonstrated effectiveness. These interventions tend to be mediated by vicarious learning processes, in which the patient receives therapeutic instruction and observes the therapist modeling and rehearsing the needed coping behaviors and social skills. Finally, newly relearned instrumental behaviors have been conceptualized in the third phase (Figure 10.1c) as the patient in his or her natural environment can experience new consequences to alternative coping responses to anxiety and depression collectively. Through the newly acquired operant coping behaviors performed by the patient in his or her own natural environment, the patient has the opportunity to experience new and more adaptive life consequences with eventual self-generating reinforcements. The following examines each of these three phases in integrative psychotherapy and the critical learning that takes place within them in greater detail.

THE THERAPEUTIC ALLIANCE: CRITICAL FRONT-END INTERVENTION

Historically, the therapeutic relationship has been considered a critical factor in well-conducted psychotherapy, although the theoretical explanations for its importance have been varied (see Figure 10.1a). Psychoanalytic theorists have referred to what takes place for the patient in the therapist–patient relationship as a "corrective emotional experience" with a caring human being (F. Alexander & French, 1946). Attachment theorists, in particular, have suggested that the therapeutic relationship could be thought of as a holding (or facilitating) environment, metaphorically likening it to the safety and security of the holding that takes place in a healthy parental relationship (Winnicott, 1965). They postulated that secure attachment to a stable figure provides the assurance needed for the child in a family (or the patient in therapy) to be daring enough to test or explore new avenues in the world knowing that there will be the availability, responsiveness, and assistance should he or she encounter adverse, demoralizing, or frightening circumstances (Bowlby, 1969, 1988). To help create this level of emotional security in the therapeutic context, psychotherapists in the client-centered tradition (Rogers, 1951; Truax & Carkhuff, 1967b) suggested that genuineness, empathy, and positive regard by the therapist were essential elements in the therapeutic relationship. In addition, clinicians interested in integrating insight-oriented and behavioral approaches to treatment have noted the many subtleties involved in the concept of safe and optimally therapeutic communication (e.g., P. L. Wachtel, 1993). Strupp and Hadley (1979) were the first to subsume these elements under the term nonspecific factors in treatment, later referred to as common factors (e.g., Garfield, 1992a), such as emotional presence, empathy, and the instillation of hope. Such factors play an important role in all forms of psychotherapy, including cognitive–behavioral therapy (e.g., Ilardi & Craighead, 1994, 1999; Tang & DeRubeis, 1999a). In addition, the therapist's sincere consideration of a given patient's readiness (e.g., Prochaska & DiClemente, 1992a) and preparation (Tang & DeRubeis, 1999b) for all aspects of the technical interventions phase of treatment is part of the careful consideration in the alliance-building phase of treatment.

Howard et al. (1993) referred to what takes place in this phase as *remoralization*, or the enhancement of the psychotherapy patient's subjective state of well-being. Patients frequently enter psychotherapy in a demoralized state, feeling as though they are powerless to change their circumstances, exercise control over their lives, and feel as though they are unable to meet the expectations of self or others (Frank & Frank, 1993). "The evidence is strong that symptomatic improvement in psychiatric outpatients is positively related to aspects of the therapeutic setting that arouse their hopes of help" (Frank, 1968, p. 387). These interpersonal and therapeutic processes exert their influence in the treatment setting even before the formal, technical aspects of psychotherapy begin. Accordingly, the initial phase of treatment is characterized by the therapist being perceived by the patient as being trustworthy and competent, the patient and therapist arriving at a consensus surrounding the problem definition, and the establishment of an implicit treatment contract or agreement that results in a sufficient therapeutic alliance (Goldman & Milman, 1978).

Family therapists have also recognized the need to form a working alliance. Because this treatment modality requires the formation of multiple therapeutic relationships with several family members to form a therapeutic system rather than a therapeutic relationship with a single identified patient, this process has been termed *joining* with the family (Minuchin, 1974; Minuchin & Fishman, 1981). To be effective in couple and family therapy, the therapist must gain acceptance and admittance to the family by validating the family's strengths, values, hierarchy, and each family member's importance to the family unit (Simon et al., 1985). Regarding this phase of family treatment, Minuchin et al. (1978) observed the following:

> The therapist must join the field of stabilized family interactions in order to observe them. He must gain experiential knowledge of the controlling power that the system exerts. *Only then can he challenge*[italics added] the family interactions with any knowledge of the range of thresholds that the system can tolerate. (p. 94)

Although adept cognitive–behavioral clinicians have clearly incorporated a working knowledge of the therapeutic relationship into their everyday professional life, a systematic framework for integrating the concept of the therapeutic alliance and technical interventions has not been fully outlined (Safran & Segal, 1996; Scaturo, 2002d; P. L. Wachtel, 1982). An overall framework that would better articulate in systematic terms the relationship between specific technical factors of cognitive–behavioral interventions and the nonspecific factors of the therapeutic alliance is a worthy aspiration of the field at this point in its history. Safran (1998), for example, has embedded cognitive–behavioral therapy within the context of Sullivan's (1953) interpersonal theory to widen the scope of cognitive–behavioral therapy to incorporate factors pertaining to the therapeutic alliance. One problem in attempting to conceptualize these varied explanations and curative factors in treatment has been the lack of a common "theoretical language" within which to conceptualize these various aspects of treatment. These seemingly disparate theoretical languages and conceptual frameworks include, but are not limited to, psychodynamic theory, object relations theory, interpersonal theory, learning theory, social learning theory, cognitive–social learning theory, family systems theory, and likely a number of others. However, it is indeed possible to conceptualize the significance of these various therapeutic elements within the broader context of a learning theoretical perspective.

In the initial alliance-building phase of therapy, the patient gradually "tests" the professional–interpersonal relationship that he or she is beginning to establish with the psychotherapist. The anxious patient tends to test for safety in the therapeutic relationship, whereas the depressed patient looks for hope and viability from the therapist. In each instance, though, the patient progressively discloses more of his or her worries and fears, often about which the patient may initially associate powerful feelings of shame or guilt. The anxious patient scans the therapist and the therapeutic environment for any possible signs of shock or disapproval on the part of the psychotherapist. The depressed patient scans the therapeutic context to see if there are any signs of hope to be had. In particular, the patient is also scanning the environment to see if the hope offered has some genuine viability attached to it or if what is being proffered appears to be more on the order of "false hope" in his or her estimation. In what at times may be a lengthy process of trial and error, the patient gradually pairs or associates his or her discussion of the difficulties with a sense of safety and viability. Because of the subtlety and gradualness of many patients' "behavioral tests" of trust in the therapeutic relationship and the associative learning processes to which the "test results" are linked, the alliance-building phase of treatment may be one of the more time-intensive aspects of the therapy.

COGNITIVE AND BEHAVIORAL TECHNICAL INTERVENTIONS: VICARIOUS LEARNING THROUGH OBSERVATION AND INSTRUCTION

The principles of conditioning, or what Barlow (1988, p. 224) termed "emotional learning," in the acquisition of anxiety are supported by strong historical evidence (e.g., Miller, 1948; Mowrer, 1947) but are insufficient to fully account for the full range of learning that takes place in the psychotherapeutic situation. Likewise, the emotional aspects of the therapeutic alliance are necessary but insufficient to fully account for the positive behavior change that takes place in psychotherapy. The therapeutic relationship alone is unable to incorporate the importance of cognitive variables (i.e., instructional and observational behaviors) involved in relearning (Seligman &

Johnston, 1973) and the fact that cognitive and emotional processes are inextricably intertwined in learning (Barlow, 1988).

The learning of pathological responses through the observation of others has been subsumed under the rubric of vicarious learning. The acquisition of anxiety and fear through observing a model's fear of a given situation has been thoroughly demonstrated in both humans (e.g., Bandura & Rosenthal, 1966) and primates (e.g., Mineka, Davidson, Cook, & Keir, 1984). In the social psychological laboratory, for example, Bandura and Rosenthal (1966) were able to demonstrate that participants who observed a model feigning pain in a mock aversive-conditioning study acquired intense emotional responses to the sound of a buzzer that was paired with the noxious electric shock without direct contact with the stimulus. In the natural environment, one can acquire phobic reactions through the observation of fear demonstrated in a trusted model (e.g., mother) to a harmless stimulus (e.g., insects). Likewise, a father's repeated instructional warnings to avoid a given behavior (e.g., admonishments to drive defensively) lest some calamitous event may take place can invoke anxiety in a given circumstance (e.g., being in the driver's seat).

Correspondingly, psychotherapy predicated on modeling techniques (Bandura, 1971; Rosenthal & Bandura, 1978) and observational learning provides one of the active ingredients in cognitive–behavioral therapy that initiates relearning of fearful and depressive–helpless responses. For example, assertiveness training (e.g., Alberti & Emmons, 1975) through the process of behavior rehearsal (e.g., Lazarus, 1966) in which the therapist first models alternative coping behavior and the patient then practices it is one such approach to lessening learned helplessness in social contexts. In addition to modeling techniques in psychotherapy, there is considerable experimental evidence to demonstrate that instructional learning on response-reinforcement contingencies in specific situations can markedly accelerate behavioral changes (Bandura, 1969). For example, psychoeducational instructions at the outset of panic control treatment (Barlow & Cerny, 1988; Scaturo, 1994) or stress inoculation procedures (Meichenbaum, 1977) are an essential part of cognitive–behavioral directives to initiate change.

Howard et al. (1993) found the technical interventions phase of psychotherapy to be the most difficult stage of treatment to operationalize for empirical study, in part because of the multifaceted nature of the interventions that take place at this point in treatment. Generically, they have termed this phase of treatment *remediation*, involving the mobilizing of the patient's existing coping skills or the encouragement and teaching of more effective skills, regardless of the specific symptomatology being treated (e.g., anxiety or depression). Also somewhat generically, family therapists have termed the technique involved in this phase *enactment*, in which the family therapist behaviorally intervenes or directs the family members to experience a new pattern of relating to one another within the actual therapy session

(Simon et al., 1985). Enactment is the behavioral technique in which the therapist asks the family members to relate to one another and observes the dysfunctional behavior patterns played out in his or her presence (Minuchin & Fishman, 1981). The therapist then attempts to facilitate a new, more functional family transaction surrounding the presenting problem. For example, the family therapist may use a "family lunch session" to help modify the family's behavior surrounding a teenage child's anorexia (Rosman, Minuchin, & Liebman, 1975). Subsequently, the newly enacted pattern may be assigned as behavioral homework for the family to repeat outside of the session. Thus, the in-session behavioral enactment directed by the therapist paves the way for the restructuring of the family's interaction patterns within their natural home environment. Like Howard et al.'s concept of remediation, the family therapy technique of enactment occurs in the second, technical interventions phase of therapy after the family therapist has "joined" with the family and is relatively generic with respect to presenting symptomatology (e.g., anorexia, anxiety, depression). With regard to more symptom-specific technical interventions, Figure 10.1b provides a number of examples of well-established cognitive–behavioral techniques that utilize vicarious learning processes in the treatment of both anxiety and depression.

Technical Interventions for Anxiety

Among the cognitive–behavioral techniques basic to any structured treatment program for the treatment of anxiety is the learning of progressive muscular relaxation, which can be taught by the therapist as a coping alternative to fear and loss of control (E. Jacobson, 1964). From the outset of behavioral treatments for anxiety, the relaxation training was typically the first step in the early use of systematic desensitization that combines instructional learning with associative learning to hierarchically recondition the patient's responses to anxiety provoking stimuli (Wolpe, 1958). Relaxation has also been used as a critical component in more recent cognitive–behavioral exposure therapy programs for both generalized anxiety (e.g., Barlow & Craske, 2001) and more specific panic disorders (e.g., Barlow & Cerny, 1988; Craske et al., 2000). Also in this technical intervention phase, cognitive restructuring (e.g., Lazarus, 1971) aimed at eliminating negative and anxiety-provoking expectations is targeted, as well as psychotherapy by the therapist modeling (Bandura, 1971) interpersonal behaviors such as appropriate conversational behavior for patients with social anxiety. Finally, a variety of family interventions including, for example, spouse-assisted behavior therapy for anxiety and panic can be coached during this phase of treatment (e.g., Barlow et al., 1984; Cerny et al., 1987).

Mowrer (1947) was one of the first theorists to recognize the presence of multiple forms of learning in the acquisition and maintenance of neurotic (i.e., anxious) behavior. According to his *two-factor learning theory* (Mowrer,

1947), neurotic anxiety, or fear of a harmless situation, is acquired and maintained by means of a two-step learning process. Two-factor learning theory of anxiety encompassed a combination of associative learning processes via classical conditioning and instrumental learning via operant conditioning. Mowrer noted the importance of associative learning in the initial *acquisition* of a fear response to a previously unfeared or nonthreatening stimulus. In addition, he cited instrumental learning in which the organism then learns to avoid the feared stimulus as critical in *maintaining* the feared response. In other words, the learned avoidance of the stimulus prevents the modification of the acquired fear through subsequent experiences with alternative consequences to its exposure. One of the clearest illustrations of two-learning factors in the etiology of anxiety is that of panic disorder with agoraphobia (Scaturo, 1994). In the first step, the panic disorder patient associates the intense physiological discomfort of a panic attack with the setting within which it first takes place (e.g., a shopping mall). Second, by means of operant or instrumental conditioning, the patient subsequently learns to remove him- or herself from the feared situation, developing a phobic avoidance to the previously harmless situation (i.e., the mall, or marketplace [*agora* in the Greek language]). Because the avoidance deprives the patient of the opportunity and exposure to unlearn the feared expectation or to relearn any alternative consequences to this situation, the acquired neurotic anxiety is resistant to extinction or change.

Correspondingly, multiple forms of learning are likely involved in a treatment process that incorporates learning principles in both the development of the therapeutic alliance and the technical aspects of the treatment. Accordingly, the most efficacious component in the cognitive–behavioral treatment for anxiety is generally regarded as the gradual, hierarchically, and systematically self-paced form of *exposure* to the feared stimuli without its feared catastrophic consequences (e.g., Barlow, 1988). From a learning theoretical standpoint, the extinction of fear is more crucial to actual anxiety reduction over time than the behavioral coping strategies (e.g., progressive relaxation techniques) intended to manage the ongoing stress of an anxiety state. Although extinction of fear may indeed constitute the primary curative element in the abatement of anxiety, what is it about the patient–psychotherapist interaction, being the focal point of change, that allows the patient to make an initial approach response—even for a single instance—toward the confrontation of his or her fears? Certainly, the desire for symptom relief is one obvious motivation, but research on how psychotherapy patients view their treatment has shown that symptom relief is only a small part of why patients seek treatment (Scaturo, 1994; Strupp, Fox, & Lesser, 1969). The therapist's ability to help the patient approach the problem in a graduated way with some learned coping techniques to manage the accompanying stressors is also a part of the picture. However, despite the safe, incremental nature of this approach, why is the patient willing and able to consider approaching the behavioral threshold for the in vivo portion of his or her treatment for the first time? Even in recent research which suggests that early cognitive changes in therapy lead to sudden gains in treatment and ultimately to good outcome in cognitive–behavioral therapy for depressed patients, Tang and DeRubeis (1999b, p. 902) noted that the crucial unanswered question is, "What leads to the cognitive changes?"

The answer to this question likely lies somewhere in what Safran and colleagues (Safran, 1993; Safran & Greenberg, 1993, 1998; Safran & Muran, 1998; Safran & Segal, 1996) have studied concerning the qualities of the therapeutic alliance in cognitive–behavioral therapy. This issue also concerns the therapeutic alliance's link to what Mowrer (1947) referred to as associative learning, in contrast to the instrumental learning that takes place in the *behavioral activation* phases of the treatment. In this instance, associative learning primarily accounts for the trust (Truax & Carkhuff, 1967b) and security of Winnicott's (1965) facilitating environment experienced within the therapeutic relationship. In other words, the patient associates safety with the therapist and the psychotherapeutic context in which a trusted figure gradually encourages the patient by way of discussion to move forward to approach the previously feared and paralyzing situation (i.e., to make an initial approach response). The security that the patient feels in that environment is integrally related to a number of factors. Of course, one such factor includes trust of the therapeutic environment and the principles of professional ethics and integrity (e.g., beneficence, nonmaleficence) that the clinician brings to that context (e.g., Beauchamp & Childress, 1994). As important, however, is the patient's sense of emotional security that is also affected by the qualities of the therapeutic relationship (e.g., Rogers, 1951; Truax & Carkhuff, 1967b) and by the person of the clinician (e.g., Keith et al., 1993).

The interpersonal trust that the patient places in, and alliance with, the psychotherapist is understandably the more subtle, elusive, and ethereal aspect of treatment. The alliance, of course, may be the more time-intensive aspect of treatment, because the attainment of interpersonal trust is not instantaneous but, in fact, earned in a relationship (personal or professional) over some period of time. Most patients do not endow an anonymous therapist with trust simply because the clinician holds a degree from an impressive university or has been credentialed by an established health care system or managed care company. Although these formalities and requirements may be essential to the professional practice of health care, they are not sufficient for the psychotherapy patient; neither would our research on interpersonal behavior support this notion, nor would most reputable psychotherapists recommend it. Understandably, the process of building trust varies from patient to patient. Some patients are able to develop sufficient trust and confidence because they perceive the therapist to be a well-intended human being. Others, not unlike most members of our own profession, require more empirical evidence for this, are more cautious, and may take time to test the therapist's responses in various ways prior to establishing this needed bond. However, once the associational phase of treatment has taken place in the context of the therapeutic alliance, it catalyzes and allows the behavioral aspect of treatment to become effective.

Technical Interventions for Depression

Although it has been argued that some symptoms of anxiety and depression are highly correlated with a general emotional distress, called *negative affect*, as inherent at the core of both of these affective states (e.g., Clark & Watson, 1991), the phenomenology and related ideational content of depression are in some important ways characteristically distinct from that of anxiety (Beck, 1976; Burns & Eidelson, 1998). Rather than being fearful of some imagined and dreaded consequence, the depressed patient's pretherapeutic state is more that of demoralization and helplessness (Seligman, 1974, 1975) with a related expectation that nothing that one may do would make any appreciable difference or improvement in one's life structure.

As a result, what immobilizes the depressed patient is more the belief in the relative degree of *viability* for potential coping behaviors or courses of action under discussion with the psychotherapist rather than fear over these courses of action. The concerns over viability relate in large measure to elements of the patient's explanatory style regarding misfortune (Seligman, 1990), attribution concerning these events (Weiner et al., 1971), and generalized expectancies regarding their control over these events (Rotter, 1966). The trust that the patient places in the therapeutic relationship and alliance largely relates to his or her likelihood to engage in any initial attempt at a potential behavioral solution or the cognitive challenge to his or her long-held pessimistic explanation as to why such solutions are unlikely to work. This scenario largely explains the need for the therapist to adopt Seligman's (1990) concept of *flexible optimism* in his or her work. A flexible stance allows the therapist to initially identify and express an understanding of the reasons for the depressed patient's pessimistic stance toward the world, while gradually infusing the therapeutic context with *realistic optimism* (Schneider, 2001) to allow for the possibility of behavioral changes that are likely to generate new outcomes for the patient. Thus, the long history of therapeutic concern in this field over factors involving the patient–therapist relationship is equally relevant to depression, albeit in a different form, as it is to anxiety in the treatment context.

Some of the commonly used technical interventions for depression are listed in Figure 10.1b. Since Lewinsohn's (1974) early behavioral work in having depressed patients actively schedule pleasant events in their daily lives to combat depression, behavioral activation has been demonstrated to be an integral component in cognitive–behavioral therapy for depression

(N. S. Jacobson et al., 1996). The active use of role-playing, or behavior rehearsal (Lazarus, 1966), by the patient with the therapist in teaching new, unfamiliar, and underutilized social and interpersonal behavior strategies makes use of vicarious learning through observation of and modeling by the therapist, as well as direct instruction on the part of the psychotherapist. A classic example of such behavioral instruction has been demonstrated in the area of assertiveness training (Alberti & Emmons, 1975) as an alternative to passivity, on the one hand, and hostility, on the other, in lessening the patient's sense of learned helplessness in becoming more socially effective. Other cognitive therapy techniques, such as thought-stopping (Cautela & Wisocki, 1977), are a form of distraction techniques in which the patient makes a conscious effort to interrupt a specific negative thought and engage in an alternative activity that will help him or her divert attention from the pessimistic rumination as a coping behavior in the short run. In the long run, a more effective strategy is for the patient to engage in a cognitive disputation by marshalling evidence against the negative or self-critical thought pattern and actively arguing against it (Beck et al., 1979). Finally, as therapy progresses, the cognitive therapist can assist the patient in recognizing his or her maladaptive "depressogenic assumptions" about the world that give rise to one's sense of helplessness about his or her life (e.g., "To be happy, I must be successful at absolutely everything that I do") and to therapeutically argue against such extremist views of the world in a counterpropagandistic way (e.g., Ellis, 1962). It is also during this technical interventions phase that some patients have exhibited a critical session early on and somewhat sudden gains in the cognitive–behavioral therapy for depression (Tang & DeRubeis, 1999b).

RELEARNING: THE CORRECTIVE BEHAVIORAL EXPERIENCE

Whether the changes made by the patient are cognitive, affective, or behavioral in form, or more likely an amalgam of all three, the sine qua non of effective psychotherapy involves that which the patient has "relearned" and the applications that the patient has taken with him or her into his or her own life space and natural environment. Figure 10.1c outlines a number of examples of conceptual elements in the literature that signify the psychological and behavioral changes made by the patient in his or her life outside the therapeutic context following psychotherapeutic intervention. So, in the treatment of anxiety, for example, by means of gradual and safe exposure, first through imagery and contemplation (Prochaska & DiClemente, 1992a) while in the therapist's office, then in vivo, the anxious patient learns to acquire a new emotional response to the feared situation first in a classic systematic desensitization method of behavior therapy predicated on the notion of counterconditioning (Wolpe, 1958), and subsequently through the instrumental initiatives taken by the patient in his or her own life. Thus, following the behavior therapist's technical interventions, the patient is able to elicit and reassociate an unfeared response to the previous symptomatically feared situation. The operant steps that the patient takes to expose him- or herself to the previously feared situation in his or her everyday life become instrumental in the ultimate deconditioning or extinction of the patient's previously fearful reactions to the situation and in the reacquisition of a new response to the provoking stimuli. Thus, treatment unfolds gradually in this intertwined three-phase process of relearning.

As noted previously, although critical to the process of effective psychotherapy, the latter two phases of treatment involving technical interventions and relearning fall short of explaining the early learned reactions in the psychotherapist's consulting room that account for the initial approach responses taken by the patient. These initial approach responses are needed in order for the patient to operantly take hold of and modify his or her environment for relearning to occur. The initial "front-end" learning involves the impact of the therapeutic alliance and is associational in form, as is the "back-end" relearning that takes place in the patient's natural environment, following the cognitive–behavioral technical interventions, and is instrumental in form. However, the relearning that occurs in the patient's life and natural environment in response to the technical interventions provides the patient with what might be termed a *corrective behavioral experience*, in conjunction with the *corrective emotional experience* (F. Alexander & French, 1946) acquired in the therapeutic relationship.

Howard et al. (1993) have termed what takes place in this third phase of treatment as *rehabilitation*. In essence, rehabilitation involves unlearning maladaptive behavior patterns and establishing new methods of coping with life. The therapy itself, for whatever period of time that it continues during this phase, takes on a less intensive, more supportive maintenance function as the patient is more effectively able to navigate life stressors on his or her own. Learning-based therapists (e.g., Goldstein, 1995) see this as a time for *generalization enhancement* of the skills learned in the treatment context to transfer to real-life settings over time. It is also during this period of treatment that Tang and DeRubeis (1999b) have observed a gradually increasing, general *upward spiral* in depressed patients who have undergone cognitive–behavioral therapy. For Bandura (1977a, 1997), this is a time when the patient's sense of self-efficacy, or belief that his or her capabilities to organize and execute the behavior that is required to manage impinging life stressors and situations, is beginning to take hold. Likewise, for Seligman, this is a phase during which the patient's sense of learned helplessness (Seligman, 1975), or belief that nothing one does in the face of life adversity makes any difference, is giving way to a gradually increasing sense of realistic learned optimism (Seligman, 1990) that is a prelude to constructive action and serves as a protective function against the inaction of depressive states. Similarly, feminist therapists have postulated a general construct of empowerment (e.g.,

Kaschak, 1999) that takes place during the process of treatment that transfers from the therapist to the patient as a result of the work done together in treatment.

In family therapy, after the family therapist has "joined" with the family in the alliance-building phase of treatment and has assisted the family with enacting more adaptive interactional patterns in therapy sessions during the technical interventions phase of therapy, then the therapist is able to encourage the repetition of these newly acquired patterns, thereby *restructuring* (Minuchin & Fishman, 1981) the family in this final relearning phase of treatment. For example, in a family with an overly close, enmeshed relationship between a substance-abusing son and his mother who excuses his behavior, the family therapist may enact changes during the therapy session in which he or she temporarily interrupts the close contact between the mother and son to foster more contact between the son and his disengaged father. As this experience is repeated, at first through homework assignments, and later as it becomes more self-reinforcing, the family begins to restructure in a way that is more adaptive for all of its members. The spouses are more strongly allied with one another so that a better balance exists between the support, structure, and nurturance provided by both members of the couple to their child. The therapeutic changes are aimed at altering the family's interaction patterns that serve to maintain the problem behavior while fostering more adaptive patterns that eliminate the need for the symptom(s) in the family's everyday life.

CONCEPTUAL AND EMPIRICAL SUPPORT

Empirical support for this triphasic learning conceptualization of psychotherapy processes can be found in Howard et al.'s (1993) three-phase model of psychotherapy outcome. Their model postulates three phases of treatment outcome involving the concepts of remoralization, remediation, and rehabilitation. On a large sample ($N = 529$) of patients at the time of their initial intake interview before beginning individual psychotherapy at the Institute of Psychiatry at Northwestern University's Memorial Hospital, self-report data of the patients' subjective well-being, symptomatic distress, and life functioning were collected and readministered again following Sessions 2, 4, and 17, whenever possible. Although the sample sizes for the reported analyses varied because some patients did not complete the questionnaire data at each index session for a variety of reasons, sophisticated statistical analyses revealed that changes in subjective well-being, symptomatic distress, and overall life functioning scores over this period of time lent strong empirical support to the three-phase model described by the authors.

The present triphasic learning conceptualization of integrative psychotherapy processes shares important similarities as well as important differences with Howard et al.'s (1993) model of psychotherapy outcome. Howard et al.'s notion of *progressive* clinical improvement from one phase to the next is clearly shared in the present view. The notion that improvement in one phase *potentiates* improvement in the subsequent phases is integral to this learning perspective. In other words, initial phases in psychotherapy treatment appear to act as prerequisites for effectiveness in succeeding phases of treatment. Although there is an overall general agreement of the functions provided by each of these three phases of psychotherapeutic treatment, there is some disparity in the explanatory processes to which behavior change is attributed, particularly in the first and somewhat in the second phase of treatment. In the first phase of treatment, the building and maintenance of the therapeutic alliance is considered to be the primary element that is operative in early clinical improvement. No doubt remoralization is an important part of what is provided by an effective therapeutic alliance, but it serves only one such function. While demoralization (i.e., absence of perceived viability in one's available behavioral alternatives) is likely present in a large portion of patients seeking psychotherapy (J. D. Frank & Frank, 1993), the instillation of hope may be more salient to those patients experiencing depressive states in particular. For patients coming to treatment in a wide range of anxiety states, the question of fear in exercising one's perceived alternatives and the degree of safety (e.g., Bowlby, 1973; Winnicott, 1965) associated with them are likely to be more salient than a sense of demoralization. Thus, the adequacy of the therapeutic alliance in providing a combined sense of trust, safety, and viability is seen as the most critical element in this phase of treatment.

The safety and viability that the patient is able to associate with the therapeutic context provide a degree of readiness (e.g., Prochaska & DiClemente, 1992a) for proactive cognitive and behavioral interventions that take place at this time. Although remediation may indeed be the overall function of this second phase of treatment, it is during this phase that the therapeutic learning processes in the directive aspects of cognitive and behavioral interventions (i.e., observation and instruction) exercise their strength. Then, the relearning that takes place in the patient's natural environment in the third phase of treatment as a result of the application of the newly acquired cognitive and behavioral strategies in the present conceptualization is generally similar to Howard et al.'s (1993) notion of rehabilitation. However, and perhaps most important, the present approach differs from Howard et al.'s model of therapeutic outcome through the linkages made between each of the three phases of treatment and the incorporation of three types of learning processes—associative, vicarious, and instrumental learning—that occur with one another to produce therapeutic change, thereby providing a common theoretical language for therapeutic process by which one may understand the relationship between a number of broad theoretical perspectives and their respective relevancies to the process of psychotherapy.

Additional conceptual and empirical support for this approach can be found variously throughout the psychotherapy literature. Persons and Burns (1985), in a study examining the mechanisms of action in cognitive therapy among both depressed and anxious patients, found that mood changes were a function of three types of factors, two of which correspond to each of the first two phases outlined in the present three-phase model of integrative psychotherapy and a third relates to given patient characteristics (i.e., the presence or absence of a personality disorder). First, the cognitive therapy technical intervention involving the therapist's correction or removal of distortions in automatic thoughts was significantly related to the alleviation of negative mood. Second, a good patient–therapist relationship was also found to contribute significantly to improvement in the patient's mood. Taken together, these two treatment factors, which correspond to the factors discussed in the first and second phase of the present model, were found to make independent and additive contributions to therapeutic outcome.

Additionally, in outlining the training needs of cognitive therapists, Dobson and Shaw (1993) pointed out that the manualization of cognitive therapy has taught us that three key aspects are relevant to the selection and training of cognitive therapists. Providing further conceptual support for the present approach, two of these three key aspects of training are relevant to the critical therapeutic activities highlighted in the first and second phase of the current three-phase conceptualization of treatment, namely, *relationship-building factors* and *therapeutic techniques*. Dobson and Shaw's third key aspect of training, namely, the therapist's demonstrated ability for *case conceptualization*, is more specifically an assessment activity of the therapist and relates to the adequacy of the therapist's training, education, and understanding of psychopathology. The two therapeutic activities highlighted as significant to the training of cognitive therapists, once again, correspond well to the first two activities identified by the first two phases of the present model, namely, the importance of alliance-building and the use of technical interventions.

Finally, the third phase of the current model, that is, the relearning that occurs for the patient within his or her own natural environment, has not received as much separate attention in the psychotherapy literature as have the first two phases involving the therapeutic alliance and technical interventions. However, the problem has received specific notice among those who have conceived of psychotherapy as a structured learning process involving the training of psychological and social skills (e.g., Goldstein, 1973, 1981; Sprafkin et al., 1993). As noted previously in chapter 7 on group therapy, structured learning therapy is a psychoeducational form of group treatment to teach patients a variety of interpersonal and social skills (e.g., assertiveness or empathy skills) and consists of four major components: (a) modeling of a specific behavior by the group therapist; (b) role-playing the behavior with the assistance of other group members; (c) social reinforcement, verbal reward, and corrective feedback from the therapist and the group; and (d) transfer training to enhance the generalization of these newly learned skills to the patient's social environment outside of the group setting. The need for transfer training and generalization enhancement (Goldstein, 1995) of newly learned skills and interpersonal behaviors in psychotherapy is a direct application of the relearning phase in the current model of integrative psychotherapy. The generalization that takes place in this final phase of treatment encompasses both the transfer of new behaviors to the patient's natural environment (i.e., setting generalization) and the maintenance of these newly learned skills over time (i.e., temporal generalization).

CONCLUDING REMARKS

Psychotherapy, in whatever form, is primarily a verbal medium. Although it may be demonstrated that the actual performance of a feared response in the absence of its feared anticipated consequences is the final curative step prior to the relearning that takes place in an anxious patient's natural environment, it is the verbal discussion of this possibility with the psychotherapist in an atmosphere of emotional safety that is the first curative step in therapy. Likewise, while some behavioral or social activation in the life of a depressed patient may be the eventual curative technical step in alleviating the patient's depressive symptomatology, it is the discussion surrounding the viability of such an action with a trusted therapeutic figure that potentiates such a response. A confiding therapeutic alliance allows for the meaningful construction and assignment of behavioral homework that is designed to accomplish the critical secondary and tertiary steps in treatment. The patient's sense of security and validation in this setting is, in fact, what arouses the necessary curative actions to behavioral threshold.

In recent years, a fresh look has been taken at the concept of the therapeutic alliance as it relates to empirically validated cognitive–behavioral therapy. When one examines the functions of a sound therapeutic alliance, such as the safety of the holding or facilitating environment, positive regard, and interpersonal trust, the therapeutic environment can serve as a safe and valid context in which to discuss fearful or demoralizing life experiences and in which these can be reassociated with an element of safety and hope. Within this context, new and previously untried behavioral solutions that are discussed and considered by the anxious or depressed patient, and that precede an attempt at such exploratory behaviors, can be associated and reconditioned as more neutral in valence. The contemplation and imagery of novel problem-solving behaviors is particularly relevant to the *cognitive* component of cognitive–behavioral therapy. As the patient then goes out and does the in vivo steps through homework assignments that are the *behavioral* forte of cognitive–behavioral treatment and acquires new and more positive or neutral experiences with the previously avoided situations, then new learning can occur instrumentally.

The historical polemics surrounding the curative factors in psychotherapy have been a matter of debate from its early beginnings. Psychotherapists who regarded the therapeutic relationship as primary, at times, have argued that nonspecific factors such as empathy, genuineness, and positive regard were both necessary and sufficient and, by implication, to the exclusion of other more directive factors in treatment (e.g., Rogers, 1957). Behavioral critics, such as Skinner (Rogers & Skinner, 1956) and Bandura (1969), responded to this view with a criticism of the nondirective method that suggested that the entirety of such an approach was neither sufficient nor necessary. In the current learning perspective, the associative learning that incorporates the safety and viability of the therapeutic alliance, the vicarious learning involved in the armamentarium of cognitive–behavioral technical interventions, and the new instrumental learning that occurs in the psychotherapy patient's natural environment each comprises a necessary condition for effective relearning in an integrative psychotherapeutic approach. In and of themselves, each of the components is necessary but insufficient for effective treatment. Taken together, we may begin to arrive at a conceptualization in which the therapeutic relationship, in tandem with cognitive and behavioral activation techniques that allow for instrumental behaviors to take place in the patient's daily life, more closely approximates the necessary and sufficient conditions for constructive change.

Although difficult enough in theory, attempts at psychotherapy integration and the management of its associated dilemmas are even more complex in actual clinical practice. The following chapter provides just such an example with the diagnoses of panic disorder and agoraphobia. A case illustration of a patient with such a disorder serves to clarify and amplify these complexities and clinical dilemmas in the natural treatment environment.

11

INTEGRATIVE PSYCHOTHERAPY IN CLINICAL PRACTICE: AN ILLUSTRATION OF DILEMMA MANAGEMENT

Integrative psychotherapy requires a certain degree of theoretical and technical "diplomacy" on the part of the psychotherapist. That is to say, many therapists who regard themselves as integrationists in the theory and practice of psychotherapy have come to believe that most of the established approaches to treatment have some degree of validity and applicability to some patients under certain circumstances. For the most part, integrative psychotherapists have found it more useful to examine the *clinical rationales* for applying certain techniques or approaches to therapy under varying treatment conditions rather than arguing dogmatically for single-theory or single-method approaches. In this respect, they have argued, somewhat diplomatically, not simply for détente between the various approaches to psychotherapy but for a genuine integration and pluralism among them that will ultimately enhance therapeutic effectiveness.

This chapter is an adaptation of "Integrative Psychotherapy for Panic Disorder and Agoraphobia in Clinical Practice," by D. J. Scaturo, 1994, *Journal of Psychotherapy Integration, 4*, 253–272. Copyright 1994 by Kluwer Academic. Adapted with permission.

Over three decades ago, Paul (1969) posed what he regarded as "the ultimate question" to guide behavior therapy research: "What treatment, by whom, is most effective for this individual, with that specific problem, under which set of circumstances, and how does it come about?" (p. 62). Expectably, this comprehensive question is equally relevant to research on other psychotherapeutic approaches, behavioral and nonbehavioral alike (Arkowitz, 1992b). Furthermore, this is a question that confronts every psychotherapist in clinical practice as one makes treatment-oriented decisions that guide further questions, interpretations, and directives. The clinical dilemmas posed by this multifaceted dilemma are applicable to any psychotherapist regardless of his or her treatment approach, including those who ascribe to single-theory or single-method approaches (Scaturo, 2001).

As elaborated earlier in chapter 2, the rules of the psychotherapeutic framework and the psychoanalytic technique were, for the early psychoanalysts, rather rigidly outlined (see Langs, 1973), such that the analyst might have frequently found these limitations too confining and unresponsive to a given patient's clinical needs. Similarly, for the early behavior therapists in the 1960s (see Bandura, 1969), behavioral techniques were also clearly delineated, even though many behavioral therapists strained against the technical limitations of behavioral protocols in the course of their clinical work, frequently feeling that additional dimensions of the patient's functioning needed to be addressed. Likewise, for many of the early family therapists (e.g., J. Haley, 1970), at a time when family therapy was in its adolescence as a discipline and attempting to establish its professional identity, it was rigidly held that therapy had to be conducted with the entire family unit, or at least with everyone living in the household present, in order for treatment to occur.

In each of these examples, the clinicians, regardless of their particular theoretical orientations, have found the constraints of their own theoretical frameworks to be too limiting to adequately address the complicated treatment needs of certain patients with particular psychological disorders. In essence, the clinical dilemmas posed by Paul's (1969) question of what to do, when, with whom, and why are too complex for any single theoretical framework to address adequately. In this chapter, two multifaceted forms of anxiety disorder provide an illustration of the clinical dilemmas that typically arise for psychotherapists in actual clinical practice. Patients with panic disorder and agoraphobia frequently present to the practitioner with complex clinical needs for which an integrated, pluralistic approach to treatment more thoroughly addresses the multiplicity of treatment factors than any particular single-theory or single-method approach (Scaturo, 1994).

This chapter is divided into two parts. The first part outlines the various components for inclusion in the treatment of panic disorder and agoraphobia, addresses their respective behavioral and psychodynamic origins in the understanding of anxiety, and discusses theoretical bases for integration among these elements. The second part discusses concepts from family systems theory, which help to provide an understanding of the reverberating effects of panic disorder on the identified patients' most significant social support group (i.e., the family) and how an integration of individual, couple, and family treatment modalities can enhance the treatment process. Finally, an illustrative case vignette is presented.

INTEGRATING BEHAVIORAL AND
PSYCHODYNAMIC INTERVENTIONS

The following is a description of an integrative pattern of treatment with anxiety and panic disorders that has been developed for clinical practice (Scaturo, 1994). Various elements of this approach have been drawn from behavioral, psychodynamic, and family systems schools of treatment. The integration in this approach hinges largely on the clinical rationale, a critical concept in integrative psychotherapy, for utilizing a given paradigm in a specific phase of treatment. Without a carefully deliberated rationale, attempts at integration become haphazard at best and based on therapeutic methods that might be considered "fashionable" (Dryden, 1984), rather than those that are in the patient's clinical best interest. In the current approach, the clinical decision making is predicated jointly on the patient's clinical needs at each phase of treatment as well as the goodness of fit with which a given theoretical framework addresses those needs at a given point in treatment.

Schacht (1984, p. 127) observed that "integration may grow first in the preintellectual awareness of therapists who have practical working knowledge of both [behavioral and psychodynamic] approaches." What is described in the following paragraphs has been derived from an initial "preintellectual awareness" of accumulated clinical experiences with a psychological disorder that presents with pressing symptom management concerns at the outset of treatment, but is also strongly linked to psychodynamic origins that typically emerge as behavioral control is established over the patient's intrusive symptomatology.

Clinical Considerations: Facets of an Integrative Approach to Treatment

Panic disorder and panic disorder with agoraphobia are clinical syndromes that make a strong case for psychotherapy integration, in part because the outset of treatment is usually characterized by a *crisis phase*. Although the patient's history might be filled with a range of limited-symptom panic attacks in the months or years preceding the first contact with a psychotherapist, there is usually some *critical incident*, that is, a full-blown panic attack or some particularly intrusive or disturbing experience with panic, that forms the precipitating event for the patient to reach a motivational threshold to call the therapist for help. If the panic disorder has been compounded by agoraphobic avoidance, then the intrusion of symptoms and functional impairment on the patient's life can be considered to be even more profound. The intensity of these fears, and the intrusion of symptomatic behavior on the life of the patient and his or her family members, make it incumbent on the clinician to do something active at the outset of treatment to help the patient cope, beyond simply exploring the parameters of the problem. The patient is literally asking the therapist to "throw a life preserver."

Receiving some type of "life preserver" from the clinician may be a necessity for survival (i.e., remaining in treatment to the next phase). It is the more active or directive forms of our clinical armamentarium that provide the patient with the needed coping techniques. Two active interventions useful at the outset in the treatment of panic are (a) patient education and psychoeducational material and (b) cognitive–behavioral therapy interventions. Before outlining these interventions it is important to make note of two pretreatment considerations that, although often considered to be "givens" in therapy, are so critical in nature that to not mention them here would be an important omission.

Pretreatment Considerations

Therapeutic Alliance. The first of these pretreatment considerations is, of course, to establish an effective therapeutic alliance with the patient. Adequate rapport is necessary to establish a basic sense of trust in the therapeutic relationship. Trust is so critical—particularly among fearful, panic disorder patients—that therapy is literally unable to proceed without it. Wolfe (1989, 1992a, 1992b) regarded the therapeutic alliance as the first of four components in his integrative model of treatment for anxiety disorders.

Referral For a Physical Examination. The other given in panic disorder treatment is addressing the patient's physiological symptoms. Not surprisingly, many referrals for the psychological treatment of panic disorder originate from the patient's primary care physician (e.g., T. M. Brown & Baron, 1992). The severe physical symptoms associated with panic (e.g., shortness of breath, chest pain, abdominal distress) make contact with a physician a logical first choice for these patients. These referrals have the advantage of the physician having already ruled out organic factors for the symptomatology. However, for referrals for the treatment of panic that have not originated from a physician, making a referral to the patient's primary care physician for a physical examination to rule out any physical disorder that might account for the patient's symptoms should always be the first step. Additionally, the patient's physician may also be prescribing antianxiety medication or antidepressants, in which case an ongoing dialogue about the patient's symptomatology and changes observed as the treatment progresses is generally in the patient's best interest. Typically, the patient is very receptive to this coordinated intervention and feels quite "cared for" by the team approach taken by the psychotherapist and the physician. Once organic factors have been ruled out, then the diagnosis of panic disorder can be more comfortably considered. Having any physical causes ruled out can also help patients with panic disorder more readily accept the psychological bases for their symptoms.

Integrative Components for Psychotherapy

Psychoeducational Intervention. At the outset of psychotherapy, following a rather traditional consultative interview to gather significant aspects of the patient's psychosocial history, after a physician has ruled out any organic involvement, and after the diagnosis of panic disorder can be made with a reasonable certainty, the treatment should begin with a reasonably full explanation of panic disorder and its symptoms so that the patient can begin to have an understanding of what is happening and have some hope in its "treatability." Such an explanation helps to provide the patient with a sense of "normalization" of his or her symptoms. It is generally useful to provide the patient with accurate and authoritative information on panic disorder (e.g., Barlow & Craske's, 2001, *Client Workbook*). Such information helps to provide a rationale to the patient for the behavior therapy components that follow and that serve to invoke some basic level of coping skill over the patient's seemingly overwhelming symptoms.

Cognitive and Behavioral Interventions. Basic to any behavioral approach to the treatment of anxiety disorders is the use of relaxation as a coping device. Relaxation in the form of deep diaphragmatic breathing, muscular relaxation techniques, and imagery techniques is generally provided. Interventions predicated on cognitive therapy aimed at the cognitive restructuring of catastrophic ideas and belief systems help interrupt the patient's anxiety-escalating cycles. Both cognitive and behavior management techniques are provided at this phase of treatment to enable the patient to better cope with the anxiety-provoking material that he or she ultimately must address in therapy, as well as in his or her daily life. However, the components outlined thus far could be regarded at best as necessary but insufficient components in the comprehensive treatment of panic disorder.

Graduated Fear Exposure: Contemporaneous Focus. Facing one's fears, both in and outside of the treatment sessions, and surviving (i.e., enduring) them without the anticipated catastrophic consequence is the ultimate requirement for symptom reduction (e.g., Barlow & Waddell, 1985). Achieving this in a gradual manner that can be tolerated by the patient is the therapeutic task at this stage of treatment. The panic disorder patient's fears can be divided into two categories: fears of the present (or contemporaneous fears) and fears of the past.

For many patients, the fears will have already been elicited in the initial exploration of their presenting problems early on in treatment. However, in this phase of treatment, patients can begin to feel safe enough with the therapist and in control enough with their learned coping techniques to begin to confront their fears in the session in a more experiential way. Confronting their contemporaneous fears can take several forms. For patients experiencing agoraphobic avoidance, a systematic desensitization hierarchy or a less structured guided imagery session can help them experience a "walk through" their feared events with the therapist present. With respect to the panic disorder per se, experiencing the symptoms and bodily sensations that typically signal impending doom to patients, without the actual experience of catastrophe, constitutes the first real sense of control. Barlow and Cerny's (1988) panic control treatment program utilizes a number of exercises to induce the sensations of panic and, thereby, help the patients move safely through their fears. Likewise, a probing interview that focuses on a detailed description by the patients of their feared experiences and sensations can serve a similar function. Ultimately, being able to experience an oncoming panic attack in the patients' natural environment, and to safely endure and survive this, disempowers the grip that panic disorder has on their lives.

Graduated Fear Exposure: Historical Focus. By this phase in treatment, a number of patients are likely to be well on their way to reducing or controlling their intrusive panic symptomatology. In addition, the constriction of agoraphobia may be all but abated. Despite this level of symptomatic improvement, however, comprehensive treatment is not fully complete. Although symptom removal is an important criterion for success in psychotherapy, it is certainly not the only criterion. Furthermore, from the standpoint of the mental health services consumer (e.g., "Mental Health: Does Therapy Help?," 1995), there is evidence to suggest that symptom removal may not even be the most important criterion of success. In a now classic study by Strupp, Fox, and Lesser (1969) on how psychotherapy patients viewed their treatment, these researchers concluded the following:

> Most noteworthy perhaps was the relatively minor emphasis on alleviation of common neurotic symptoms, such as anxiety, depression, and physical disturbances. . . . The view of therapeutic change taken by the people in our survey thus coincides with that of all analytically oriented therapists: it is not seen in terms of "symptom removal" but as occurring on a broad spectrum of life experience. . . . One of the striking accomplishments of psychotherapy with this population (as is probably the case with most patients) was the transformation of what seemed to be mysterious and mystifying symptoms into phenomena with explainable antecedents. (pp. 120–121)

Arriving at an adequate understanding of how symptoms relate to history is one of the major contributions of exploratory–psychodynamic psychotherapy. By anchoring patients' experiences to the reality of their past, for the panic disorder patient, the emergence of panic symptoms becomes understood by the patient as a reasonable, but no longer necessary (i.e., archaic), adaptation to what were very real and terrifying life events.

Abandonment and Separation Anxiety. What constellation of early life experiences is likely to be relevant to a patient who presents with symptoms of panic induced by a sense of impending catastrophe? Freud regarded the experiences of abandonment and separation from one's primary caregiver to be one of the few primary sources of anxiety (Yalom, 1980). From an object relations theoretical perspective (e.g., Fairbairn, 1954), separation anxiety has been considered to be the basic anxiety that forms the prototype to which all other future losses resonate (Framo, 1992). My own clinical work with panic disorder and the work of others have led me to believe that abandonment and separation anxiety are the primary sources of anxiety for these patients (e.g., Friedman, 1985; Sable, 1994, 2000; Scaturo, 1994). Although there has been some dispute over this hypothesis in the literature (e.g., Thyer, Himle, & Fischer, 1988), there is evidence to suggest that the hypothesis has particular validity with respect to women with panic disorder and agoraphobia (e.g., Casat, 1988; Zitrin & Ross, 1988).

Bowlby (1988), in his lifelong study of separation anxiety, asked a critical question for understanding this phenomenon: Why should "mere separation" cause anxiety? He concluded that both humans and animals respond with fear to given circumstances, not simply because there is a high risk of danger but because such situations signal an increased risk. Clearly, the absence of one's primary caregiver signals just such an increased risk to one's safety. According to Bowlby, this is why threats to abandon a child, which are often used as a means of behavioral control by desperate parents, typically evoke terror into children. He noted that such threats, as well as threats of suicide by a parent, are common sources of intense separation anxiety. Furthermore, Bowlby (1988, p. 30) held that the "extraordinary neglect [of separation anxiety and abandonment] in clinical theory is due . . . to a failure to give proper weight to the powerful effects, at all ages, of real-life events."

Frequently, panic disorder patients observed in clinical practice have had some intense experience with abandonment or the threat of abandonment, emotionally or otherwise, as the interpersonal issue at the core of their panic symptoms. To leave this issue unexamined is to accept a less than complete and a less than adequate course of psychotherapy with these patients. To provide a more complete course of therapy, yielding both symptom reduction and an emotional understanding of the experience described thus far requires an integration of behavioral and psychodynamic theory and practice, which has been the most frequently examined area of theoretical interest in psychotherapy integration (Arkowitz, 1992a).

Theoretical Considerations: Evolution of an Integrative Process in Clinical Practice

A number of authors have grappled with these clinical issues from a more conceptual point of view. Conceptually, the present form of psycho-therapy integration discussed in this chapter is most similar to the earlier work of Rhoads (1984), whose writings reflect the "preintellectual" clinical awareness noted earlier by Schacht (1984). Rhoads outlined four ways in which behavioral and psychodynamic interventions can coexist or comple-ment one another: (a) Behavior therapy can be regarded as an introduction to more exploratory therapy to provide a certain degree of rapid symptom relief. (b) Behavior therapy can serve as an adjunct to psychodynamic therapy, ameliorating specific target behaviors throughout the course of therapy. (c) Psychodynamic therapy can serve as an adjunct to behavior therapy in dealing with "resistances" to a given behavior therapy protocol. (d) An inte-grated approach in which a shift from one approach to another, usually from a more structured behavioral approach to a less structured psychodynamic therapy, can occur. These "hybrid" approaches to integration are also repre-sented in the early work of Birk (1970; Birk & Brinkley-Birk, 1974).

According to Rhoad's (1984) schema, my approach with panic disorder and agoraphobia began with the use of behavior therapy as an introduction to treatment. As Rhoads (1984, p. 198) observed: "Many patients . . . [panic disorder patients clearly among them] are so distressed by their symptoms that they find it difficult to focus on other issues in their lives." Thus, I gen-erally begin therapy with these patients, as I would with any patient present-ing with intrusive and disruptive symptomatology such as panic, with a be-havioral approach that is embedded in the broader context of a psychodynamic conceptualization and genetic understanding of the patient's problem his-tory. As P. L. Wachtel (1991, p. 53) noted, "most efforts at integration have a 'flavor' that derives from the therapist's original orientation," my own ori-entation tending toward a more interpersonal and object relations view of the presenting problem.

My early efforts at striving toward integration in clinical work could probably have been characterized by a sense of "shifting" from one modality to another, as is common among clinicians with a developing interest in integrative treatment (e.g., Goldfried, 1997, 2000; P. L. Wachtel, 1991). As such, the early stage of my integration had some similarity to the methods of Shapiro, Barkham, Reynolds, Hardy, and Stiles (1992) that combined pre-scriptive (i.e., cognitive–behavioral) and exploratory (i.e., psychodynamic–interpersonal) psychotherapy in which the decision to work within predomi-nantly an exploratory versus a prescriptive mode was often made at the outset of a given session (e.g., "Today we'll be doing relaxation training"). Progres-sively, though, the interweaving of notions from alternative theoretical frame-works was clearly a more subtle process than this initial perspective would

appear, as was apparent to me from an examination of my intrasession patient–therapist interactions and interventions. In addition, my tendency to
utilize more structured interventions when the patient presented as more
disorganized by his or her symptomatology is consistent with Shapiro et al.'s
(1992) proposition that interventions should be responsive to the variations
over time in the patient's requirements. Finally, my integrative work is com-
patible with Shapiro et al.'s proposition that the goal of psychotherapy is to
advance the patient's assimilation of his or her problematic experiences in
life. It is this therapeutic goal that is enhanced by the inclusion of an exploratory psychotherapy.

Schacht (1984) proposed another schema by which types of integrative
experiences in psychotherapy can be categorized. Six different models are
identified within which the relationship between behavioral and psychodynamic therapy can be conceptualized. One model is that of a separatist approach in which behavioral and psychodynamic therapy are viewed as essentially incompatible and disparate. A second model involves the translation
of concepts and languages between the two approaches. The third model
views behavioral and psychodynamic therapy as separate but complementary
in their respective functions. The fourth model involves the notion of a synergistic effect between the two approaches in which either form of therapy
enhances the operation of the other. The fifth model involves the concept of
emergence in which the integration of the two approaches yields a new and
hybrid therapeutic approach. Finally, the sixth model can be regarded as a
metatheoretical approach that involves theoretical synthesis and a
reconceptualization of human behavior and functioning.

Within Schacht's (1984) classificatory system, my initial clinical work
with panic disorder and agoraphobia originated from a complementary view
of behavioral and psychodynamic therapy (Model 3). As a result, I struggled
for some time with the periodically awkward notion of "shifting" from desensitization work, for example, in the initial phase of therapy to more
exploratory work in the latter consolidation phase of therapy as, I believe,
do many clinicians who attempt to implement elements of both approaches
in a single course of therapy with a patient. As I persisted with the integration of these approaches and concepts, I began to achieve glimpses of what
P. L. Wachtel (e.g., P. L. Wachtel & McKinney, 1992) has referred to as a
synergistic effect between the two modalities. For example, I found that progressively working through the steps of a desensitization hierarchy would
bring forth associations by the patient of earlier anxiety-provoking experiences that were closer to the core of the original source of his or her vulnerabilities. Correspondingly, an exploration of the patient's earlier experiences with, say, separation anxiety would enhance his or her ability and
motivation to confront and persist with behavioral homework. Thus, over
time, I found myself increasingly striving toward Schacht's synergistic model
(Model 4).

In the course of developing an integrative process, I have found my clinical experience with psychotherapy integration to be consistent with P. L. Wachtel's (1991, p. 44) observation that "for most of us integration remains more a goal than a constant daily reality. Eclecticism in practice and integration in aspiration is an accurate description of what most of us in the integrative movement do much of the time."

TOWARD AN INTEGRATION OF TREATMENT MODALITIES: WHO IS TO ATTEND WHICH SESSIONS AND WHY?

Individual Psychotherapy

All of the therapeutic activities described thus far, both behaviorally and psychodynamically, are able to be conducted within an individual psychotherapy format, addressing primarily the patient's intrapsychic sphere. However, the present conceptualization of panic disorder and agoraphobia views the traumas associated with these disturbances, as well as the emotional conflicts surrounding them, as essentially interpersonal in nature (Wolfe, 1989, 1992a, 1992b). The reciprocal impact and intrusion of panic disorder on the patients and their significant others is profound. To address the panic disorder patient's interpersonal world, one can further articulate and refine the treatment process by integrating the concepts of a third major theoretical paradigm, family systems theory, that is of great practical importance in helping the clinician to decide who in the family, or in the patient's interpersonal network, is to attend which sessions and why.

Couple Therapy

It is of particular significance that Barlow and his colleagues (Barlow, O'Brien, & Last, 1984; Barlow & Waddell, 1985; Cerny et al., 1987) have demonstrated that the inclusion of a spouse in the cognitive–behavioral treatment for agoraphobia yielded a substantial advantage over the nonspouse group not only in treatment outcome but also in the maintenance over these gains at the time of a 2-year follow-up. These findings compel the clinician to consider what mechanism might be in operation in this and other forms of couple treatment for these types of disorders

Couple therapy in general can have three substantial effects on the treatment of a patient with panic disorder. First, by including the spouse in treatment, the therapist is able to enlist the spouse's support in the treatment process and in the completion of the behavioral portion of the treatment program, which enables the identified patient to cope more effectively with the symptoms of panic and agoraphobic avoidance. Second, in the psychodynamic exploration of the origins of the index patient's panic, having the spouse present to listen to the patient's history (some of which the spouse may be hearing for the first time), articulating the emotional pain involved, and discussing its relevance to the panic symptoms can serve to augment the spouse's empathy and compassion toward the patient and the now understandable origins of the patient's previously perplexing difficulties. Third, having the spouse offer significant portions of his or her own family history often helps the clinician discover the complementary emotional issue in the spouse's early life, which enables the couple to discover their "interlocking pathology" (Ackerman, 1958) or complementarity in their marital system. Such a discovery often helps to articulate and strengthen the couple's emotional attachment and bond to one another and that, in turn, impacts significantly on the presenting problem of panic disorder. Framo (1970) articulated this theoretical perspective, outlining the clinical utility of this approach from an object relations view of marital and family systems. A brief elaboration of these aspects of couple therapy may serve to clarify these points.

Enlisting Spousal Support

Involving the spouse in the psychoeducational and behavioral portion of the treatment, as well as improving marital communication surrounding the management of panic-related symptoms, is remarkably helpful in generating support for the index patient. For example, J. O. Wilson (1989) developed a set of "Guidelines for Support Persons" that is a kind of generic "Do's and Don'ts" list for spouses who are attempting to assist their agoraphobic spouse in overcoming their anxiety and panic in the patient's natural environment and everyday life. It is this type of symptom-oriented approach that appears to be the focus of Barlow, O'Brien, and Last's (1984) couple treatment for agoraphobia. Thus, while Barlow et al.'s inclusion of the patient's spouse in the treatment program might be best characterized as "spouse-assisted behavior therapy" rather than as relationship-oriented therapy for couples, it is nevertheless significant to note that simply improving couples' communication surrounding the symptom management of the agoraphobic behavior has yielded an impressive advantage over individual behavior therapy in the treatment of this disorder.

Understanding the Historical Origins of Panic

Explaining the generic aspects of panic disorder and how symptoms tend to be manifested in most panic patients helps to normalize the spouse's view of the index patient's panic-related behavior. Only through a shared exploration of the patient's history and traumatic origins (e.g., early abandonment experiences) of the panic can the spouse understand and appreciate how the panic has provided a protective function against even more catastrophic fears and expectations in the patient's life. True empathy by the spouse can only come about fully through a recognition of and identification with the patient's emotional pain. Given this understanding, a joint exploration of the spouse's own psychosocial history in search of the emotional basis of the couple's attachment to one another, and the spouse's "mirror issue" to the index patient's panic disorder, is clinically useful.

Articulating Spousal Attachments

As noted previously in chapter 5 on marital and couple therapy, people typically select partners who have matching levels of emotional maturity but who have differing defense mechanisms (Goldenberg & Goldenberg, 1980). As a result, it should not be surprising that the panic disorder patient's spouse has typically experienced some degree of emotional trauma in his or her history that is roughly comparable with the interpersonal trauma that forms the core issue for the panic disorder in the index patient. However, because spouses defend against their experiences differently, it would not be expected that the sequelae to their own traumatic experiences be manifested also through a panic disorder, but rather manifested in some other type of disturbance— perhaps through a numbing response to one's emotional life, for example. Whatever the form of its manifestation in the spouse, helping the couple to understand the basis for their emotional connection to one another serves to establish a genuine empathy between them and often validates and solidifies their emotional bond to one another. Augmenting their attachment in this way often serves to lessen the tendency toward abandonment fears in the identified patient and thus lessens the vulnerability toward panic attacks and symptoms. An understanding and application of object relations theory is often useful in conducting this type of therapeutic work with couples (e.g., D. E. Scharff & Scharff, 1991; Siegel, 1992).

Family Therapy and Intervention

Family therapy with members of the household other than the patient's spouse has not been utilized typically in the treatment of panic disorder and agoraphobia. However, it is not difficult to speculate about a clinical scenario in which at least some form of family consultation or intervention might be advisable. E. F. Wachtel and Wachtel (1986) and Feldman (1989, 1992) have provided general guidelines under which the clinician might integrate individual and family treatment. More specifically, in the treatment of panic disorder and agoraphobia, whenever someone else other than the spouse is intimately involved in helping the patient manage his or her anxiety, involving that person in the therapy in some capacity might be helpful.

For example, Barlow (1988) developed a list and collection of common talismans, or safety cues, which agoraphobic patients have used to help them cope or ward off their panic attacks. These have included an unused or even an empty bottle of antianxiety medications, bracelets, religious symbols, and even family pets. The other category of talisman, however, is that of "safe people," most often a spouse who knows of the patient's panic disorder. When the "safe person" is a spouse and a co-equal in the family hierarchy, then involving him or her in the treatment as a support person is typically quite helpful, as noted above. However, it is also not uncommon for a child to be a talisman, for example, for his or her mother, who may be unwilling to leave the house without this particular child present.

When a child becomes the talisman, though, this poses a particular type of family problem. Unlike the spouse, the child is not a co-equal in the family hierarchy. When a young child is delegated an excessive degree of care-taking responsibility to an adult in the family, this places the child at risk for becoming parentified (J. Haley, 1976) by the family and, over time, at risk for losing a significant portion of his or her youth to functioning in this role. Under these circumstances, then, it may well be advisable to get the child in (to the session) in order to get him or her out (of the clinical picture), which is a common family intervention with other types of clinical problems as well. Doing so is, however, a delicately negotiated family intervention in which the clinician attempts to dismiss the child from the responsibility of the clinical management of the parent's condition, while working with the parent to find other, more adaptive ways to have the child be involved and attached to the parent around other issues not involving the parent's panic. Children, frequently the oldest child, who are drafted into the ranks by the family for this type of care-taking behavior, often derive tremendous gratification by having a helping role in the family, which they regard as special with the identified patient. Once having intervened in this way, the clinician then may often be left working with the couple, which may be the hierarchically critical clinical unit.

A CASE VIGNETTE

At the time she sought therapy, Ms. A. was a 35-year-old woman, married for the past 10 years. She and her husband had one child, a daughter, age 5. Although currently unemployed, she had worked until the birth of their child.

Ms. A. began experiencing panic attacks about 2 years earlier, initially at a shopping mall, when her husband had been required to be out of town for a 3-month period for his job. For 6 months after her husband's return home, Ms. A. did not tell him about her panic attacks and increasing agoraphobic avoidance, until it ultimately became apparent to him that "something was wrong." At that time, she had seen an individual psychotherapist, who insisted that the husband remain in the waiting room during her sessions. About 6 months later, with her symptoms unabated, Ms. A. was referred by her family physician, who had been prescribing both an antianxiety agent and an antidepressant.

Significant in Ms. A.'s history was that her mother had died of a sudden heart attack when Ms. A. was only 10 years of age, and that she had been able to remember very little of the time spent with her mother. In addition, Ms. A reported feeling quite dependent on her husband and that she became quite anxious in his absence. She was not only relieved when the present therapist indicated that it was fine for him to accompany her to the appointment but also surprised (given her previous experience in therapy) when her husband was invited into the session along with her.

It is of note that Ms. A.'s husband was also quite depressed since the death of his mother a few months before the initial session. Interestingly, her mother-in-law's funeral had been the first funeral that Ms. A. had ever attended, because she had been emotionally unable to attend the funeral of her own mother 25 years ago. Mr. A. was also very close to his father, a combat veteran of the Second World War, who was immersed in trauma-related issues pertaining to death, loss, and his emotional sequelae from the war. Ms. A.'s husband was acutely aware of these emotional difficulties of his father and attended combat unit reunions with his father on a number of occasions.

Course in Therapy

In the beginning phase of therapy, the couple reviewed Barlow and Craske's (2001) workbook, as well as J. O. Wilson's (1989) guidelines for support persons, to help them work through the in vivo goals for conquering the patient's agoraphobia. While relaxation training is generally taught within an individual therapy format, the relaxation techniques in this case were taught with both members of the couple present. Instead of making an audiotape of this session for in-home practice as typically done, the couple was given a written copy of the relaxation instructions and asked to read aloud to each other for 2 weeks of practice to help the patient with her anxiety and to assist her husband with the insomnia that he reported at the outset of treatment.

A rank-ordered hierarchy of steps to be taken in successive approximation was identified and targeted to help overcome the agoraphobia. As the hierarchy was worked through, increased discussion of Ms. A.'s fears of abandonment of the present (e.g., her husband leaving home for 3 months) and from the past (e.g., her mother's untimely death) ensued. Increasingly, the patient began to grieve the loss of her mother for the first time.

Her agoraphobia and panic gradually abated. Occasionally, when her husband was unable to attend a session on a given week, the patient was able to drive herself to the session rather than canceling as she had done earlier on in treatment. She returned to the mall, at first with her husband present as a support person, and then on her own. The feeling of impending panic became less intense and less frequent with greater durations in between episodes. Her ability to control and ride out the feelings when they occurred increased progressively over time.

The couple was seen weekly for 4 months, then at intervals of 2, 4, 6, and 8 weeks. At the time of follow-up, Ms. A.'s maternal grandmother had died. It was this grandmother who had raised Ms. A. after her mother had died 25 years ago. Despite the salience of increased feelings of abandonment surrounding this recent loss of a surrogate mother, Ms. A. grieved her grandmother's loss more readily and required only a brief increase in the frequency of very few sessions at this time.

Case Discussion

The case reviewed above contains a number of elements commonly seen in panic disorder patients and couples. The precipitating event (in this case, the patient's first panic attack at the shopping mall) generally foments within a context that is reminiscent of the historical interpersonal trauma. In this instance, Ms. A.'s husband having been out of town for several months prior to her panic attack provided a context that heightened her vulnerability (and, correspondingly, lowered her threshold) to panic through its symbolic link with the earlier feelings of abandonment originally experienced at the time of her mother's death.

In addition, Ms. A.'s initial experience with a therapist working within a single-theory or single-method approach (e.g., psychoanalytically oriented individual psychotherapy) was also not uncommon. Within the confines of such a framework, it would not be unusual for her to find her husband being asked to remain in the waiting room while the treatment is conducted with the index patient. Only by conceptualizing the case more broadly and integratively can the clinician recognize that the husband's absence was at least part of the presenting problem and that his presence in the sessions was at least part of the treatment. That is to say, Ms. A.'s panic disorder and agoraphobia were simultaneously an intrapsychic and interpersonal problem.

The inclusion of Ms. A.'s husband in the treatment process carried with it all of the three advantages outlined in the section above on the topic of couple therapy. First, Mr. A.'s involvement, particularly at the outset of treatment, clearly helped to enlist his support in the completion of the behavioral homework (i.e., the desensitization hierarchy) as he was instructed to stay with his wife as she initially ventured outside of their home, only subsequently repeating these steps on her own. Second, although Mr. A. had known the facts of his wife's family history, observing her emotional reaction in the session as she discussed her mother's death and its impact on her provided for Mr. A. a deeper sense of understanding and compassion toward his wife and began to make her previously perplexing panic attacks more comprehensible to him. Finally, as Mr. A. discussed some of the contemporaneous and historical reasons for his own periods of depression, Ms. A. was better able to understand their mutual attachment to one another and was gradually able to feel less vulnerable to fears of abandonment in her marital relationship.

The present case also contained elements of what P. L. Wachtel (e.g., P. L. Wachtel & McKinney, 1992) referred to as a *synergism* between behavioral and psychodynamic interventions. As Ms. A. began to confront the possibility of attempting some of the steps in the desensitization hierarchy without the assistance of her husband, this tearfully brought to mind her fearful feelings during his absence, which in turn brought to mind memories of her feelings at the time of her mother's death. Likewise, as Ms. A. began to more fully understand the impact of her mother's death on her life, and the longevity of the difficulties associated with her mother's loss throughout her life cycle, she strengthened her resolve to complete the behavioral assignments and to become more functional once again. That is to say, Ms. A.'s panic disorder and agoraphobia were simultaneously a contemporaneous and a historical problem.

CONCLUDING REMARKS

To paraphrase Paul's (1969) ultimate question in psychotherapy research noted at the beginning of this chapter, the crucial recurring technical dilemma for the clinician in any given psychotherapy session is, "What to do, when, with whom, and why?" Since the publication of P. L. Wachtel's (1977) now classic work on the integration of psychoanalysis and behavior therapy, there has been a recognition by many in the field of psychotherapy of the need to arrive at some integrated understanding, or at least détente, with respect to the major schools of thought regarding behavioral and psychological change. In part, this has taken place because these two theoretical systems focus on the polar opposites of one another—the "yin and yang" of the psychological structure. Behavior therapy has focused traditionally on confrontation of the contemporaneous symptomatology and the strengthening of more adaptive psychological defenses. Psychoanalytic therapy attempts to work through the defensive structure to resolve the historical bases of the underlying neurotic conflict. Behavior therapists have argued that psychoanalysis and psychoanalytic methods require enormous periods of time during which the patient's presenting complaint remains unattended. Psychoanalysts have argued that the behavioral focus on symptomatology does not provide lasting or meaningful change. Of course, both arguments are, in part, true. Furthermore, attention to the psychological structures that are addressed differentially by these two theoretical systems improves the quality and meaningfulness of psychotherapy for people undergoing emotional conflict.

In addition to the integration needed among the theoretical systems (e.g., behavioral and psychoanalytic) that help to conceptualize the emotional problems, integrative work is also needed that would serve to better conceptualize the treatment systems (e.g., individual and family systems) interacting within the psychotherapeutic context. Individual psychodynamic psychotherapy has focused traditionally on the internal, intrapsychic world of the patient. However, since Harry Stack Sullivan's (1938, 1953) early work to the present-day proliferation of ideas surrounding family psychology and interventions, there has been an increasing recognition of the saliency of the interpersonal context of the identified patient's emotional difficulties and the degree to which the significant others' involvement can either serve to maintain or help ameliorate maladaptive behavior patterns surrounding the symptomatology. Truly integrative psychotherapy takes into consideration (a) the intrapsychic world addressed in individual psychotherapy, (b) the unique involvement of the dyadic subsystem that marital and couple therapy can address, and (c) the additional subsystems of children and extended family addressed in family consultations and intervention.

Finally, to more fully appreciate the pervasiveness of dilemmas in the life of the patient and in the process of psychotherapy, it is helpful to understand the broad base of such bidimensionality in the history of psychology. Often represented in terms of *dialecticism* and its corresponding need for *synthesis*, the necessity for integration of the various dimensions of psychotherapy and its conceptualization is well represented by numerous examples in the field of psychology with even more broadly based roots in both Eastern and Western philosophy. In the following final chapter, this trend is traced throughout psychology, providing an abundance of illustrations of how fundamental the notions of dilemmas and their integration, dialecticism, and synthesis are to understanding the psychological functioning of human beings, and ultimately to the work that we do as clinicians.

12

DILEMMAS, DIALECTICISM, AND INTEGRATION IN THE HISTORY OF PSYCHOLOGY: TOWARD SYNERGY AND SYNTHESIS

Historically, there have been a number of avenues and attempts to integrate the knowledge base in the field of psychotherapy (Arkowitz, 1992b). Perhaps the first systematic approach was in the area of *theoretical integration* in which concepts from two or more theories of treatment are combined, the amalgam of which is hoped to provide an improvement. The earliest attempt at such integration was likely Dollard and Miller's (1950) reconceptualization of psychoanalytic concepts (e.g., anxiety, repression, psychotherapy) into learning theoretical, stimulus–response terminology. A subsequent hallmark for this kind of approach was P. L. Wachtel's (1977) classic work on the blending of psychoanalytic and behavioral theories of treatment. A second approach was the search for *common factors* that exist between different treatment approaches (Arkowitz, 1992a; Garfield, 1992a), including various nonspecific factors (e.g., compassion, the arousal of hope; Strupp & Hadley, 1979), the criticality of the therapeutic alliance (e.g., Safran, 1993), and the facilitative factors (e.g., empathy, genuineness, positive regard) involved in the therapeutic relationship (Rogers, 1951). A third approach has been known as *technical eclecticism*, utilizing an amalgam of therapeutic techniques on a pragmatic basis and overarching clinical rationale in which each serves its own purpose in a broader program of treatment, as exemplified by Lazarus's (1992) multimodal therapy. And, yet a fourth approach might be characterized as the *integration of treatment modalities* (Norcross & Goldfried, 1992), most notably the work in integrating individual and family treatment regimens, isolating the identified patient versus including other participants in the family system within which that person interacts (e.g., Feldman, 1989, 1992).

PSYCHOTHERAPY INTEGRATION: A PERSONAL JOURNEY

For most practitioners, though, the integration of what they have learned from their formal education and accrual of clinical experiences is necessarily a very personal expedition. The vehicle by which integration takes place, in the end, is always incorporated within the self, or person, of the given psychotherapist. As clinicians, we learn interview techniques, how to establish rapport with the patient, and various techniques to accomplish specific therapeutic goals, but ultimately what makes sense to the particular patient in understanding his or her personal difficulties and potential solutions is what gets conveyed to the patient about what makes sense to, or how the problem is understood by, his or her clinician. As neophyte clinicians, we attempt to absorb the "style" and, often, mannerisms of our most respected mentors. At some point, at least one of our clinical supervisors will say to us that we must develop our "own therapeutic style," without us ever knowing precisely what that means until years to come.

In the last chapter, I commented on the evolution of an integrative process in my own clinical practice. My own interest in psychotherapy integration began about 10 years after I had completed my formal education in the field. At that point, I met weekly with a group of seasoned clinicians who appeared to be grappling with some of the same concerns in their clinical work. These concerns involved specific decision-making processes and rationales at nodal points in a given patient's treatment. Such matters of unease involved questions such as how to conduct interviews with the patient's significant others, when it seems in the patient's best interest, without breaking thoroughly from a given individually oriented therapeutic framework, or questions of how to address the inner conflicts of one member of a couple when the lion's share of the clinical work pertained to the pattern of interactions between the couple? As one thinks through and tries to anticipate the potential implications for the patient in any give course of clinical action, questions like these, to clinicians seriously interested in conducting effective and comprehensive clinical work, inevitably lead to a broadly based discussion of one's accumulation of formal educational experiences, professional readings, clinical experiences, philosophy about the world, and personal understanding of life often based on one's own life struggles. In my own experience, as I suspect it is for many others, it has been a highly personal encounter in which one attempts to understand and combine the broad, and often disparate, elements of what one has learned about psychology, psychotherapy, one's patients, and one's own life over a period of years.

Philosophically Speaking

An extensive philosophical basis exists for the integration of the various aspects of psychotherapy. Throughout the course of Eastern and Western civilizations, the notion of the "dilemma," as well as the dialecticism involved in its resolution, has been seen as one of the many paradoxes of life. Psychotherapeutically, the process of integrating the disparate elements in living is an essential ingredient for approximating some degree of harmony and abatement of clinical symptomatology. A comprehensive perspective on human psychological functioning and psychopathology is fundamental to an understanding of clinical dilemmas. The remainder of this chapter examines the recurrence of these concepts throughout the history of philosophical thought and psychological theorizing, commenting wherever possible on the relevance to the various clinical dilemmas discussed in earlier chapters.

In Eastern culture, the well-known Taoist symbol of the yin and yang represents the dynamic flow of opposites in the static form of black and white. This dualism represents balance, harmony, and equality. More important, the equilibrium is not considered to be a placid coexistence. Rather, it exists as a dynamic tension and recurrent struggle for ascendancy, one over the other, as is much of life. The symbol represents the struggle between co-equal opposites: the negative and the positive, the dark and the light, the sun and moon, hot and cold, masculine and feminine, the heavens and the earth, the ascending and the descending, the teacher and the student, and the seasoned and the unseasoned (Watts, 1977). It is the view of life as a dynamic struggle, as is psychotherapy integration. The balance of opposites is "not some bland, 'wouldn't it be nice if there was no disagreement, no struggle . . . ' notion" (Palmer, 1997, p. ix). Likewise, the Buddhist endorsement of the individual to take the Middle Way in life so as to avoid the deleterious effects of extreme stances is not a nondescript recommendation for moderation, but more an encouragement of a dynamic balance requiring constant adjustments and course corrections in determining the safest path (e.g., J. L. Garfield, 1995; Humphreys, 1984; Safran, 2003). The ultimate solution in Eastern thought lies in accepting a broader context for definition of the presenting problem.

In chapter 11, it was suggested that integrative psychotherapy required a certain degree of diplomacy in its practice. In retrospect, it appears that this statement contains only a partial truth. In a diplomatic sense, the integrationist perspective, consistent with Eastern thought, recognizes the inherent value and validity in each of the established approaches to psychotherapy. However, unlike the common perception of diplomacy, a *passive compromise* is neither desirable nor the goal. Rather, integrative psychotherapy is best likened to the *active diplomatic process* of debate and struggle as the means by which recognition of each alternate perspective becomes realized and incorporated into a meaningful understanding and whole. The Eastern perspective on balance and equilibrium emerges from managing tension and conflict, thereby creating harmony out of chaos. So, too, the concept of dilemma management (Scaturo & McPeak, 1998) in psychotherapy integration is the process by which the conditions for more harmonious existence are approached and approximated.

Duality in Western culture is perhaps best represented by the notion of the *dialectic*. Socrates believed that the greatest potential good for a human being was to engage others in examination of the questions about fundamental concepts of life, self, and value in the world (Stokes, 1997), as is denoted by the Socratic dictum, "The unexamined life is not worth living." Undertaking such a self-examination of one's life is to become engaged in a dialectic. In the Socratic method of inquiry (Carey & Mullan, 2004), Socrates would ask his students a question such as, "What is truth (or justice, courage, or the like)?" Socrates, himself, would remain skeptical, disavowing knowledge of the answer (Overholser, 1995). Parenthetically, it is interesting to note that many an impatient psychoanalytic patient has often accused his or her psychoanalyst of "claiming to have no knowledge" of the answers to the patient's questions (with the patient disconcertingly believing otherwise); this parallel position for the psychotherapist is the therapeutic stance of technical neutrality, as discussed in chapter 9. Ultimately, Socrates and his students would, together, flesh out a multifaceted answer that would articulate the original question's complexity (Huffman, 2002). Later in Western civilization, Hegel, the 19th-century German philosopher, outlined a dialectical theory of history (Gadamer, 1976) in which he suggested that any development in history tends to be confronted, followed, and replaced by a phase that represents elements that are largely opposed to the elements of the previous phase. Subsequently, the opposing phase tends to be replaced by a period that is representative of some resolution of the previous two phases. The three phases of dialectical development, denoted by the terms *thesis, antithesis*, and *synthesis*, represent mankind's striving for some form of integration and resolution of dissonant and contradictory elements. The progression and historical sequencing of various contradictions and resolutions that evolve into greater levels of complexity and maturity of thought have had broad applicability to states of consciousness, worldviews, ethical positions, religious perspectives, social organization, as well as shifts in dominant scientific paradigms (Kuhn, 1970; Soll, 2002).

In the history of psychology and psychotherapy, the notion of conflict and dilemmas is ever present in the various areas of study in psychology in general and in the various approaches to psychotherapy in particular. This theme emerges from psychoanalytic thought and is seen also in conceptualizations of personality, psychopathology, attachment, family systems, social psychology, and cognition. A brief review and examination of these areas of study readily reveals the broad relevance and applicability of this concept to a wide range of subareas within the discipline of psychology. Observations of duality, dilemmas, and dialecticism across these broader areas of theory and investigation provide a type of *convergent validity* of their significance to the field. Conflict between a vast number of constructs appearing in bipolar opposition to one another seems to be a common state of affairs in the study of psychology. The psychological literature is replete with examples of such conceptual dichotomies that are thoroughly intermingled in the course of everyday clinical practice (e.g., Keith et al., 1993): mind versus body, intrapsychic versus interpersonal, insight versus behavior, acute versus chronic, individual versus family, and autonomy versus affiliation, to name only a few.

Conflict in Psychodynamic Conceptualization

Freud's (1894/1962) conceptualization of psychodynamic functioning and disturbance involved the notion of emotional conflict between the desired wish for the expression of some pleasurable activity or state and the dreaded fear of negative consequences or disapproval of such expression from one's conscience or social milieu. In this view, the patient's defensive and symptomatic behavior is representative of a compromise in this dilemma between the expressive forces of gratification, on the one hand, and the self-protective, repressive forces within oneself, on the other (Auld & Hyman, 1991). In essence, Freud saw conflict in a person as a struggle to negotiate the gratification of needs to survive in the world as a biological organism, on the one hand, and the concessions that one makes to coexist with others in the world as a social animal, on the other (Aronson, 1998). In the course of navigating the conflicting demands of life, one arrives at characteristic strategies in coping with such conflicts.

Theorizing Personality

Personality, then, consists in part of one's repertoire of desires, fears, and attempts to negotiate the field between these two states (Horowitz, 1988). Accordingly, personality develops by the repeated use of a coping style that had worked well in mastering previously stressful situations and applying these response patterns to subsequent stressors. Dimensions of personality are often described as varying in degree along continuums of bipolar opposites appearing to be in conflict with one another. Many personality dimensions exist (e.g., London & Exner, 1978), including such characteristics as high versus low authoritarianism, dependence versus independence, introversion versus extroversion, and internal versus external locus of control of reinforcement. In each case, however, what underlies a particular expression of personality along any given dimension tends to be the way in which variation in neurotic conflict is manifested. For example, Horowitz (1988) discussed two well-formulated, prototypic character styles of coping and relating to others: the *histrionic* style and the *compulsive* style. In the hysterical, or histrionic, defensive style, there is a general avoidance of knowledge (i.e., repression) and, thereby, personal responsibility for behavior in one's life. Strongly experienced, but poorly modulated, emotional states lead to a globalized and scattered focus on "the big picture" (Horowitz, 1977). Thus, a repression of information to the histrionic person is instrumental in the avoidance of responsibility of thoughts and actions that he or she might find objectionable. In contrast, an obsessional or compulsive style of defense is characterized by rigid thought patterns while stifling emotional experience. An excessively sensitized and sharp attention to the details of a problem may derail the focus away from the more important or central emotional theme. The mutual attraction and complementarity of these common, but opposite styles of coping with the world has been discussed earlier in chapter 5 on dilemmas in marital and couple therapy.

Personality differences, such as histrionic and compulsive styles, were often found to be associated with individual differences in a concept known as *perceptual defense* (Bell & Byrne, 1978). For example, Bruner and Postman (1947) gave a word association test (Jung, 1918) to a group of participants and recorded reaction times to each word on the list. The list incorporated a number of anxiety-related words such as *death, penis,* and *blush.* The words were presented rapidly and at increasingly slower speeds with the use of a tachistoscope. As is typical in word association tasks (e.g., Scaturo, 1977), reaction time has been used as a measure of emotionality with the assumption that the longer the reaction time, the more threatening is the word. Participants in this study formed a bimodal group with respect to the anxiety-based words: In one group of participants, the greater the threat value of the word, the more difficult it was for them to perceive it (i.e., perceptual defense). In the other group, the greater the threat value of the word, the faster the recognition time (i.e., perceptual vigilance). The two differing perceptual patterns were interpreted in terms of the specific ego defenses that were developed by given individuals to cope with perceived threat.

These two rather opposite personality *styles,* and in their more extreme forms personality *disorders,* are fueled by two conflicting strategies of psychological defense that vary along a continuum from repression to sensitization (e.g., Bell & Byrne, 1978; Byrne, 1964); that is, repressers avoid, whereas sensitizers approach. The original hypothesis regarding defensive behavior assumed a curvilinear relationship. Thus, individuals scoring in the middle of the Repression–Sensitization Scale (R-S Scale) were expected to be better adjusted than those falling at either of the extreme ends of the scale. Unfortunately, the data supporting this appealing hypothesis have been more perplexing than originally anticipated. Personality data on these two defensive styles tend to show that repressors score better on measures of self-concept, dogmatism, perceived hostility, aggression, and medical disorders. Somewhat contrary to initial expectations, with respect to their descriptions of family environments, repressors reported a warmer, more relaxed, and even-tempered affectionate family atmosphere, whereas sensitizers characterized their family relationships as more stressful, unhappy, critical, angry, and emotionally distant. Of course, in part because repression on the R-S Scale is strongly associated with social desirability, it is entirely possible that the nature of the defenses used by repressor families may account for the unrealistically positive and socially acceptable recollections of family of origin. Bell and Byrne (1978, p. 473) also pointed out that there are bits of evidence to suggest that "all may not be as rosy with repressors as they keep telling us." For example, when samples of normal college students were compared with samples of disturbed psychiatric patients, the students tended to cluster toward the middle of the R-S Scale, whereas the mental patients clustered around both of the two extremes. In addition, sensitizers have been found to possess a greater capacity for cognitive complexity than do their repressor counterparts. So, the argument for integration of extremes from a mental health perspective continues to show some support in this area of study. Also, these differences between these two styles of coping with perceived threat have also given rise to the speculation surrounding theoretical inclinations of different clinicians and the significance of integration in clinical work as discussed previously in chapter 2.

Research using the repression–sensitization dimension appears to have dwindled considerably since the 1970s. However, another more recent line of research on a conceptually similar topic—Seligman's (1990) research on the *optimism–pessimism dimension*—has shown remarkably similar empirical findings. Predicated on his years of research attempting to understand the explanatory factors related to clinical depression, Seligman (1974, 1975) attributed much of depression to one's belief that personal control is unattainable, that is to say, a state of learned helplessness. According to Seligman, both perceived helplessness (i.e., a pessimistic outlook) and perceived control (i.e., an optimistic viewpoint) are learned phenomena and are essentially bipolar opposite constructs affecting one's emotional life—*learned pessimism* and *learned optimism*. Furthermore, like Byrne's (1964) analysis of repression–sensitization, Seligman's (1990) review of the "balance sheet" of optimism and pessimism shows, at first glance, an imbalance in the ledger: Pessimism (in contrast to optimism, but not unlike sensitization) advances clinical depression, produces a state of inertia in the face of misfortune, feels bad as an emotional state, is related more frequently to failure in tasks and goals, is related to poor physical health, and has been shown to lead to the defeat of political candidates.

As a result, although the evolutionary role of optimism seems more readily apparent, Seligman (1990) considered what the "survival value" of pessimism has been also from an evolutionary perspective. That is to say, why hasn't evolution selected out pessimism from existence long ago, given its many disadvantages? The answer to this question lies in the fact that pessimism corrects for something that optimism does poorly; that is, pessimism provides a more accurate picture of reality. Ironically enough, social psychological research has shown that depressed, pessimistic people tend to judge reality more accurately, whereas nondepressed optimists tend to distort reality in self-serving ways (Seligman, 1990). Thus, there appears to be an important place for pessimism in society and social systems. In the world of business, for example, a company needs the optimistic planners and visionaries who undertake the growth-promoting strivings of the business. However, the company also needs the more pessimistic financial officers and risk management specialists who have a realistic sense of the dangers and limitations, who counsel caution, essential for the business' survival. Likewise, in the political arena, although excessive pessimism may have indeed accounted for the failure of certain political candidates in an election year, such as the Dukakis campaign of 1988 (see Seligman, 1990, for a discussion), it is also the case that inappropriate optimism and ignoring the risks are significant parts of the "groupthink" process that is involved in the suspension of critical thinking and moral judgment from group pressures that has historically contributed to some enormous policy fiascoes such as the Bay of Pigs invasion, the attack on Pearl Harbor, and the escalation of the Vietnam War (Janis, 1983). Accordingly, much like the Taoism expressed in the yin and yang, Seligman (1990, p. 114) concluded: "The genius of evolution lies in the dynamic tension between optimism and pessimism continually correcting each other."

Reminiscent of the Buddhist concept of the Middle Way, Seligman's (1990) proposed solution to this apparent dilemma is a concept that he has termed *flexible optimism*. Essentially, he recommended a *situational analysis* of the degree of the risk and the cost failure involved in a given situation. According to Seligman, if the cost of failure is high, then the use of optimism is clearly the wrong strategy to invoke. For example, the person who has had several drinks at a party and is trying to decide whether he or she is capable of safely driving home is well advised to err on the side of pessimism and assume he or she is in greater danger rather than less. The risk of inappropriate optimism could be at the cost of one's life. Alternatively, the person at the party experiencing social anxiety and trying to decide whether to attempt to open up a conversation with someone whom the person finds attractive and, thereby, risk social rejection is likely to stand to gain more in interpersonal connectedness by optimistically assuming acceptance than he or she has to lose by being rebuffed.

Dialecticism in Psychopathology

Borderline Personality Disorder

Inflexible, compartmentalized, and unintegrated thought processes are present in both severe and less severe forms of psychopathology. For example, the phenomenon of *splitting* is generally considered to be a primitive defense mechanism that is characterized by a polarization of affect: positive and negative feelings, love and hate, attachment and rejection (Goin, 1998). Splitting is frequently regarded as a pathognomonic symptom of borderline personality disorder, a severe characterological disturbance the diagnostic features of which include a persistent pattern of instability of interpersonal relations, emotional dysregulation, identity disorganization, profound impulsivity, and self-destructive and self-defeating behavior. The defense itself is intended to provide protection against overwhelming anxiety, often stemming from fears of abandonment, and intense emotional states. Rather than offering any real protection though, splitting instead is linked to serious self-destructive behavior and tumultuous interpersonal relationships. The interpersonal disruption often emanates from a profound sense of confusion that the splitting process creates among individuals, both professional and nonprofessional, whose intention it is to help the borderline person. Thus, splitting is regarded as a "primitive" or immature mechanism in the sense that one may observe this phenomenon in small children whose emotional development has matured only to the point of determining whether or not something or someone is "either good or bad" (Vaillant, 1992). Subsequent psychological development provides an increasingly greater ability to tolerate seemingly paradoxical emotions and an ability to synthesize and integrate contradictions in thought, and a more complex view of reality (Goin, 1998).

The term *splitting* has been derived from psychoanalytic origins that encompass ego psychology and object relations theory (e.g., Freud, 1940/1964c; Kernberg, 1975, 1976, 1984). Accordingly, the borderline patient is seen as having undergone a range of severe negative childhood experiences (e.g., psychological trauma) that are retained as predominantly negative object relations representations. Likewise, these representations are stored separately from any positive object relations units acquired by the patient. The rigid personality organization that is kept in place by these primitive defensive operations, and that is the psychoanalytic basis of borderline pathology, is the target of psychodynamic psychotherapy with these patients (Swenson, 1989). The goal of psychodynamic treatment is for the psychotherapist to provide a sense of empathy and constancy for the borderline patient, while simultaneously providing firm limits and interpersonal boundaries. Affecting this balance between acceptance of the borderline patient's emotional turmoil, while not being overwhelmed by the patient's neediness, impulsivity, parasuicidal behavior, and anxiety, is a major challenge for the psychotherapist (Goin, 1998).

Historically, the vast majority of psychotherapeutic treatments for borderline conditions have been psychoanalytically based. More recently, however, a manualized cognitive–behavioral form of treatment program for borderline personality disorder has emerged (Linehan, 1993). Although firmly identified as a cognitive–behavioral therapy for borderline conditions, Linehan (1987a, 1987b, 1987c) had originally termed this treatment approach dialectical behavior therapy (DBT), a term that has continued to endure. "'Dialectical' refers to the importance accorded, throughout the course of therapy, to countering the rigid, black-and-white thinking of these patients and to resolving, via synthesis rather than polarization, the multiple tensions that exist in their lives" (Swenson, 1989, p. 27). Although cognitive–behavioral and psychodynamic therapies may differ in the structure of their respective therapeutic frames, the nature of the therapeutic alliance, and range of therapeutic techniques, it is clear that these two forms of treatment also hold a number of treatment goals in common. Many of these goals for therapy surround the dialectic that exists in these patients' lives, such that a more effective regulation of positive and negative affects and a better integration and synthesis of the positive and negative aspects of self and others, with its corresponding stabilization of the patients' interpersonal spheres, are ultimately achieved by whatever route is taken.

The importance of a dialectical perspective in Linehan's approach to treatment of the borderline patient stimulated the integration of Zen practice (Aitken, 1982; Kapleau, 1989a) and Eastern thought (Kapleau, 1989b) along with the behavioral aspects of therapy. Heard and Linehan (1994, p. 55) noted that "the process and goal of psychotherapy integration parallel the process and goal of psychotherapy itself," namely, to foster synthesis in the patient. Synthesis may be achieved in a variety of forms, including the integration of incongruent parts of one's self or the assimilation of new social and interpersonal skills into one's behavioral repertoire, the overall objective of which is to enhance the patient's personal effectiveness in managing life itself. Three primary characteristics of dialectical philosophy have been identified as relevant to DBT in particular and to psychotherapy in general (Heard & Linehan, 1994): interrelatedness–unity, opposition–heterogeneity, and ongoing change. In brief, the basic interrelatedness and unity of life emphasizes the relationship between life's apparent contradictions, the complexity of causality, and the overall Gestalt as more than the sum of its parts. The recognition of frequent opposing forces in life, forces that are not static in nature but that are in a dynamic tension with balance occurring as only a temporary phenomenon at any given point in time, underscores the complexity of the whole. The fundamental opposition in psychotherapy involves the conflict between the motivation for behavior change, on the one hand, and the phenomenon of radical acceptance, validation, and toleration of the reality of the moment in one's life without change, on the other. Finally, change is a process of continuous transition of the person through resolving the opposing forces of life through some form of synthesis. In sum, learning such integrative processes is essential to borderline patients for whom extreme compartmentalization of life experience, and the detrimental aspects of these extremes, has been a way of life and survival.

The notion of the radical acceptance of one's self in the moment in Eastern thought (e.g., Aitken, 1982) has its counterpart in Western existential thought as well. In Frankl's (1946/1985, 1966) existential approach known as *logotherapy*, derived from the Greek word *logos*, which denotes "meaning," a meaning-focused orientation to psychotherapy defocuses the patient's attention off of the common self-centered concerns that typically fuel neurotic anxiety. This existential approach to treatment, like Zen philosophy, recognizes that much of the suffering from traumatic experiences in life (i.e., frequent precipitants to borderline and other emotional pathology) is essentially *unavoidable*. Furthermore, although suffering is not considered a prerequisite for meaning in life (and to endure avoidable suffering is regarded as irrational), meaning for the patient is nevertheless seen as possible, despite suffering. Writing on the existential dilemmas in therapy as far back as the 1950s, Weisskopf-Joelson (1955) noted that the "modern" view of mental health emphasizes the notion that "people ought to be happy" and that apparent unhappiness is reflective of some character flaw within the person. She observed that such a system of values in society at large, perhaps even more present in the new millennium, contributes to the burden felt by those with unavoidable unhappiness from experiencing of tragedy in their lives. Thus, the patient is "not only unhappy, but ashamed about being unhappy" as well, with little opportunity to find pride and meaning in one's suffering, that is, to find it "ennobling rather than degrading" (Weisskopf-Joelson, 1958, p. 195). To find meaning in psychological suffering from unavoidable tragedy is to necessarily accept a more complex view of causality in life.

Chronic Depression and Dysthymia

Although rigid compartmentalization may contribute to the interpersonal and characterological disturbances seen in relatively severe forms of psychopathology such as borderline personality disorder noted above, less extreme forms of polarized thought are likewise present in less severe forms of psychological disturbance, such as moderate levels of chronic depression or dysthymia. Such cognitive distortions have been the focus of many cognitive therapy programs for patients with dysthymic disorders (Schuyler, 2002). There are a number of cognitive errors that play a role in depressogenic thoughts and assumptions, or personal explanations about how we explain what happens to us during life in general, and how we explain misfortune in our lives in particular (Beck et al., 1979). One such distortion, most often called *dichotomous thinking*, is also known by the descriptive terms of *black-and-white thinking*, *polarized thinking*, or *bipolar thinking*. Like splitting, everything tends to be seen in terms of bipolar extremes, such as good or bad, black or white. Unlike splitting in borderline pathology, dichotomous thinking in chronic depression tends to be less extreme, less rigid, and more amenable to therapeutic intervention. Cognitive therapy interventions aimed at dichotomous thinking for depression attempt to demonstrate to the depressed patients that events that happen to them in their lives can be construed along a continuum rather than in tight polarized compartments. So, for example, with depressed patients who are prone to excessive self-blame for misfortune in their lives, the cognitive therapist might challenge the belief that the patients are somehow 100% responsible for each and every negative thing that happens to them in their lives (Beck et al., 1979) and may urge them to realistically assign percentages or weights to the various possible causes for calamities, thereby helping these patients to arrive at a more complex and accurate view of causality.

Dialecticism in Social Psychology: The Resolution of Dissonance

Many of the techniques of cognitive therapy are predicated on the assumptions of the theoretical and empirical work demonstrating the saliency of *cognitive consistency* in the social psychology of normative interpersonal behavior (Heider, 1958). Cognitive consistency theories and research are based on the general proposition that inconsistent cognitions generate an unpleasant psychological state leading to behaviors that are designed to achieve consistency among thoughts and actions (Shaw & Costanzo, 1982). Various terms have been applied to the study of this phenomenon, including *cognitive imbalance* (Heider, 1946), *asymmetry* (Newcomb, 1953), *incongruity* (Osgood & Tannenbaum, 1955), and *dissonance* (Aronson, 1997; Festinger, 1957). Cognitive consistency theories are closely related to the principles of Gestalt psychology, to the recognition that the whole is more than the sum of its parts, and to the dynamic aspects of Lewin's (1935, 1951) field theory of personality and social psychology.

Dissonance theory (Festinger, 1957) holds that people are generally motivated to change their behavior and act more consistently with their perceptions, values, and beliefs about the world. When a disagreement, or inconsistency, exists between two portions of information, the conflict between them produces cognitive dissonance. Dissonance is an uncomfortable state of dynamic tension that generally motivates the person to find ways of reducing it. Frequently, the emotional dilemma between the conflicting aspects of information prevents action and causes the person to "freeze" from indecision. The resolution of dissonance takes place when one alternative course of action begins to appear more attractive than the other. As dissonance is resolved, the individual is more able to act in accord with behaviors that are associated with that particular behavioral choice or course of action (K. M. Brown, 1999). The broad scope and utility of cognitive consistency is apparent not only from the standpoint of psychopathology but also as a foundation of cognitive–behavioral interventions as noted in chapter 4, as the basis of interpersonal learning that takes place in interactional group psychotherapy as discussed in chapter 7, and as an important element of normative interpersonal relations as well.

Family Psychology and Attachment Theory: A Universal Human Dilemma

As a final example, in the area of intimate personal relationships involving family and kinship ties (i.e., one's primary social group), a number of early family therapists and theorists have identified, in differing terminology, what has been regarded as a fundamental human dilemma. Framo (1970, p. 163) postulated that "the universal human conflict between autonomy . . . on the one hand and the need to be accepted by intimate others on the other hand would have to be included in any comprehensive explanation of the development of psychopathology." Bowen (1978) articulated this family dilemma as the choice somewhere between the extremes of fusion with significant others and the differentiation of the individual from one's family of origin. Likewise, Bowlby (1969) applied the terms of attachment and separation to this same conflict. Humankind, as perhaps the most social of all animals (Aronson, 1998), not only requires the attachment to family for protection in the early years as vital to survival but is also dependent on parental care for a much longer period of time. Thus, the fear of separation and abandonment from the protection of significant others in life produces overwhelming anxiety. A remnant of these attachment needs, and the anxiety and panic that may ensue in their absence, resonates for most human beings throughout the course of the life cycle. As a result, people will undergo enormous sacrifices of their own sense of self and independence to circumvent the loss of this protective bond and subsequent threat to one's existence. One of the eternal questions that confronts each individual in life can be conceptualized as follows (Framo, 1976, p. 207): "How much does one owe oneself, and how much does one owe others?" Thus, an integrative treatment approach to family therapy is likely to involve the dilemmas surrounding both the index patient's family of procreation (i.e., his or her spouse and children) and family of origin (i.e., his or her parent and siblings), as discussed in chapters 5 and 6. For Framo (1976, p. 208), true integration in family therapy is approximated by the "achievement of balance between the old and the new family systems, the inner and the outer worlds."

CONCLUDING REMARKS: SYNTHESIS AND SYNERGY IN PSYCHOTHERAPY INTEGRATION

The historical sampling from broad and diverse areas in psychology provides a cogent illustration of the pervasiveness of dilemmas and dialecticism that is at the heart of this discipline. The "thesis" of internal psychodynamic functioning proposed by Freud laid the groundwork (and need) for the "antithesis" of behaviorism that, in turn, paved the way for a "synthesis" of covert dialogues and cognitions with overt observable behaviors in an integrated cognitive–behavioral conceptualization. Such a progression represents only one of many areas in which this dialectical process is exemplified in psychology at a theoretical level of understanding. At the day-to-day level of clinical reality for the psychotherapist, synthesis in the practice and process of psychotherapy is gradually approximated through a thorough dialectical examination of the patient's dilemmas in life, as well as the dilemmas that they pose for the therapist in the process of treatment. A genuine integration in psychotherapy calls for a synthesis rather than simply an eclecticism of different approaches in the practice of psychotherapy, in which the combined effect is truly more than, and characteristically different from, the sum of its individual parts.

Initially, the divergent eclectic perspectives provide the prerequisites for an eventual synthesis. The seemingly disparate aspects of therapeutic dilemmas mutually and synergistically provide complementary information about the patient and enlighten the clinician about the complexity of the patient's problems. The behavioral and symptomatic aspects of the patient's difficulties tell only one side of a multifaceted story. The intrapsychic and emotional life of the patient reveals a different facet of this behavioral picture. Finally, family relationships with significant others within the patient's interpersonal sphere both influence the problem and are another expression of it, and they serve to round out the patient's story and dilemmas. Ultimately, grappling with clinical dilemmas in psychotherapy teaches us that integration is an ongoing dialectic rather than an endpoint, an aspiration rather than an achievement, and, like the lives of the patient and the psychotherapist, a process rather than a goal.

REFERENCES

Ackerman, N. W. (1958). Interlocking pathology in family relationships. In S. Rado & G. Daniels (Eds.), *Changing concepts in psychoanalytic medicine* (pp. 135–150). New York: Grune & Stratton.

Adler, K. (1972). Techniques that shorten psychotherapy: Illustrated with five cases. *Journal of Individual Psychology, 28,* 155 168.

Adler, W. (1981). *The war of the Roses.* New York: Warner Books.

Ainsworth, M. D. S. (1985a). Patterns of infant–mother attachment: Antecedents and effects upon development. *Bulletin of New York Academy of Medicine, 61,* 771–791.

Ainsworth, M. D. S. (1985b). Attachments across the life-span. *Bulletin of New York Academy of Medicine, 61,* 792–812.

Aitken, R. (1982). *Taking the path of Zen.* New York: North Point Press.

Alberti, R. E., & Emmons, M. L. (1975). *Your perfect right: A guide to assertive behavior.* San Luis Obispo, CA: Impact.

Alexander, F., & French, T. M. (1946). *Psychoanalytic therapy: Principles and applications.* New York: Ronald Press.

Alexander, J. F., Holtzworth-Munroe, A., & Jameson, P. (1994). The process and outcome of marital and family therapy: Research review and evaluation. In A. E. Bergin & S. L. Garfield (Eds.), *Handbook of psychotherapy and behavior change* (4th ed., pp. 595–630). New York: Wiley.

Allen, S. N., & Bloom, S. L. (1994). Group and family treatment of post-traumatic stress disorder. *Psychiatric Clinics of North America, 8,* 425–438.

American Psychiatric Association. (1994). *Diagnostic and statistical manual of mental disorders* (4th ed.). Washington, DC: Author.

American Psychological Association. (2002). Ethical principles of psychologists and code of conduct. *American Psychologist, 57,* 1060–1073.

Andersen, T. (1987). The reflecting team: Dialogue and meta-dialogue in clinical work. *Family Process, 26,* 415–428.

Andersen, T. (Ed.). (1991). *The reflecting team: Dialogues and dialogues about dialogues.* New York: Norton.

Andersen, T. (1992). Reflections on reflecting with families. In S. McNamee & K. J. Gergen (Eds.), *Therapy as social construction* (pp. 54–68). Newbury Park, CA: Sage.

Andersen, T. (1993). See and hear: And be seen and heard. In S. Friedman (Ed.), *The new language of change* (pp. 303–322). New York: Guilford Press.

Arkowitz, H. (1992a). A common factors therapy for depression. In J. C. Norcross & M. R. Goldfried (Eds.), *Handbook of psychotherapy integration* (pp. 402–432). New York: Basic Books.

Arkowitz, H. (1992b). Integrative theories of therapy. In D. K. Freedheim (Ed.), *History of psychotherapy: A century of change* (pp. 261–303). Washington, DC: American Psychological Association.

Aronson, E. (1997). A theory of cognitive dissonance. *American Journal of Psychology, 110,* 127–137.

Aronson, E. (1998). *The social animal* (8th ed.). New York: Freeman.

Asendorpf, J. B., Wallbott, H. G., & Scherer, K. R. (1983). Der verflixte represser: Ein vorschlag zu einer zweidimensionalen operationalisierung von repression–sensitization [The troublesome repressor: A suggestion for the two-dimensional operationalization of repression–sensitization]. *Zeitschrift fur Differentielle und Personlichkeitspsychologie, 4,* 113–128.

Auld, F., & Hyman, M. (1991). *Resolution of inner conflict: An introduction to psychoanalytic therapy.* Washington, DC: American Psychological Association.

Authier, J., Gustafson, K., Guerney, B., & Kasdorf, J. A. (1975). The psychological practitioner as teacher: A theoretical–historical and practical review. *The Counseling Psychologist, 5*(2), 31–50.

Bachelor, A. (1988). How clients perceive therapist empathy: A content analysis of "received" empathy. *Psychotherapy, 25,* 227–240.

Balint, M. (1957). *The doctor, his patient, and the illness.* New York: International Universities Press.

Balint, M. (1966). Psychoanalysis and medical practice. *International Journal of Psychoanalysis, 47,* 54–62.

Balint, M., Ornstein, P., & Balint, E. (1972). *Focal psychotherapy: An example of applied psychoanalysis.* London: Tavistock.

Bandura, A. (1961). Psychotherapy as a learning process. *Psychological Bulletin, 58,* 143–159.

Bandura, A. (1969). *Principles of behavior modification.* New York: Holt, Rinehart & Winston.

Bandura, A. (1971). Psychotherapy based upon modeling principles. In A. E. Bergin & S. L. Garfield (Eds.), *Handbook of psychotherapy and behavior change: An empirical analysis* (pp. 653–708). New York: Wiley.

Bandura, A. (1977a). Self-efficacy: Toward a unifying concept of behavior change. *Psychological Review, 84,* 191–215.

Bandura, A. (1977b). *Social learning theory.* Englewood Cliffs, NJ: Prentice-Hall.

Bandura, A. (1978). The self system in reciprocal determinism. *American Psychologist, 33,* 344–358.

Bandura, A. (1997). *Self-efficacy: The exercise of control.* New York: Freeman.

Bandura, A., & Rosenthal, T. L. (1966). Vicarious classical conditioning as a function of arousal level. *Journal of Personality and Social Psychology, 3,* 54–62.

Barlow, D. H. (1988). *Anxiety and its disorders: The nature and treatment of anxiety and panic.* New York: Guilford Press.

Barlow, D. H. (1992). The development of an anxiety research clinic. In D. K. Freedheim (Ed.), *History of psychotherapy: A century of change* (pp. 429–431). Washington, DC: American Psychological Association.

Barlow, D. H., & Cerny, J. A. (1988). *Psychological treatment of panic*. New York: Guilford Press.

Barlow, D. H., & Craske, M. G. (2001). *Mastery of Your Anxiety and Panic (MAP–3): Client workbook* (3rd ed.). New York: Academic Press.

Barlow, D. H., Hayes, S. C., & Nelson, R. O. (1984). *The scientist practitioner: Research and accountability in clinical and educational settings*. New York: Pergamon Press.

Barlow, D. H., O'Brien, G. T., & Last, C. G. (1984). Couples treatment of agoraphobia. *Behavior Therapy, 15*, 41–58.

Barlow, D. H., & Waddell, T. (1985). Agoraphobia. In D. H. Barlow (Ed.), *Clinical handbook of psychological disorders* (pp. 1–68). New York: Guilford Press.

Bateson, G. (1935). Culture contact and schismogenesis. *Man, 35* (Article 99), 178–183. (Reprinted in *Steps to an ecology of mind*, pp. 61–72, by G. Bateson, 1972, New York: Ballantine Books)

Bateson, G. (1972). *Steps to an ecology of mind*. New York: Ballantine Books.

Beattie, M. (1987). *Codependent no more*. New York: Ballantine Books.

Beauchamp, T., & Childress, J. (1994). *Principles of biomedical ethics* (4th ed.). New York: Oxford University Press.

Beck, A. T. (1970). Cognitive therapy: Nature and relation to behavior therapy. *Behavior Therapy, 1*, 184–200.

Beck, A. T. (1976). *Cognitive therapy and the emotional disorders*. New York: Meridian.

Beck, A. T., Freeman, A., & Associates. (1990). *Cognitive therapy of personality disorders*. New York: Guilford Press.

Beck, A. T., Rush, A. J., Shaw, B. F., & Emery, G. (1979). *Cognitive therapy of depression*. New York: Guilford Press.

Bell, P. A., & Byrne, D. (1978). Repression–sensitization. In H. London & J. E. Exner Jr. (Eds.), *Dimensions of personality* (pp. 449–485). New York: Wiley.

Bellack, A. S., & Hersen, M. (Eds.). (1985). *Dictionary of behavior therapy techniques*. New York: Pergamon Press.

Bellak, L., & Siegel, H. (1983). *Handbook of brief and emergency psychotherapy*. Larchmont, NY: C.P.S.

Bem, D. J. (1970). *Beliefs, attitudes, and human affairs*. Belmont, CA: Brooks/Cole.

Benjamin, L. T., Jr., & Baker, D. B. (2000). Boulder at 50: Introduction to the section. *American Psychologist, 55*, 233–236.

Berrien, F. K. (1968). *General and social systems*. New Brunswick, NJ: Rutgers University Press.

Bersoff, D. N. (2003). *Ethical conflicts in psychology* (3rd ed.). Washington, DC: American Psychological Association.

Beutler, L. E., Crago, M., & Arrizmendi, T. G. (1986). Research on therapist variables in psychotherapy. In S. L. Garfield & A. E. Bergin (Eds.), *Handbook of psychotherapy and behavior change* (pp. 257–310). New York: Wiley.

Birk, L. (1970). Behavior therapy: Integration with dynamic psychiatry. *Behavior Therapy, 1*, 522–526.

Birk, L., & Brinkley-Birk, A. (1974). Psychoanalysis and behavior therapy. *American Journal of Psychiatry, 131*, 499–510.

Blanchard, E. B., & Hickling, E. J. (1997). *After the crash: Assessment and treatment of motor vehicle accident survivors.* Washington, DC: American Psychological Association.

Blatt, S. J. (1995). The destructiveness of perfectionism: Implications for the treatment of depression. *American Psychologist, 50*, 1003–1020.

Blatt, S. J., & Erlich, H. S. (1982). A critique of the concepts of resistance in behavior therapy. In P. L. Wachtel (Ed.), *Resistance: Psychodynamic and behavioral approaches* (pp. 197–203). New York: Plenum Press.

Blos, P. (1941). *The adolescent personality.* New York: Appleton-Century-Crofts.

Boszormeyi-Nagy, I., & Framo, J. L. (Eds.). (1965). *Intensive family therapy.* Hagerstown, MD: Hoeber Medical Division, Harper & Row.

Boszormeyi-Nagy, I., & Spark, G. (1973). *Invisible loyalties: Reciprocity in intergenerational family therapy.* New York: Harper & Row Medical Department.

Bowen, M. (1959). Family relationships in schizophrenia. In A. Auerback (Ed.), *Schizophrenia: An integrated approach* (pp. 147–178). New York: Ronald Press.

Bowen, M. (1960). A family concept of schizophrenia. In D. D. Jackson (Ed.), *The etiology of schizophrenia* (pp. 346–370). New York: Basic Books.

Bowen, M. (1965). Family psychotherapy with schizophrenia in the hospital and in private practice. In I. Boszormenyi-Nagy & J. L. Framo (Eds.), *Intensive psychotherapy* (pp. 213–243). Hagerstown, MD: HarperCollins.

Bowen, M. (1974). Alcoholism and the family. In F. Seixas, R. Cadoret, & S. Eggleston (Eds.), *Annals of the New York Academy of Sciences, 233*, 115–122.

Bowen, M. (1976). Theory in the practice of psychotherapy. In P. Guerin (Ed.), *Family therapy* (pp. 42–90). New York: Gardner Press.

Bowen, M. (1978). *Family therapy in clinical practice.* New York: Jason Aronson.

Bowen, M. (1985). Toward the differentiation of self in one's family of origin. In M. Bowen, *Family therapy in clinical practice* (pp. 529–547). New York: Jason Aronson.

Bowlby, J. (1969). *Attachment and loss: Vol. 1. Attachment.* New York: Basic Books.

Bowlby, J. (1973). *Attachment and loss: Vol. 2. Anxiety and anger.* New York: Basic Books.

Bowlby, J. (1988). *A secure base: Parent–child attachment and health human development.* New York: Basic Books.

Brody, E. M., & Farber, B. A. (1989). Effects of psychotherapy on significant others. *Professional Psychology: Research and Practice, 20*, 116–122.

Brooks, J. L. (Producer), Milchan, A. (Producer), & Devito, D. (Director). 1989. *The War of the Roses* [Motion picture]. United States: Twentieth Century Fox.

Brown, K. M. (1999). *Cognitive consistency theory: Overview.* Retrieved June 5, 2003, from University of South Florida, Community and Family Health Web Site: http://hsc.usf.edu/~kmbrown/Cognitive_Consistency_Overview.htm

Brown, T. M., & Baron, D. A. (1992). Anxiety disorders seen in primary care. *Journal of American Osteopathic Association, 92*, 95–101.

Bruner, J. S., & Postman, L. (1947). Emotional selectivity in perception and reaction. *Journal of Personality, 16*, 69–77.

Budman, S. H., & Gurman, A. S. (1988). *Theory and practice of brief therapy*. New York: Guilford Press.

Budman, S. H., & Steenbarger, B. (1997). *The essential guide to group practice in mental health*. New York: Guilford Press.

Bugental, J. (1964). The third force in psychology. *Journal of Humanistic Psychology, 4*, 19–26.

Burlingame, G. M., & Fuhriman, A. (1990). Time-limited group therapy. *The Counseling Psychologist, 18* (1), 93–118.

Burns, D. D., & Eidelson, R. J. (1998). Why are depression and anxiety correlated? A test of the tripartite model. *Journal of Consulting and Clinical Psychology, 66*, 461–473.

Buss, D. M. M. (1999). *Evolutionary psychology: The new science of the mind*. New York: Allyn & Bacon.

Butler, S. F., & Strupp, H. H. (1986). Specific and nonspecific factors in psychotherapy: A problematic paradigm for psychotherapy research. *Psychotherapy, 23*, 30–40.

Byrne, D. (1964). Repression–sensitization as a dimension of personality. In B. A. Maher (Ed.), *Progress in experimental personality research* (pp. 169–220). New York: Academic Press.

Byrne, D. (1966). *An introduction to personality: A research approach*. Englewood Cliffs, NJ: Prentice-Hall.

Carey, K., & Burgess, J. F. (2000). Hospital costing: Experience from the VHA. *Financial Accountability and Management, 16*, 289–308.

Carey, T. A., & Mullan, R. J. (2004). What is Socratic questioning? *Psychotherapy: Theory, Research, Practice, Training, 41*, 217–226.

Carkhuff, R. R., & Berenson, B. G. (1967). *Beyond counseling and therapy*. New York: Holt, Rinehart & Winston.

Carroll, L., Gilroy, P. J., & Murra, J. (1999). The moral imperative: Self-care for women psychotherapists. *Women & Therapy, 22*, 133–143.

Carter, B., & Peters, J. K. (1996). *Love, honor, and negotiate*. New York: Pocket Books.

Carter, C. A. (1971). Advantages of being a woman therapist. *Psychotherapy: Theory, Research, and Practice, 8*, 297–300.

Casat, C. D. (1988). Childhood anxiety disorders: A review of the possible relationship to adult panic disorder and agoraphobia. *Journal of Anxiety Disorders, 2*, 51–60.

Cautela, J. R., & Wisocki, P. A. (1977). The thought stopping procedure: Description, application, and learning theory interpretations. *Psychological Reports, 27*, 255–264.

Cerny, J. A., Barlow, D. H., Craske, M. G., & Himadi, W. G. (1987). Couples treatment of agoraphobia: A two-year follow-up. *Behavior Therapy, 18*, 401–415.

Chambless, D. L. (1996). In defense of dissemination of empirically supported psychological interventions. *Clinical Psychology: Science and Practice, 3*, 230–235.

Chambless, D. L., Baker, M. J., Baucom, D. H., Beutler, L. E., Calhoun, K. S., Crits-Christoph, P., et al. (1998). Update on empirically validated therapies: II. *The Clinical Psychologist, 51*(1), 3–16.

Chambliss, C. H. (1999). *Psychotherapy and managed care: Reconciling research and reality.* New York: Allyn & Bacon.

Clark, L. A., & Watson, D. (1991). Tripartite model of anxiety and depression: Psychometric evidence and taxonomic implications. *Journal of Abnormal Psychology, 100*, 316–336.

Clarkson, P. (2000). *Ethics: Working with ethical and moral dilemmas in psychotherapy.* London: Whurr Publishers.

Conroy, P. (1986). *The prince of tides.* New York: Houghton Mifflin.

Coon, D. (1980). *Introduction to psychology: Exploration and application* (2nd ed.). St. Paul, MN: West.

Cooper, J. O., Heron, T. E., & Heward, W. L. (1987). *Applied behavior analysis.* Columbus, OH: Merrill.

Corrigan, P. W. (2005). *On the stigma of mental illness.* Washington, DC: American Psychological Association.

Craske, M. G., Barlow, D. H., & Meadows, E. A. (2000). *Mastery of Your Anxiety and Panic (MAP–3): Therapist guide for anxiety, panic, and agoraphobia* (3rd ed.). New York: Academic Press.

Cummings, N. A. (1990). Brief intermittent psychotherapy throughout the life cycle. In J. K. Zeig & S. G. Gilligan (Eds.), *Brief therapy: Myths, methods, and metaphors* (pp. 169–184). New York: Brunner/Mazel.

Cummings, N. A. (1991). Brief intermittent therapy throughout the life cycle. In C. S. Austad & W. H. Berman (Eds.), *Psychotherapy in managed health care* (pp. 35–45). Washington, DC: American Psychological Association.

Cummings, N. A., & Cummings, J. L. (2000). *The essence of psychotherapy: Reinventing the art in the new era of data.* San Diego, CA: Academic Press.

Cummings, N. A., & VandenBos, G. R. (1979). The general practice of psychology. *Professional Psychology, 10*, 430–440.

Cushman, P. (1992). Psychotherapy to 1992: A historically situated interpretation. In D. K. Freedheim (Ed.), *History of psychotherapy: A century of change* (pp. 21–64). Washington, DC: American Psychological Association.

Damon, M., & Affleck, B. (1997). *Good Will Hunting: A screenplay.* New York: Hyperion.

Danieli, Y. (1984). Psychotherapists' participation in the conspiracy of silence about the Holocaust. *Psychoanalytic Psychology, 1*, 23–42.

Davanloo, H. (Ed.). (1978). *Basic principles and techniques in short-term dynamic psychotherapy.* New York: Spectrum.

Davanloo, H. (Ed.). (1980). *Short-term dynamic psychotherapy*. New York: Jason Aronson.

Davanloo, H. (1988). The technique of unlocking the unconscious: Part I. *International Journal of Short-Term Psychotherapy, 3*, 99–212.

Davanloo, H. (1990). *Unlocking the unconscious: Selected papers of Habib Davanloo, M.D.* Chichester, England: Wiley.

Davidson, L. M., & Baum, A. (1993). Predictors of chronic stress among Vietnam veterans: Stressor exposure and intrusive recall. *Journal of Traumatic Stress, 6*, 195 212.

Davison, G. C., & Neale, J. M. (1998). *Abnormal psychology* (7th ed.). New York: Wiley.

Deci, E. L., & Ryan, R. M. (1985). *Intrinsic motivation and self-determination in human behavior*. New York: Perseus.

Deci, E. L., & Ryan, R. M. (Eds.). (2002). *Handbook of self-determination research*. Rochester, NY: University of Rochester Press.

DeRubeis, R. J., & Crits-Christoph, P. (1998). Empirically supported individual and group psychological treatments for adult mental disorders. *Journal of Consulting and Clinical Psychology, 66*, 37–52.

Deutch, F., & Murphy, W. F. (1955a). *The clinical interview: Vol. 1. Diagnosis, a method of teaching associative exploration*. New York: International Universities Press.

Deutch, F., & Murphy, W. F. (1955b). *The clinical interview: Vol. 2: Therapy, a method of teaching sector psychotherapy*. New York: International Universities Press.

Dickens, C. (1992). *Great expectations*. Ware, England: Wordsworth Editions. (Original work published 1861)

Dies, R. R. (1973). Group therapist self-disclosure: An evaluation by clients. *Journal of Counseling Psychology, 20*, 344–348.

Disraeli, I. (1861). *Curiosities of literature* (Vol. IV). Boston: Crosby, Nichols, Lee.

Dobson, K. S., & Shaw, B. F. (1993). The training of cognitive therapists: What have we learned from treatment manuals? *Psychotherapy, 30*, 573–577.

Doherty, W. J. (1995). *Soul searching: Why psychotherapy must promote moral responsibility*. New York: Basic Books.

Doherty, W. J., & Baird, M. A. (1983). *Family therapy and family medicine: Toward the primary care of families*. New York: Guilford Press.

Dollard, J., & Miller, N. E. (1950). *Personality and psychotherapy*. New York: McGraw-Hill.

Drowns-Allen, K. S., Allen, R. M., & Larson, D. B. (1980). *How to perform a structured mental status interview: A self-instructional program*. Carrboro, NC: Health Sciences Consortium.

Dryden, W. (1984). Issues in the eclectic practice of individual psychotherapy. In W. Dryden (Ed.), *Individual therapy in Britain* (pp. 341–363). London: Harper & Row.

Dryden, W. (1997). *Therapists' dilemmas* (Rev. ed.). London: Sage.

Edelwich, J., & Brodsky, A. (1991). *Sexual dilemmas for the helping professional* (Rev. and expanded ed.). New York: Brunner/Mazel.

Eissler, K. R. (1953). The effect of the structure of the ego on psychoanalytic technique. *Journal of the American Psychoanalytic Association, 1*, 104–143.

Ekstein, R. (1956). Psychoanalytic techniques. In D. Bower & L. E. Abt (Eds.), *Progress in clinical psychology* (Vol. 2, pp. 79–97). New York: Grune & Stratton.

Ellis, A. (1962). *Reason and emotion in psychotherapy*. New York: Lyle Stuart.

Endler, M. S., & Magnusson, D. (1976). Toward an interactional psychology of personality. *Psychological Bulletin, 83*, 956–974.

Enright, R. D., & Fitzgibbons, R. P. (2000). *Helping clients forgive: An empirical guide for resolving anger and restoring hope*. Washington, DC: American Psychological Association.

Epston, D., & White, M. (1992). *Experience, contradiction, narrative, and imagination: Selected papers of David Epston and Michael White, 1989–1991*. Adelaide, South Australia: Dulwich Center.

Epston, D., Winslade, J., Crocket, K., & Monk, G. (1996). *Narrative therapy in practice: The archeology of hope*. San Francisco: Jossey-Bass.

Erikson, E. H. (1950). *Childhood and society*. New York: Norton.

Eron, J. B., & Lund, T. W. (1998). *Narrative solutions in brief therapy*. New York: Guilford Press.

Fairbairn, W. R. D. (1954). *An object-relations theory of personality*. New York: Basic Books.

Fay, A., & Lazarus, A. A. (1993). Cognitive–behavioral group therapy. In A. Alonzo & H. I. Swiller (Eds.), *Group therapy in clinical practice* (pp. 449–469). Washington, DC: American Psychiatric Press.

Feachem, R. G. A., Sekhri, N. K., & White, K. L. (2002). Getting more for their dollar: A comparison of the NHS with California's Kaiser Permanente. *British Medical Journal, 324*, 135–143.

Feather, B. W., & Rhoads, J. M. (1972). Psychodynamic behavior therapy: II. Clinical aspects. *Archives of General Psychiatry, 26*, 503–511.

Feldman, L. B. (1989). Integrating individual and family therapy. *Journal of Integrative and Eclectic Psychotherapy, 8*, 41–52.

Feldman, L. B. (1992). *Integrating individual and family therapy*. New York: Brunner/Mazel.

Feldman, L. B., & Powell, S. L. (1992). Integrating therapeutic modalities. In J. C. Norcross & M. R. Goldfried (Eds.), *Handbook of psychotherapy integration* (pp. 503–560). New York: Basic Books.

Feminist Therapy Institute, Inc. (1990). Feminist Therapy Institute code of ethics. In H. Lerman & N. Porter (Eds.), *Feminist ethics in psychotherapy* (pp. 37–40). New York: Springer Publishing Company.

Festinger, L. (1957). *A theory of cognitive dissonance*. Stanford, CA: Stanford University Press.

Fiese, B. H., & Scaturo, D. J. (1995). The use of self-help terminology in focus-group discussions with adult children of alcoholics: Implications for research and clinical practice. *Family Therapy, 22(1)*, 1–8.

Figley, C. R. (1985). From victim to survivor: Social responsibility in the wake of catastrophe. In C. R. Figley (Ed.), *Trauma and its wake* (pp. 398–415). New York: Brunner/Mazel.

Foa, E. B., & Emmelkamp, P. M. G. (Eds.). (1983). *Failures in behavior therapy*. New York: Wiley.

Foa, E. B., Keane, T. M., & Friedman, M. J. (2000). *Effective treatments for PTSD: Practice guidelines from the International Society of Traumatic Stress Studies*. New York: Guilford Press.

Fox, R. (2002). Efficiency in the NHS. *Journal of the Royal Society of Medicine, 95*, 579–579.

Framo, J. L. (1968). My family, my families. *Voices: The Art and Science of Psychotherapy, 4*, 18–27.

Framo, J. L. (1970). Symptoms from a family transactional viewpoint. In N. W. Ackerman, J. Leib, & J. K. Pearce (Eds.), *Family therapy in transition* (pp. 271–308). Boston: Little, Brown.

Framo, J. L. (1976). Family of origin as a resource for adults in marital and family therapy: You can and should go home again. *Family Process, 15*, 193–210.

Framo, J. L. (1977). In-laws and out-laws: A marital case of kinship confusion. In P. Papp (Ed.), *Family therapy: Full-length case studies* (pp. 167–181). New York: Gardner Press.

Framo, J. L. (1980). Marriage and marital therapy: Issues and initial interview techniques. In M. Andolfi & I. Zwerling (Eds.), *Dimensions of family therapy* (pp. 49–71). New York: Guilford Press.

Framo, J. L. (1992). *Family-of-origin therapy: An intergenerational approach*. New York: Brunner/Mazel.

Framo, J. L. (1993, November 19). *Family of origin in couples therapy*. Paper presented at the Family Therapy Training Program, University of Rochester, Rochester, NY.

Frank, J. D. (1961). *Persuasion and healing*. Baltimore: Johns Hopkins University Press.

Frank, J. D. (1968). The role of hope in psychotherapy. *International Journal of Psychiatry, 5*, 383–395.

Frank, J. D. (1971). Therapeutic factors in psychotherapy. *American Journal of Psychotherapy, 25*, 350–361.

Frank, J. D., & Frank, J. B. (1993). *Persuasion and healing: A comparative study of psychotherapy* (3rd ed.). Baltimore: Johns Hopkins University Press.

Frankl, V. E. (1960). Paradoxical intention: A logotherapeutic technique. *American Journal of Psychotherapy, 14*, 520–535.

Frankl, V. E. (1966). Logotherapy and existential analysis: A review. *American Journal of Psychotherapy, 20*, 252–260.

Frankl, V. E. (1985). *Man's search for meaning*. New York: Washington Square Press. (Original work published 1946)

Freedheim, D. K. (Ed.). (1992). *History of psychotherapy: A century of change*. Washington, DC: American Psychological Association.

Freeman, J., Epston, D., & Lobovits, D. (1997). *Playful approaches to serious problems: Narrative therapy with children and their families*. New York: Norton.

Freud, S. (1958a). The dynamics of transference. In J. Strachey (Ed. & Trans.), *The standard edition of the complete psychological works of Sigmund Freud* (Vol. 12, pp. 97–108). London: Hogarth Press. (Original work published 1912)

Freud, S. (1958b). On the beginning of treatment: I. Further recommendations on the technique of psycho-analysis. In J. Strachey (Ed. & Trans.), *The standard edition of the complete psychological works of Sigmund Freud* (Vol. 12, pp. 121–144). London: Hogarth Press. (Original work published 1913)

Freud, S. (1958c). Recommendations to physicians practicing psychoanalysis. In J. Strachey (Ed. & Trans.), *The standard edition of the complete psychological works of Sigmund Freud* (Vol. 12, pp. 109–120). London: Hogarth Press. (Original work published 1912)

Freud, S. (1958d). "Wild" psycho-analysis. In J. Strachey (Ed. & Trans.), *The standard edition of the complete psychological works of Sigmund Freud* (Vol. 11, pp. 219–230). London: Hogarth Press. (Original work published 1910)

Freud, S. (1959a). Inhibitions, symptoms, and anxiety. In J. Strachey (Ed. & Trans.), *The standard edition of the complete psychological works of Sigmund Freud* (Vol. 20, pp. 179–258). London: Hogarth Press. (Original work published 1926)

Freud, S. (1959b). The question of lay analysis. In J. Strachey (Ed. & Trans.), *The standard edition of the complete psychological works of Sigmund Freud* (Vol. 20, pp. 179–258). London: Hogarth Press. (Original work published 1926)

Freud, S. (1962). The neuro-psychoses of defence. In J. Strachey (Ed. & Trans.), *The standard edition of the complete psychological works of Sigmund Freud* (Vol. 3, pp. 43–61). London: Hogarth Press. (Original work published 1894)

Freud, S. (1963). Introductory lectures on psycho-analysis: Part 3. In J. Strachey (Ed. & Trans.), *The standard edition of the complete psychological works of Sigmund Freud* (Vol. 16, pp. 431–447). London: Hogarth Press. (Original work published 1917)

Freud, S. (1964a). Analysis terminable and interminable. In J. Strachey (Ed. & Trans.), *The standard edition of the complete psychological works of Sigmund Freud* (Vol. 23, pp. 209–253). London: Hogarth Press. (Original work published 1937)

Freud, S. (1964b). An outline of psychoanalysis. In J. Strachey (Ed. & Trans.), *The standard edition of the complete psychological works of Sigmund Freud* (Vol. 23, pp. 141–207). London: Hogarth Press. (Original work published 1940)

Freud, S. (1964c). Splitting of the ego in the process of defence. In J. Strachey (Ed. & Trans.), *The standard edition of the complete psychological works of Sigmund Freud* (Vol. 23, pp. 275–278). London: Hogarth Press. (Original work published 1940)

Friedman, S. (1985). Implications of object-relations theory for the behavioral treatment of agoraphobia. *American Journal of Psychotherapy, 39*, 525–540.

Friesen, J. D. (1985). *Structural-strategic marriage and family therapy*. New York: Gardner Press.

Fuhriman, A., & Burlingame, G. M. (2001). Group psychotherapy training and effectiveness. *International Journal of Group Psychotherapy, 51*, 399–416.

Furst, L. R. (1999). *Just talk: Narratives of psychotherapy*. Lexington: University of Kentucky Press.

Gadamer, H.-G. (1976). *Hegel's dialectic* (P. C. Smith, Trans.). New Haven, CT: Yale University Press.

Gardner, R. A. (1986). *Child custody litigation: A guide for parents and mental health professionals*. Cresskill, NJ: Creative Therapeutics.

Garfield, J. L. (Ed. & Trans.). (1995). The fundamental wisdom of the middle way: Nagarjuna's Mulamadhuamakakarika. Oxford, England: Oxford University Press.

Garfield, S. L. (1992a). Eclectic psychotherapy: A common factors approach. In J. C. Norcross & M. R. Goldfried (Eds.), *Handbook of psychotherapy integration* (pp. 169–201). New York: Basic Books.

Garfield, S. L. (1992b). Major issues in psychotherapy research. In D. K. Freedheim (Ed.), *History of psychotherapy: A century of change* (pp. 335–359). Washington, DC: American Psychological Association.

Garfield, S. L. (1996). Some problems associated with "validated" forms of psychotherapy. *Clinical Psychology: Science and Practice, 3*, 218–229.

Gay, P. (1998). *Freud: A life for our time*. New York: Norton.

Gill, M. M. (1982). *The analysis of transference*. New York: International Universities Press.

Gill, M. M. (1984). Differing views of transference. In H. Arkowitz & S. B. Messer (Eds.), *Psychoanalytic therapy and behavior therapy: Is integration possible?* (pp. 213–217). New York: Plenum Press.

Giora, Z. (1997). *The unconscious and its narratives*. New York: Jason Aronson.

Gladding, S. T. (2002). *Family therapy: History, theory, and practice* (3rd ed.). Upper Saddle River, NJ: Merrill Prentice Hall.

Goffman, E. (1961). *Asylums: Essays on the social situation of mental patients and other inmates*. New York: Anchor Press.

Goffman, E. (1986). *Stigma: Notes on the management of spoiled identity*. New York: Simon & Schuster.

Goin, M. K. (1998). Borderline personality disorder: Splitting countertransference. *Psychiatric Times, XV*(11). Retrieved June 4, 2003, from http://www.psychiatrictimes.com/p981153.html

Goldenberg, I., & Goldenberg, H. (1980). *Family therapy: An overview*. Monterey, CA: Brooks/Cole.

Goldfried, M. R. (1997). In vivo intervention or transference? An interview with Marvin Goldfried. In W. Dryden (Ed.), *Therapists' dilemmas* (Rev. ed., pp. 63–75). London: Sage.

Goldfried, M. R. (Ed.). (2000). *How therapists change: Personal and professional reflections*. Washington, DC: American Psychological Association.

Goldman, G. D., & Milman, D. S. (1978). The initial phase of treatment. In G. D. Goldman & D. S. Milman (Eds.), *Psychoanalytic psychotherapy* (pp. 20–33). Reading, MA: Addison-Wesley.

Goldstein, A. P. (1973). *Structured learning therapy: Toward a psychotherapy for the poor*. New York: Academic Press.

Goldstein, A. P. (1981). *Psychological skill training: The structured learning technique*. New York: Pergamon Press.

Goldstein, A. P. (1995). Coordinated multitargeted skills training: The promotion of generalization enhancement. In W. O'Donohue & L. Krasner (Eds.), *Handbook of psychological skills training: Clinical techniques and applications* (pp. 383–399). Boston: Allyn & Bacon.

Goodman, G., & Jacobs, M. K. (1994). The self-help, mutual-support group. In A. Fuhriman & G. M. Burlingame (Eds.), *Handbook of group psychotherapy: An empirical and clinical synthesis* (pp. 489–526). New York: Wiley.

Gorski, T. T., & Miller, M. (1984). Co-alcoholic relapse: Family factors and warning signs. In The U.S. Journal of Drug & Alcohol Dependency & Health Communications, Inc. (Eds.), *Co-dependency: An emerging issue* (pp. 77–82). Pompano Beach, FL: Health Communications.

Gottman, J. M. (1994). *What predicts divorce?* Hillsdale, NJ: Erlbaum.

Gottman, J. M. (Ed.). (1996). *What predicts divorce?: The measures*. Hillsdale, NJ: Erlbaum.

Gottman, J. M. (1999). *The marriage clinic: A scientifically-based marital therapy*. New York: Norton.

Greenblatt, M., & Levinson, D. J. (1967). The goals and responsibilities of the psychotherapist: Some problematic issues. In A. R. Mahrer (Ed.), *The goals of psychotherapy* (pp. 20–31). New York: Appleton-Century-Crofts.

Gurman, A. S. (1981). Integrative marital therapy: Toward the development of an interpersonal approach. In S. H. Budman (Ed.), *Forms of brief therapy* (pp. 415–457). New York: Guilford Press.

Gurman, A. S., & Fraenkel, P. (2002). The history of couple therapy: A millennial review. *Family Process, 41*, 199–260.

Gurman, A. S., Kniskern, D. P., & Pinsof, W. M. (1986). Research on the process and outcome of marital and family therapy. In S. L. Garfield & A. E. Bergin (Eds.), *Handbook of psychotherapy and behavior change* (3rd ed., pp. 565–626). New York: Wiley.

Gustafson, J. P. (1995). *The dilemmas of brief psychotherapy*. New York: Plenum Press.

Haley, J. (1963). *Strategies of psychotherapy*. New York: Grune & Stratton.

Haley, J. (1970). Family therapy. *International Journal of Psychiatry, 9*, 233–242.

Haley, J. (1973). *Uncommon therapy: The psychiatric techniques of Milton H. Erikson, M.D.* New York: Norton.

Haley, J. (1976). *Problem-solving therapy: New strategies for effective family therapy*. San Francisco: Jossey-Bass.

Haley, J. (1981). *Reflections on therapy and other essays*. Chevy Chase, MD: Family Therapy Institute of Washington, DC.

Haley, S. A. (1974). When the patient reports atrocities: Specific treatment considerations of the Vietnam veteran. *Archives of General Psychiatry, 30*, 191–196.

Hall, C. S., Lindzey, G., & Campbell, J. B. (1997). *Theories of personality* (4th ed.). New York: Wiley.

Hatcher, S. L., & Hatcher, R. L. (1983). Set a place for Elijah: Problems of the spouses and parents of psychotherapy patients. *Psychotherapy: Theory, Research, and Practice, 20*, 75–80.

Havens, L., & Frank, J. (1971). Review of psychoanalysis and interpersonal psychiatry. *American Journal of Psychiatry, 127*, 1704–1705.

Heard, H. L., & Linehan, M. M. (1994). Dialectical behavior therapy: An integrative approach to the treatment of borderline personality disorder. *Journal of Psychotherapy Integration, 4*, 55–82.

Heidegger, M. (1962). *Being and time*. New York: Harper & Row.

Heider, F. (1946). Attitudes and cognitive organization. *Journal of Psychology, 21*, 107–112.

Heider, F. (1958). *The psychology of interpersonal relations*. New York: Wiley.

Heller, J. (1961). *Catch-22*. New York: Simon & Schuster.

Hemingway, E. (1964). *A moveable feast*. New York: Scribner's.

Henry, W. P., Schacht, T. E., & Strupp, H. H. (1990). Patient and therapist introject, interpersonal process, and differential psychotherapy outcome. *Journal of Consulting and Clinical Psychology, 38*, 768–774.

Henry, W. P., & Strupp, H. H. (1992). The Vanderbilt Center for Psychotherapy Research. In D. K. Freedheim (Ed.), *History of psychotherapy: A century of change* (pp. 436–442). Washington, DC: American Psychological Association.

Herman, J. L. (1992). *Trauma and recovery*. New York: Basic Books.

Hermans, H. J. M., & Hermans-Jansen, E. (1995). *Self-narratives: The construction of meaning in psychotherapy*. New York: Guilford Press.

Horowitz, M. J. (Ed.). (1977). *Hysterical personality*. New York: Jason Aronson.

Horowitz, M. J. (1988). *Introduction to psychodynamics: A new synthesis*. New York: Basic Books.

Horowitz, M. J., & Marmar, C. (1985). The therapeutic alliance with difficult patients. In A. J. Frances & R. E. Hales (Eds.), *Review of psychiatry* (pp. 573–585). Washington, DC: American Psychiatric Press.

Horowitz, M. J., & Zilberg, N. (1983). Regressive alterations in the self concept. *American Journal of Psychiatry, 140*, 284–289.

Howard, K. I., Lueger, R. J., Maling, M. S., & Martinovich, Z. (1993). A phase model of psychotherapy outcome: Causal mediation of change. *Journal of Consulting and Clinical Psychology, 61*, 678–685.

Hoyt, M. F. (1995). *Brief therapy and managed care: Readings for contemporary practice*. San Francisco: Jossey-Bass.

Huffman, C. A. (2002). Socrates. *World Book Online Americas Edition*. Retrieved November 4, 2004, from http://aolsvc.worldbook.aol.com/wbol/wbPage/na/ar/co/518000

Hugo, V. (1982). *Les miserables*. London: Penguin Books. (Original work published 1862)

Humphreys, C. (1984). *Studies in the Middle Way: Being thoughts on Buddhism applied*. Wheaton, IL: Theosophical Publishing House.

Illardi, S. S., & Craighead, W. E. (1994). The role of nonspecific factors in cognitive–behavior therapy for depression. *Clinical Psychology: Science and Practice, 1*, 138–156.

Illardi, S. S., & Craighead, W. E. (1999). Rapid early response, cognitive modification, and nonspecific factors in cognitive behavior therapy for depression: A reply to Tang and DeRubeis. *Clinical Psychology: Science and Practice, 6*, 295–299.

Ivey, A. E., & Simek-Downing, L. (1980). *Counseling and psychotherapy: Skills, theories, and practice*. Englewood Cliffs, NJ: Prentice-Hall.

Jackson, D. D. (1957). The question of family homeostasis. *Psychiatric Quarterly, Supplement 31*, 79–90.

Jackson, D. D. (1965). Family rules: Marital quid pro quo. *Archives of General Psychiatry, 12*, 589–594.

Jacobson, E. (1964). *Anxiety and tension control: A psychobiologic approach*. Philadelphia: Lippincott.

Jacobson, N. S. (1991a). Behavioral versus insight-oriented marital therapy: Labels can be misleading. *Journal of Consulting and Clinical Psychology, 59*, 142–145.

Jacobson, N. S. (1991b). To be or not to be behavioral when working with couples: What does it mean? *Journal of Family Psychology, 4*, 436–445.

Jacobson, N. S. (1991c). Toward enhancing the efficacy of marital therapy and marital therapy research. *Journal of Family Psychology, 4*, 373–393.

Jacobson, N. S., Dobson, K. S., Truax, P. A., Addis, M. E., Koerner, K., Gollan, J. K., et al. (1996). A component analysis of cognitive–behavioral treatment for depression. *Journal of Consulting and Clinical Psychology, 64*, 295–304.

Jacques, E. (1965). Death and the mid-life crisis. *International Journal of Psychoanalysis, 46*, 502–514.

Janis, I. L. (1983). *Groupthink: Psychological studies of policy decisions and fiascoes* (2nd ed., rev.). Boston: Houghton Mifflin.

Janoff-Bulman, R. (1992). *Shattered assumptions: Toward a new psychology of trauma*. New York: Free Press.

Jaspers, K. (1994). *Philosophy of existence*. Philadelphia: University of Pennsylvania Press.

Johnson, A. H. (2001). The Balint movement in America. *Family Medicine, 33*, 174–177.

Johnson, A. H., Brock, C. D., Hamadeh, G., & Stock, R. (2001). The current status of Balint groups in US family practice residencies: A 10-year follow-up study, 1990–2000. *Family Medicine, 33,* 672–677.

Jones, E. (1955). *The life and work of Sigmund Freud* (Vol. 2). New York: Norton.

Jones, E. E., & Nisbett, R. E. (1971). The actor and the observer: Divergent perceptions of the causes of behavior. In E. E. Jones, D. E. Kanouse, H. H. Kelley, R. E. Nisbett, S. Valins, & B. Weiner (Eds.), *Attribution: Perceiving the causes of behavior* (pp. 79–94). Morristown, NJ: General Learning Press.

Jung, C. G. (1918). *Studies in word-association.* London: Heinemann.

Kahn, M. (1997). *Between therapist and client: The new relationship* (Rev. ed.). New York: Freeman.

Kapleau, P. (1989a). *The three pillars of Zen: Teaching, practice, and enlightenment* (25th Anniversary ed.). New York: Anchor Books.

Kapleau, P. (1989b). *Zen: Merging of East and West.* New York: Anchor Books.

Karasu, T. B. (1990). *Psychotherapy for depression.* Northvale, NJ: Jason Aronson.

Karasu, T. B. (1992). *Wisdom in the practice of psychotherapy.* New York: Basic Books.

Kaschak, E. (1999). Beyond the rule book. *Women & Therapy, 22,* 1–5.

Kaschak, E., & Hill, M. (Eds.). (1999). *Beyond the rule book: Moral issues and dilemmas in the practice of psychotherapy.* New York: Hayworth Press.

Keith, D. V., Scaturo, D. J., Marron, J. L., & Baird, M. A. (1993). A Balint-oriented case consultation group with residents in family practice: Considerations for training, mentoring, and the doctor–patient relationship. *Family Systems Medicine, 11,* 375–383.

Keller, S. A. (1999). Split loyalties: The conflicting demands of individual treatment goals and parental responsibility. *Women & Therapy, 22,* 117–131.

Kendler, H. H. (1968). *Basic psychology* (2nd ed.). New York: Appleton-Century-Crofts.

Kernberg, O. F. (1975). *Borderline conditions and pathological narcissism.* New York: Jason Aronson.

Kernberg, O. F. (1976). *Object relations theory and clinical psychoanalysis.* New York: Jason Aronson.

Kernberg, O. F. (1977). Contrasting approaches to the psychotherapy of borderline conditions. In J. F. Masterson (Ed.), *New perspectives on psychotherapy of the borderline adult* (pp. 75–104). New York: Brunner/Mazel.

Kernberg, O. F. (1984). *Severe personality disorders.* New Haven, CT: Yale University Press.

Kierkegaard, S. (1957). *The concept of dread.* Princeton, NJ: Princeton University Press.

Klerman, G. L., Weissman, M. M., Rounsaville, B. J., & Chevron, E. S. (1984). *Interpersonal psychotherapy of depression.* New York: Basic Books.

Kohut, H. (1971). *The analysis of the self.* New York: International Universities Press.

Kohut, H. (1979). The two analyses of Mr. Z. *International Journal of Psychoanalysis,* *60,* 3–27.

Kuehlwein, K. T. (2000). Enhancing creativity in cognitive therapy. *Journal of Cognitive Psychotherapy, 14,* 175–187.

Kuhn, T. S. (1970). *The structure of scientific revolutions* (2nd ed.). Chicago: University of Chicago Press.

Lambert, M. J. (Ed.). (1983). *Psychotherapy and patient relationships.* Homewood, IL: Dorsey Press.

Lambert, M. J. (1992). Psychotherapy outcome research: Implications for integrative and eclectic therapists. In J. C. Norcross & M. R. Goldfried (Eds.), *Handbook of psychotherapy integration* (pp. 94–129). New York: Basic Books.

Lambert, M. J., & Barley, D. E. (2001). Research summary of the therapeutic relationship and psychotherapy outcome. *Psychotherapy, 38,* 357–361.

Lambert, M. J., & Bergin, A. E. (1992). Achievements and limitations of psychotherapy research. In D. K. Freedheim (Ed.), *History of psychotherapy: A century of change* (pp. 360–390). Washington, DC: American Psychological Association.

Langs, R. (1973). *The techniques of psychoanalytic psychotherapy* (Vol. 1). New York: Jason Aronson.

LaPuma, J. (1998). *Managed care ethics: Essays on the impact of managed care on traditional medical ethics.* New York: Hatherleigh Press.

Lazarus, A. A. (1966). Behavior rehearsal vs. non-directive therapy vs. advice in effecting behavior change. *Behaviour Research and Therapy, 4,* 209–212.

Lazarus, A. A. (1967). In support of technical eclecticism. *Psychological Reports, 21,* 415–416.

Lazarus, A. A. (1971). *Behavior therapy and beyond.* New York: McGraw-Hill.

Lazarus, A. A. (1976). *Multimodal behavior therapy.* New York: Springer Publishing Company.

Lazarus, A. A. (1992). Multimodal therapy: Technical eclecticism with minimal integration. In J. C. Norcross & M. R. Goldfried (Eds.), *Handbook of psychotherapy integration* (pp. 231–263). New York: Basic Books.

Lazarus, A. A., & Fay, A. (1982). Resistance or rationalization? A cognitive–behavioral perspective. In P. L. Wachtel (Ed.), *Resistance: Psychodynamic and behavioral approaches* (pp. 115–132). New York: Plenum Press.

Leahy, R. L. (2001). *Overcoming resistance in cognitive therapy.* New York: Guilford Press.

Levinson, D. J., Darrow, C. N., Klein, E. B., Levinson, M. H., & McKee, B. (1978). *The seasons of a man's life.* New York: Knopf.

Lewin, K. (1935). *A dynamic theory of personality.* New York: McGraw-Hill.

Lewin, K. (1936). *Principles of topological psychology.* New York: McGraw-Hill.

Lewin, K. (1951). *Field theory in social science.* New York: Harper.

Lewinsohn, P. H. (1974). A behavioral approach to depression. In R. J. Friedman & M. M. Katz (Eds.), *The psychology of depression: Contemporary theory and research* (pp. 157–178). Washington, DC: Winston-Wiley.

Lindsay, G., & Clarkson, P. (1999). Ethical dilemmas of psychotherapists. *The Psychologist: Bulletin of the British Psychological Society, 12*, 182–185.

Linehan, M. M. (1987a). Dialectical behavior therapy: A cognitive behavioral approach to parasuicide. *Journal of Personality Disorders, 1*, 328–333.

Linehan, M. M. (1987b). Dialectical behavior therapy for borderline personality disorder. *Bulletin of the Menninger Clinic, 51*, 261–276.

Linehan, M. M. (1987c). Dialectical behavior therapy in groups: Treating borderline personality disorders and suicidal behavior. In V. M. Brady (Ed.), *Women in groups* (pp. 145–162). New York: Springer Publishing Company.

Linehan, M. M. (1993). *Cognitive–behavioral treatment of borderline personality disorder*. New York: Guilford Press.

Linson, A. (Producer), & Cuaron, A. (Director). (1998). *Great Expectations* [Motion picture]. United States: Twentieth Century Fox.

Litz, B. T., Blake, D. D., Gerardi, R. G., & Keane, T. M. (1990). Decision making guidelines for the use of direct therapeutic exposure in the treatment of posttraumatic stress disorder. *The Behavior Therapist, 13*, 91–93.

London, H., & Exner, J. E., Jr. (Eds.). (1978). *Dimensions of personality*. New York: Wiley.

Luborsky, L. (1977). Measuring a pervasive psychic structure in psychotherapy: The core conflictual relationship theme. In N. Freedman & S. Grand (Eds.), *Communicative structures and psychic structures* (pp. 367–395). New York: Plenum Press.

Luborsky, L., Crits-Christoph, P., McLellan, A. T., Woody, G., Piper, W., Liberman, B., et al. (1986). Do therapists vary much in their success? Findings from four outcome studies. *American Journal of Orthopsychiatry, 56*, 501–512.

Luborsky, L., McLellan, A. T., Woody, G. E., O'Brien, C. P., & Auerbach, A. (1985). Therapist success and its determinants. *Archives of General Psychiatry, 42*, 602–611.

Lynn, D. J., & Vaillant, G. E. (1998). Anonymity, neutrality, and confidentiality in the actual methods of Sigmund Freud: A review of 43 cases, 1907–1939. *American Journal of Psychiatry, 155*, 163–171.

MacKay, M., & Paleg, K. (Eds.). (1992). *Focal group psychotherapy*. Oakland, CA: New Harbinger.

Mackenzie, K. R. (1993). Time-limited group theory and technique. In A. Alonzo & H. I. Swiller (Eds.), *Group therapy in clinical practice* (pp. 423–447). Washington, DC: American Psychiatric Press.

Madanes, C. (1981). *Strategic family therapy*. San Francisco: Jossey-Bass.

Maddi, S. R. (1967). The existential neurosis. *Journal of Abnormal Psychology, 72*, 311–325.

Mahoney, M. J. (1974). *Cognition and behavior modification*. Cambridge, MA: Ballinger.

Malan, D. H. (1976). *The frontier of brief psychotherapy: An example of the convergence of research and clinical practice*. New York: Plenum Press.

Mann, J. (1973). *Time-limited psychotherapy*. Cambridge, MA: Harvard University Press.

Mann, J., & Goldman, R. (1982). *A casebook in time-limited psychotherapy*. New York: McGraw-Hill.

Markman, H. J. (1991). Constructive marital conflict is not an oxymoron. *Behavioral Assessment, 13*, 83–96.

Martin, P. J., Moore, J. E., & Karwisch, G. A. (1977). Therapists' expectations for in-therapy roles of hospitalized patients. *Journal of Clinical Psychology, 33*, 1103–1105.

Maslow, A. (1970). *Motivation and personality* (2nd ed.). New York: HarperCollins.

McCullough-Vaillant, L. (1997). *Changing character: Short-term anxiety-regulating psychotherapy for restructuring defenses, affects, and attachment*. New York: Basic Books.

McGuire, W. J. (1968). Personality and susceptibility to social influence. In E. F. Borgatta & W. W. Lambert (Eds.), *Handbook of personality theory and research* (pp. 1130–1187). Chicago: Rand McNally.

McLeod, J. (1998). *Narrative and psychotherapy*. New York: Sage.

McMullin, R. E. (1986). *Handbook of cognitive therapy techniques*. New York: Norton.

McMullin, R. E. (2000). *The new handbook of cognitive therapy techniques*. New York: Norton.

McPeak, W. R. (2003, January 27). *The system's storm*. Paper presented at the meeting of the Advanced Clinical Practicum, Department of Psychology, Syracuse University, Syracuse, NY.

Meador, B. D., & Rogers, C. R. (1979). Person-centered therapy. In R. J. Corsini (Ed.), *Current psychotherapies* (2nd ed., pp. 131–184). Itasca, IL: Peacock.

Meichenbaum, D. (1972). Cognitive modification of test anxious college students. *Journal of Consulting and Clinical Psychology, 39*, 370–380.

Meichenbaum, D. (1977). *Cognitive–behavior modification: An integrative approach*. New York: Plenum Press.

Meichenbaum, D. (1994). *A clinical handbook/practical therapist manual for assessing and treating adults with post-traumatic stress disorder (PTSD)*. Waterloo, Ontario, Canada: Institute Press.

Meichenbaum, D., & Cameron, R. (1974). The clinical potential of modifying what clients say to themselves. *Psychotherapy: Theory, Research, and Practice, 11*, 103–117.

Mental health: Does therapy help? (1995, November). *Consumer Reports*, pp. 734–739.

Merriam-Webster's collegiate dictionary (9th ed.). (1986). Springfield, MA: Merriam-Webster.

Miller, N. E. (1948). Studies of fear as an acquirable drive: I. Fear as motivation and fear reduction as reinforcement in the learning of new responses. *Journal of Experimental Psychology, 38*, 89–101.

Miller, N. E. (1959). Liberalization of basic S-R concepts: Extension to conflict behavior, motivation and social learning. In S. Koch (Ed.), *Psychology: A study of the science* (Vol. 2, pp. 196–292). New York: McGraw-Hill.

Miller, R. B. (2004). *Facing human suffering: Psychology and psychotherapy as moral engagement*. Washington, DC: American Psychological Association.

Mineka, S., Davidson, M., Cook, M., & Keir, R. (1984). Observational conditioning of snake fear in rhesus monkeys. *Journal of Abnormal Psychology, 93,* 355–372.

Minuchin, S. (1974). *Families and family therapy.* Cambridge, MA: Harvard University Press.

Minuchin, S., & Fishman, H. C. (1981). *Family therapy techniques.* Cambridge, MA: Harvard University Press.

Minuchin, S., Rosman, B. L., & Baker, L. (1978). *Psychosomatic families: Anorexia nervosa in context.* Cambridge, MA: Harvard University Press.

Mischel, W. (1973). Toward a cognitive social learning reconceptualization of personality. *Psychological Review, 80,* 252–283.

Moreno, J. L. (1946). *Psychodrama.* New York: Beacon House.

Mowrer, O. H. (1947). On the dual nature of learning: A reinterpretation of "conditioning" and "problem-solving." *Harvard Educational Review, 17,* 102–148.

Mozdzierz, G. J., Macchitelli, F., & Lisiecki, J. (1976). The paradox in psychotherapy: An Adlerian perspective. *Journal of Individual Psychology, 32,* 169–184.

Napier, A., & Whitaker, C. (1973). Problems of the beginning family therapist. In D. Bloch (Ed.), *Techniques of family psychotherapy: A primer* (pp. 109–122). New York: Grune & Stratton.

Newcomb, T. M. (1953). An approach to the study of communicative acts. *Psychological Review, 60,* 393–404.

Newman, C. F. (2000, October 5). *Cognitive therapy of depression: Fundamentals and applications in a group therapy setting.* Paper presented to the Department of Veterans Affairs, Syracuse, NY.

Nichols, M. P. (1974). Outcome of brief cathartic therapy. *Journal of Consulting and Clinical Psychology, 42,* 403–410.

Nichols, M. P. (1987a). The individual in the system. *Family Therapy Networker, 11,* 33–38, 85.

Nichols, M. P. (1987b). *The self in the system: Expanding the limits of family therapy.* New York: Brunner/Mazel.

Nichols, M. P., & Schwartz, R. C. (1998). *Family therapy: Concepts and methods* (4th ed.). Boston: Allyn & Bacon.

Norcross, J. C. (1988). The exclusivity myth and the equifinality principle in psychotherapy. *Journal of Integrative and Eclectic Psychotherapy, 7,* 415–421.

Norcross, J. C., & Goldfried, M. R. (Eds.). (1992). *Handbook of integrative psychotherapy.* New York: Basic Books.

Norcross, J. C., & Newman, C. F. (1992). Psychotherapy integration: Setting the context. In J. C. Norcross & M. R. Goldfried (Eds.), *Handbook of psychotherapy integration* (pp. 3–45). New York: Basic Books.

Orne, M. T. (1962). On the social psychology of the psychological experiment: With particular reference to demand characteristics and their implications. *American Psychologist, 17*, 776–783.

Orr, D. W. (1954). Transference and countertransference: A historical survey. *Journal of the American Psychoanalytic Association, 2*, 621–670.

Osgood, C. E., & Tannenbaum, P. H. (1955). The principle of congruity in the prediction of attitude change. *Psychological Review, 62*, 42–55.

Oskamp, S. (1991). *Attitudes and opinions* (2nd ed.). Englewood Cliffs, NJ: Prentice-Hall.

Overholser, J. C. (1988). Clinical utility of the Socratic method. In C. Stout (Ed.), *Annals of clinical research* (pp. 1–7). Des Plaines, IL: Forest Institute.

Overholser, J. C. (1995). Elements of the Socratic method: IV. Disavowal of knowledge. *Psychotherapy: Theory, Research, Practice, Training, 32*, 283–292.

Palmer, M. (1997). *Yin and yang*. London: Piaktus.

Papp, P. (1980). The Greek chorus and other techniques of paradoxical therapy. *Family Process, 19*, 45–57.

Paul, G. L. (1969). Behavior modification research: Design and tactics. In C. M. Franks (Ed.), *Behavior therapy: Appraisal and status* (pp. 29–62). New York: McGraw-Hill.

Pavlov, I. P. (1927). *Conditioned reflexes* (G. V. Anrep, Trans.). London: Oxford University Press.

Peale, N. V. (1952). *The power of positive thinking*. New York: Prentice-Hall.

Persons, J. B., & Burns, D. D. (1985). Mechanisms of action of cognitive therapy: The relative contributions of technical and interpersonal interventions. *Cognitive Therapy and Research, 9*, 539–551.

Peterson, R. L., Peterson, D. R., Abrams, J. C., & Stricker, G. (1997). The National Council of Schools and Programs of Professional Psychology educational model. *Professional Psychology: Research and Practice, 28*, 373–386.

Pinsof, W. M. (1983). Integrative problem-solving therapy: Toward a synthesis of family and individual psychotherapies. *Journal of Marital and Family Therapy, 9*, 19–35.

Piper, W. E., Debbane, E. G., Bienvenu, J. P., & Garant, J. (1984). A comparative study of four forms of psychotherapy. *Journal of Consulting and Clinical Psychology, 52*, 268–279.

Piper, W. E., & Ogrodniczuk, J. S. (1999). Therapy manuals and the dilemma of dynamically oriented therapists and researchers. *American Journal of Psychotherapy, 53*, 467–482.

Pitman, R. K., Altman, B., Greenwald, E., Longpre, R. E., Macklin, M. L., Poire, R. E., & Steketee, G. S. (1991). Psychiatric complications during flooding therapy for post-traumatic stress disorder. *Journal of Clinical Psychiatry, 164*, 17–20.

Plante, T. G., Andersen, E. N., & Boccaccini, M. T. (1999). Empirically supported treatments and related contemporary changes in psychotherapy practice: What do clinical ABPP's think? *The Clinical Psychologist, 52*(4), 23–31.

Pope, K. S. (1994). Sexual involvement with therapists: Patient assessment, subsequent therapy, and forensics. Washington, DC: American Psychological Association.

Pope, K. S., Lief, H. I., & Bouhoutsos, J. C. (1986). *Sexual intimacy between therapists and patients* (Vol. 5). Westport, CT: Greenwood Press.

Pope, K. S., Sonne, J. L., & Holroyd, J. (1993). *Sexual feelings in psychotherapy: Explorations for therapists in training*. Washington, DC: American Psychological Association.

Pope, K. S., & Vetter, V. A. (1992). Ethical dilemmas encountered by members of the American Psychological Association. *American Psychologist, 47*, 397–411.

Prochaska, J. O. (1979). *Systems of psychotherapy: A transtheoretical analysis*. Homewood, IL: Dorsey Press.

Prochaska, J. O., & DiClemente, C. C. (1984). *The transtheoretical approach: Crossing traditional boundaries of therapy*. New York: Brooks/Cole.

Prochaska, J. O., & DiClemente, C. C. (1992a). Stages of change in the modification of problem behaviors. *Progress in Behavior Modification, 28*, 183–218.

Prochaska, J. O., & DiClemente, C. C. (1992b). The transtheoretical approach. In J. C. Norcross & M. R. Goldfried (Eds.), *Handbook of psychotherapy integration* (pp. 300–334). New York: Basic Books.

Racker, H. (1968). *Transference and countertransference*. New York: International Universities Press.

Raimy, V. C. (1950). *Training in clinical psychology*. Englewood Cliffs, NJ: Prentice Hall.

Rangell, L. (1969). The psychoanalytic process. *International Journal of Psychoanalysis, 49*, 19–26.

Rennie, D. L., & Toukmanian, S. G. (1992). *Psychotherapy process research: Paradigmatic and narrative approaches*. New York: Sage.

Rhoads, J. M. (1984). Relationship between psychodynamic and behavior therapies. In H. Arkowitz & S. B. Messer (Eds.), *Psychoanalytic therapy and behavior therapy: Is integration possible?* (pp. 195–211). New York: Plenum Press.

Ricks, D. F. (1974). Supershrink: Methods of a therapist judged successful on the basis of adult outcome of adolescent patients. In D. Ricks, M. Roff, & A. Thomas (Eds.), *Life history research in psychopathology* (Vol. 3, pp. 275–297). Minneapolis: University of Minnesota Press.

Roberts, G., & Holmes, J. (Eds.). (1999). *Healing stories: Narrative in psychiatry and psychotherapy*. London: Oxford University Press.

Rogers, C. R. (1942). *Counseling and psychotherapy*. Boston: Houghton Mifflin.

Rogers, C. R. (1951). *Client-centered therapy: Its current practice, implications, and theory*. Boston: Houghton Mifflin.

Rogers, C. R. (1957). The necessary and sufficient conditions of therapeutic personality change. *Journal of Consulting Psychology, 21*, 95–103.

Rogers, C. R. (1959). Client-centered therapy. In S. Arieti (Ed.), *American handbook of psychiatry* (Vol. 3, pp. 183–200). New York: Basic Books.

Rogers, C. R. (1962). The interpersonal relationship: The core of guidance. In C. R. Rogers & B. Stevens (Eds.), *Person to person* (pp. 91–92). Lafayette, CA: Real People Press.

Rogers, C. R. (1969). *Freedom to learn: A view of what education might become.* Columbus, OH: Charles E. Merrill.

Rogers, C. R., & Skinner, B. F. (1956, November 30). Some issues concerning the control of human behavior: A symposium. *Science, 124,* 1057–1066.

Rokeach, M. (1963). The organization and modification of beliefs. *Centennial Review, 7,* 375–395.

Rose, S. D. (1999). Group therapy: A cognitive–behavioral approach. In J. R. Price, D. R. Hescheles, & A. R. Price (Eds.), *A guide to starting psychotherapy groups* (pp. 99–114). San Diego, CA: Academic Press.

Rosenthal, T. L., & Bandura, A. (1978). Psychological modeling: Theory and practice. In S. L. Garfield & A. E. Bergin (Eds.), *Handbook of psychotherapy and behavior change: An empirical analysis* (2nd ed., pp. 621–658). New York: Wiley.

Rosman, B., Minuchin, S., & Liebman, R. (1975). Family lunch session: An introduction to family therapy in anorexia nervosa. *American Journal of Orthopsychiatry, 45,* 846–853.

Rotter, J. B. (1966). Generalized expectancies for internal versus external control of reinforcement. *Psychological Monographs, 80*(Whole No. 609).

Ryan, W. (1971). *Blaming the victim.* New York: Vintage.

Ryle, A. (1979). The focus in brief interpretive psychotherapy: Dilemmas, traps and snags as target problems. *British Journal of Psychiatry, 134,* 46–54.

Sable, P. (1994). Separation anxiety, attachment, and agoraphobia. *Clinical Social Work Journal, 22,* 369–383.

Sable, P. (2000). *Attachment and adult psychotherapy.* Northvale, NJ: Jason Aronson.

Safran, J. D. (1993). Breaches in the therapeutic alliance: An arena for negotiating authentic relatedness. *Psychotherapy, 30,* 111–124.

Safran, J. D. (1998). *Widening the scope of cognitive therapy: The therapeutic relationship, emotion, and the process of change.* Northvale, NJ: Jason Aronson.

Safran, J. D. (Ed.). (2003). *Psychoanalysis and Buddhism: An unfolding dialogue.* Somerville, MA: Wisdom.

Safran, J. D., & Greenberg, L. S. (1993). The therapeutic alliance rupture as a transtheoretical phenomenon: Definitional and conceptual issues. *Journal of Psychotherapy Integration, 3,* 33–49.

Safran, J. D., & Greenberg, L. S. (Eds.). (1998). *Emotion, psychotherapy, and change.* New York: Guilford Press.

Safran, J. D., & Muran, J. C. (Eds.). (1998). *The therapeutic alliance in brief psychotherapy.* Washington, DC: American Psychological Association.

Safran, J. D., & Muran, J. C. (2001). A relational approach to training and supervision in cognitive psychotherapy. *Journal of Cognitive Psychotherapy, 15*(1), 3–15.

Safran, J. D., & Segal, Z. V. (1996). *Interpersonal processes in cognitive therapy.* Northvale, NJ: Jason Aronson. (Original work published 1990)

Sager, C. J. (1981). Couples contracts and marital therapy. In A. S. Gurman & D. P. Kniskern (Eds.), *Handbook of family therapy* (pp. 321–344). New York: Brunner/Mazel.

Sartre, J. (1956). *Being and nothingness.* New York: Philosophical Library.

Satterfield, W. A., Buelow, S. A., Lyddon, W. J., & Johnson, J. T. (1995). Client stages of change and expectations about counseling. *Journal of Counseling Psychology, 42,* 476–478.

Scaturo, D. J. (1977). Issue relevance as a source of political involvement. *Journal of Social Psychology, 101,* 59–67.

Scaturo, D. J. (1987). Toward an adult developmental conceptualization of alcohol abuse: A review of the literature. *British Journal of Addiction, 82,* 857–870.

Scaturo, D. J. (1994). Integrative psychotherapy for panic disorder and agoraphobia in clinical practice. *Journal of Psychotherapy Integration, 4,* 253–272.

Scaturo, D. J. (2001). The evolution of psychotherapy and the concept of manualization: An integrative perspective. *Professional Psychology: Research and Practice, 32,* 522–530.

Scaturo, D. J. (2002a, August). *Clinical dilemmas in marital and couple therapy: Art, science, and wisdom.* Paper presented at the 110th Annual Convention of the American Psychological Association, Chicago, IL. (ERIC Document Reproduction Service No. ED470724).

Scaturo, D. J. (2002b). Fundamental dilemmas in contemporary psychodynamic and insight-oriented psychotherapy. *Journal of Contemporary Psychotherapy, 32,* 143–163.

Scaturo, D. J. (2002c). Fundamental dilemmas in contemporary psychotherapy: A transtheoretical concept. *American Journal of Psychotherapy, 56(1),* 115–133.

Scaturo, D. J. (2002d). Technical skill and the therapeutic relationship: A fundamental dilemma in cognitive–behavioral and insight-oriented therapy. *Family Therapy, 29(1),* 1–21.

Scaturo, D. J. (2003a). Codependency. In J. J. Ponzetti Jr. (Ed.), *International encyclopedia of marriage and family* (2nd ed., Vol. 1, pp. 310–315). New York: Macmillan Reference USA.

Scaturo, D. J. (2003b). Fundamental dilemmas in contemporary psychotherapy: An overview. *Ethical Issues in Mental Health Counseling, 6(1),* 1–11.

Scaturo, D. J. (2004). Fundamental clinical dilemmas in contemporary group psychotherapy. *Group Analysis: The Journal of Group Analytic Psychotherapy, 37,* 201–218.

Scaturo, D. J., & Hardoby, W. J. (1988). Psychotherapy with traumatized Vietnam combatants: An overview of individual, family, and group treatment modalities. *Military Medicine, 153,* 262–269.

Scaturo, D. J., Hayes, T., Sagula, D., & Walter, T. (2000). The concept of codependency and its context within family systems theory. *Family Therapy, 27(2),* 63–70.

Scaturo, D. J., & Hayman, P. M. (1992). The impact of combat trauma across the family life cycle: Clinical considerations. *Journal of Traumatic Stress, 5,* 273–288.

Scaturo, D. J., & McPeak, W. R. (1998). Clinical dilemmas in contemporary psychotherapy: The search for clinical wisdom. *Psychotherapy, 35*(1), 1–12.

Schacht, T. E. (1984). The varieties of integrative experience. In H. Arkowitz & S. B. Messer (Eds.), *Psychoanalytic therapy and behavior therapy: Is integration possible?* (pp. 107–131). New York: Plenum Press.

Schacht, T. E., Binder, J. L., & Strupp, H. H. (1984). The dynamic focus. In H. H. Strupp & J. L. Binder (Eds.), *Psychotherapy in a new key: A guide to time-limited dynamic psychotherapy* (pp. 65–109). New York: Basic Books.

Schafer, R. (1992). *Retelling a life: Narration and dialogue in psychoanalysis.* New York: Basic Books.

Scharff, D. E., & Scharff, J. S. (1987). *Object relations family therapy.* Northvale, NJ: Jason Aronson.

Scharff, D. E., & Scharff, J. S. (1991). *Object relations couple therapy.* Northvale, NJ: Jason Aronson.

Scharff, J. S., & Scharff, D. E. (2003). *Primer of object relations therapy* (2nd ed.). Northvale, NJ: Jason Aronson.

Schneider, S. L. (2001). In search of realistic optimism: Meaning, knowledge, and warm fuzziness. *American Psychologist, 56,* 250–263.

Schutz, W. C. (1967). *Joy: Expanding human awareness.* New York: Grove Press.

Schutz, W. C. (1973). Encounter. In R. J. Corsini (Ed.), *Current psychotherapies* (pp. 401–443). Itasca, IL: Peacock.

Schuyler, D. (2002). Short-term cognitive therapy shows promise for dysthymia. *Current Psychiatry-Online, 1*(5). Retrieved November 9, 2003, from http://www.currentpsychiatry.com/2002_05/05_02_dysthymia.asp

Sekhri, N. K. (2000). Managed care: The US experience. *Bulletin of the World Health Organization, 78,* 830–844.

Seligman, M. E. P. (1974). Depression and learned helplessness. In R. J. Friedman & M. M. Katz (Eds.), *The psychology of depression: Contemporary theory and research* (pp. 83–113). Washington, DC: Winston-Wiley.

Seligman, M. E. P. (1975). *Helplessness: On depression, development, and death.* San Francisco: Freeman.

Seligman, M. E. P. (1990). *Learned optimism.* New York: Knopf.

Seligman, M. E. P. (1995). The effectiveness of psychotherapy: The *Consumer Reports* study. *American Psychologist, 50,* 965–974.

Seligman, M. E. P., & Johnston, J. (1973). A cognitive theory of avoidance learning. In J. McGuigan & B. Lumsden (Eds.), *Contemporary approaches to conditioning and learning* (pp. 69–110). New York: Wiley.

Shaffer, P. (1973). *Equus and Shrivings.* New York: Scribner.

Shapiro, D. A., Barkham, M., Reynolds, S., Hardy, G., & Stiles, W. B. (1992). Prescriptive and exploratory psychotherapies: Toward an integration based on the assimilation model. *Journal of Psychotherapy Integration, 2,* 253–272.

Shaw, M. E. (1964). Communication networks. In L. Berkowitz (Ed.), *Advances in experimental social psychology* (Vol. 1, pp. 111–147). New York: Academic Press.

Shaw, M. E., & Costanzo, P. R. (1982). *Theories of social psychology* (2nd ed.). New York: McGraw-Hill.

Sheldon, K. M., Joiner, T., & Williams, G. (2003). *Self-determination theory in the clinic: Motivating physical and mental health.* New Haven, CT: Yale University Press.

Siegel, J. P. (1992). *Repairing intimacy: An object relations approach to couples therapy.* Northvale, NJ: Jason Aronson.

Sifneos, P. E. (1979). *Short-term dynamic psychotherapy: Evaluation and technique.* New York: Plenum Press.

Sifneos, P. E. (1992). *Short-term anxiety-provoking psychotherapy: A treatment manual.* New York: Basic Books.

Silverman, W. H. (1996). Cookbooks, manuals, and paint-by-numbers: Psychotherapy in the 90s. *Psychotherapy, 33,* 207–215.

Simon, F. B., Stierlin, H., & Wynne, L. C. (1985). *The language of family therapy: A systemic vocabulary and sourcebook.* New York: Family Process Press.

Singer, J. (1974). *Imagery and daydream methods in psychotherapy.* New York: Academic Press.

Skinner, B. F. (1952). *Science and human behavior.* New York: Free Press.

Smith, D. A. (1999). Stuart Smalley syndrome: What is *not* cognitive–behavioral psychotherapy. *The Behavior Therapist, 22,* 5–8, 15.

Snyder, D. K., & Wills, R. M. (1989). Behavioral versus insight-oriented marital therapy: Effects on individual and interpersonal function. *Journal of Consulting and Clinical Psychology, 57(1),* 39–46.

Snyder, D. K., Wills, R. M., & Grady-Fletcher, A. (1991). Long-term effectiveness of behavioral versus insight-oriented marital therapy: A 4-year follow-up study. *Journal of Consulting and Clinical Psychology, 59,* 138–141.

Soll, I. (2002). Hegel, G. W. F. In the *World Book Online Americas Edition.* Retrieved March 25, 2002, from http://aolsvc.worldbook.aol.com/wbol/wbPage/na/ar/co/251040

Spanier, C., & Frank, E. (1993). Maintenance interpersonal psychotherapy: A preventative treatment for depression. In J. C. Markowitz (Ed.), *Interpersonal psychotherapy* (pp. 67–97). Washington, DC: American Psychiatric Press.

Spence, D. P., & Wallerstein, R. S. (1990). *Narrative truth and historical truth: Meaning and interpretation in psychoanalysis.* New York: Norton.

Sperry, L., & Prosen, H. (1998). Contemporary ethical dilemmas in psychotherapy: Cosmetic psychopharmacology and managed care. *American Journal of Psychotherapy, 52,* 54–63.

Spitz, H. I. (1995). *Group psychotherapy and managed mental health care: A clinical guide for providers* (Vol. 2). New York: Brunner/Mazel.

Sprafkin, R. P., Gershaw, N. J., & Goldstein, A. P. (1978). Teaching interpersonal skills to psychiatric outpatients: Using structured learning therapy in a community-based setting. *Journal of Rehabilitation, 44* (2), 26–36.

Sprafkin, R. P., Goldstein, A. P., & Gershaw, N. J. (1993). *Social skills for mental health: A structured learning approach*. New York: Allyn & Bacon.

Stanton, M. D. (1981). An integrated structural/strategic approach to family therapy. *Journal of Marital and Family Therapy, 7*, 427–439.

Starker, S. (1990). Self-help books: Ubiquitous agents of health care. *Medical Psychotherapy, 3*, 187–194.

Stokes, M. C. (Trans.). (1997). *Plato: Apology of Socrates*. Warminster, England: Aris & Phillips.

Storms, M. D. (1973). Videotape and the attribution process: Reversing the actor's and the observer's points of view. *Journal of Personality and Social Psychology, 27*, 165–175.

Stricker, G., & Trierweiler, S. J. (1995). The local clinical scientist: A bridge between science and practice. *American Psychologist, 50*, 995–1002.

Strupp, H. H. (1981). Clinical research, practice and the crisis of confidence. *Journal of Consulting and Clinical Psychology, 49*, 216–219.

Strupp, H. H., & Binder, J. L. (1984). *Psychotherapy in a new key: A guide to time-limited dynamic psychotherapy*. New York: Basic Books.

Strupp, H. H., Fox, R. E., & Lesser, K. (1969). *Patients view their psychotherapy*. Baltimore: Johns Hopkins University Press.

Strupp, H. H., & Hadley, S. W. (1979). Specific vs. nonspecific factors in psychotherapy: A controlled study of outcome. *Archives of General Psychiatry, 36*, 1125–1136.

Stuart, S. P. (2002, April 5). *Interpersonal psychotherapy: Effective, brief treatment for depression*. Continuing professional education presentation at the Psychotherapy Institute, Department of Psychiatry, University of Rochester School of Medicine and Dentistry, Rochester, NY.

Stuart, S. P., & Robertson, M. (2003). *Interpersonal psychotherapy: A clinician's guide*. London: Arnold.

Styron, W. (1979). *Sophie's choice*. New York: Random House.

Sullivan, H. S. (1938). Psychiatry: Introduction to the study of interpersonal relations. *Psychiatry, 1*, 121–134.

Sullivan, H. S. (1953). *The interpersonal theory of psychiatry*. New York: Norton.

Sweet, A. A. (1984). The therapeutic relationship in behavior therapy. *Clinical Psychology Review, 4*, 253–272.

Swenson, C. (1989). Kernberg and Linehan: Two approaches to the borderline patient. *Journal of Personality Disorders, 3*, 26–35.

Szasz, T. S. (1970). *Ideology and insanity: Essays on the psychiatric dehumanization of man*. Garden City, NY: Anchor.

Talmon, M. (1990). *Single session therapy: Maximizing the effect of the first (and often only) therapeutic encounter*. San Francisco: Jossey-Bass.

Tang, T. Z., & DeRubeis, R. J. (1999a). Reconsidering rapid early response in cognitive behavioral therapy for depression. *Clinical Psychology: Science and Practice, 6*, 283–288.

Tang, T. Z., & DeRubeis, R. J. (1999b). Sudden gains and critical sessions in cognitive–behavioral therapy for depression. *Journal of Consulting and Clinical Psychology, 67*, 894–904.

Thyer, B. A., Himle, J., & Fischer, D. (1988). Is parental death a selective precursor to either panic disorder or agoraphobia? A test of the separation anxiety hypothesis. *Journal of Anxiety Disorders, 2*, 333–338.

Tinsley, H. E., Workman, K. R., & Kass, R. A. (1980). Factor analysis of the domain of client expectancies about counseling. *Journal of Counseling Psychology, 27*, 561–570.

Truax, C. B., & Carkhuff, R. R. (1967a). The client-centered process as viewed by other therapists. In C. R. Rogers, E. T. Gendlin, D. Kiessler, & C. B. Truax (Eds.), *The therapeutic relationship and its impact* (pp. 419–505). Madison: University of Wisconsin Press.

Truax, C. B., & Carkhuff, R. R. (1967b). *Toward effective counseling and psychotherapy: Training and practice*. Chicago: Aldine.

Vaillant, G. E. (1992). The clinical management of immature defenses in the treatment of individuals with personality disorders. In G. E. Vaillant, *Ego mechanisms of defense: A guide for clinicians and researchers* (pp. 59–86). Washington, DC: American Psychiatric Press.

Vaillant, G. E. (2002). *Aging well: Surprising guideposts to a happier life from the landmark Harvard study of adult development*. New York: Little, Brown.

Vaillant, G. E., & Milofsky, E. S. (1980). Natural history of male psychological health: IX. Empirical evidence for Erickson's model of the life cycle. *American Journal of Psychiatry, 137*, 1348–1359.

Wachtel, E. F. (1979). Learning family therapy: The dilemmas of an individual psychotherapist. *Journal of Contemporary Psychotherapy, 10*, 122–135.

Wachtel, E. F. (1992). An integrative approach to working with troubled children and their families. *Journal of Psychotherapy Integration, 2*, 207–224.

Wachtel, E. F. (1994). *Treating troubled children and their families*. New York: Guilford Press.

Wachtel, E. F., & Wachtel, P. L. (1986). *Family dynamics in individual psychotherapy: A guide to clinical strategies*. New York: Guilford Press.

Wachtel, P. L. (1977). *Psychoanalysis and behavior therapy: Toward an integration*. New York: Basic Books.

Wachtel, P. L. (1981, January 3–10). The politics of narcissism. *The Nation, 232*, 13–15.

Wachtel, P. L. (Ed.). (1982). *Resistance: Psychodynamic and behavioral approaches*. New York: Plenum Press.

Wachtel, P. L. (1987). *Action and insight*. New York: Guilford Press.

Wachtel, P. L (1991). From eclecticism to synthesis: Toward a more seamless psychotherapy integration. *Journal of Psychotherapy Integration, 1*, 43–54.

Wachtel, P. L. (1993). *Therapeutic communication: Principles and effective practice*. New York: Guilford Press.

Wachtel, P. L. (1997). The non-improving patient: An interview with Paul Wachtel. In W. Dryden (Ed.), *Therapists' dilemmas* (Rev. ed., pp. 139–151). London: Sage.

Wachtel, P. L., & McKinney, M. K. (1992). Cyclical psychodynamics and integrative psychodynamic psychotherapy. In J. C. Norcross & M. R. Goldfried (Eds.), *Handbook of psychotherapy integration* (pp. 335–370). New York: Basic Books.

Wallerstein, J. S. (1990). Transference and countertransference in clinical intervention with divorcing families. *American Journal of Orthopsychiatry, 60*, 337–345.

Wallerstein, J. S., & Blakeslee, S. (1989). *Second chances: Men, women, and children a decade after divorce*. New York: Ticknor & Fields.

Wallerstein, J. S., Lewis, J., & Blakeslee, S. (2000). *The unexpected legacy of divorce: A 25 year landmark study*. New York: Hyperion.

Wallerstein, R. S., & Robbins, L. L. (1956). The Psychotherapy Research Project of the Menninger Foundation—Rationale, method, sample use: IV. Concepts. *Bulletin of the Menninger Clinic, 20*, 239–262.

Watson, J. B. (1913). Psychology as the behaviorist views it. *Psychological Review, 20*, 158–177.

Watson, J. B. (1925). *Behaviorism*. New York: Norton.

Watts, A. (1977). *Tao: The watercourse way*. New York: Knopf.

Weeks, G. R., & L'Abate, L. (1982). *Paradoxical psychotherapy: Theory and practice with individuals, couples, and families*. New York: Brunner/Mazel.

Weiner, B., Frieze, I., Kukla, A., Reed, L., Rest, S., & Rosenbaum, R. M. (1971). *Perceiving the causes of success and failure*. Morristown, NJ: General Learning Press.

Weiss, R. S. (1974). The provisions of social relationships. In Z. Rubin (Ed.), *Doing unto others* (pp. 17–26). Englewood Cliffs, NJ: Prentice-Hall.

Weisskopf-Joelson, E. (1955). Some comments on a Viennese School of Psychiatry. *Journal of Abnormal and Social Psychology, 51*, 701–703.

Weisskopf-Joelson, E. (1958). Logotherapy and existential analysis. *Acta Psychotherapeutica, 6*, 193–204.

Weissman, M. M., & Markowitz, J. C. (1998). An overview of interpersonal psychotherapy. In J. C. Markowitz (Ed.), *Interpersonal psychotherapy* (pp. 1–33). Washington, DC: American Psychiatric Press.

Whitaker, C. (1976). A family is a four dimensional relationship. In P. Guerin (Ed.), *Family therapy* (pp. 182–192). New York: Gardner Press.

White, J. R., & Freeman, A. S. (Eds.). (2000). *Cognitive–behavioral group therapy for specific problems and populations*. Washington, DC: American Psychological Association.

White, M., & Epston, D. (1990). *Narrative means to therapeutic ends*. New York: Norton.

Whitehouse, W. G., Orne, E. C., & Dinges, D. F. (2002). Demand characteristics: Toward an understanding of their meaning and application in clinical practice. *Prevention & Treatment, 5*, Article 34. Retrieved March 3, 2003, from http://www.journals.apa.org/prevention/volume5/pre0050034i.html

Wile, D. B. (1984). Kohut, Kernberg, and accusatory interpretations. *Psychotherapy, 21*, 353–364.

Wilson, G. T. (1984). Clinical issues and strategies in the practice of behavior therapy. In G. T. Wilson, C. M. Franks, P. C. Kendall, & J. P. Foreyt (Eds.), *Annual review of behavior therapy* (Vol. 9, pp. 309–343). New York: Guilford Press.

Wilson, J. O. (1989, August). *Guidelines for support persons from the Phobia Center of the Southwest*. Paper presented at the 97th Annual Convention of the American Psychological Association, New Orleans, LA.

Winch, R. F. (1958). *Mate selection: A study of complementary needs*. New York: HarperCollins.

Winnicott, D. W. (1965). *The maturational processes and the facilitating environment: Studies in the theory of emotional development*. London: Hogarth Press.

Wolfe, B. E. (1989). Phobias, panic and psychotherapy integration. *Journal of Integrative and Eclectic Psychotherapy, 8*, 264–276.

Wolfe, B. E. (1992a). Integrative psychotherapy of the anxiety disorders. In J. C. Norcross & M. R. Goldfried (Eds.), *Handbook of psychotherapy integration* (pp. 373–401). New York: Basic Books.

Wolfe, B. E. (1992b). Self-experiencing and the integrative treatment of anxiety disorders. *Journal of Psychotherapy Integration, 2*, 29–43.

Wolpe, J. (1958). *Psychotherapy by reciprocal inhibition*. Stanford, CA: Stanford University Press.

Wolpe, J. (1992). *The practice of behavior therapy* (4th ed.). Boston: Allyn & Bacon.

Wong, P. S. (1999). Anxiety, signal anxiety, and unconscious anticipation: Neuroscientific evidence for an unconscious function in humans. *Journal of the American Psychoanalytic Association, 47*, 817–841.

Woody, S. R., & Sanderson, W. C. (1998). Manuals for empirically supported treatments: 1998 update. *The Clinical Psychologist, 51*(1), 17–21.

Wynne, L. C. (1984). The epigenesis of relational systems: A model for understanding family development. *Family Process, 23*, 297–318.

Wynne, L. C., Ryckoff, I. M., Day, J., & Hirsch, S. I. (1958). Pseudomutuality in the family relationships of schizophrenics. *Psychiatry, 21*, 205–220.

Yalom, I. D. (1980). *Existential psychotherapy*. New York: Basic Books.

Yalom, I. D. (1983). *Inpatient group psychotherapy*. New York: Basic Books.

Yalom, I. D. (1995). *The theory and practice of group psychotherapy* (4th ed.). New York: Basic Books.

Yerkes, R. M., & Dodson, J. D. (1908). The relation of strength of stimulus to rapidity of habit-formation. *Journal of Comparative Neurology and Psychology, 18*, 459–482.

Zitrin, C. M., & Ross, D. C. (1988). Early separation anxiety and adult agoraphobia. *Journal of Nervous and Mental Disease, 176*, 621–625.

INDEX

ABOUT THE AUTHOR

Douglas J. Scaturo, PhD, is the lead psychologist and director of the APA-accredited Psychology Internship Training Program at the Behavioral Health Outpatient Clinic of the Syracuse Veterans Affairs Medical Center, which is accredited by the American Psychological Association. Dr. Scaturo holds academic appointments as a clinical associate professor in the Departments of Psychiatry and Family Medicine in the College of Medicine at the State University of New York Upstate Medical University and as clinical adjunct associate professor in the Department of Psychology at Syracuse University. His published clinical and research interests are in the areas of posttraumatic stress disorder, panic disorders and agoraphobia, codependency and alcohol abuse, the assessment and delivery of behavioral health services in primary care settings, the doctor–patient relationship in family medicine, the family life cycle, psychotherapy integration, and most recently and extensively on the clinical dilemmas that take place for psychotherapists working within a broad range of theoretical orientations and treatment modalities. He regularly lectures at national and international conferences and conducts professional workshops for clinicians in these areas of practice. Dr. Scaturo lives in central New York with his wife and son, where he also conducts a part-time private practice in individual and couple therapy in Syracuse.